THE CREATIVE WORLD OF BEETHOVEN

Also by Paul Henry Lang

THE CREATIVE WORLD

OF

Beethoven

Edited by PAUL HENRY LANG

W · W · NORTON & COMPANY · INC ·

NEW YORK

W. W. Norton & Company, Inc. is the publisher of current or forthcoming books on music by Putnam Aldrich, William Austin, Anthony Baines, Philip Bate, Sol Berkowitz, Friedrich Blume, Howard Boatwright, Nadia Boulanger, Paul Brainerd, Nathan Broder, Manfred Bukofzer, John Castellini, John Clough, Doda Conrad, Aaron Copland, Hans David, Paul Des Marais, Otto Erich Deutsch, Frederick Dorian, Alfred Einstein, Gabriel Fontrier, Harold Gleason, Richard Franko Goldman, Noah Greenberg, Donald Jay Grout, James Haar, F. L. Harrison, Daniel Heartz, Richard Hoppin, John Horton, Edgar Hunt, A. J. B. Hutchings, Charles Ives, Roger Kamien, Hermann Keller, Leo Kraft, Stanley Krebs, Paul Henry Lang, Lyndesay G. Langwill, Jens Peter Larsen, Jan LaRue, Maurice Lieberman, Irving Lowens, Joseph Machlis, Carol McClintock, Alfred Mann, W. T. Marrocco, Arthur Mendel, William J. Mitchell, Douglas Moore, Joel Newman, John F. Ohl, Carl Parrish, Vincent Persichetti, Marc Pincherle, Walter Piston, Gustave Reese, Alexander Ringer, Curt Sachs, Denis Stevens, Robert Stevenson, Oliver Strunk, Francis Toye, Bruno Walter, J. T. Westrup, Emanuel Winternitz, Walter Wiora, and Percy Young.

Library of Congress Catalog Card No. 79-159746

SBN 393 02158 0 (cloth edition)

SBN 393 00605 0 (paper edition)

PRINTED IN THE UNITED STATES OF AMERICA

1 2 3 4 5 6 7 8 9 0

CONTENTS

48771

ILLUSTRATIONS

THE CREATIVE WORLD OF BEETHOVEN

THE CREATIVE WORLD OF ... (faint mirror-image text)

INTRODUCTION

By PAUL HENRY LANG

Musical historiography, especially in the nineteenth century, delighted in assigning exceptional positions to certain composers. Such men, like the Earth in the Ptolemaic system, were regarded as the energy center around which the rest of the musical world revolved. This tendency to idealize creative artists has grown during the last hundred years, reaching its height in the case of Beethoven, who has long since become the heroic representative not only of his period but of all music, a symbol for all ages. No other composer in the history of Western music is accorded this universal admiration, this respect bordering on veneration. So, as we celebrate the bicentenary of his birth, perhaps we should preface this fine collection of scholarly essays with some reflections concerning Beethoven's exceptional position in musical history as well as in men's hearts.

Beethoven was the first among the great masters to divorce the creative from the performing artist, the first to whom composing was a bitterly relentless affair, "perhaps the only language of his soul," as Marx says in his early biography. And the Beethoven of his last period attains to that degree of universality in which tendencies and forms lose their significance, melting into a vision that encompasses all that is human. Those who in the early nineteenth century heard his agitated and yearning themes, who were struck by the irresistible propulsive force of the allegros, the majesty of the adagios, the menacing humor of the scherzos, and the wild rhythms of the finales, recognized that this music, compared to that of his predecessors, is somewhat raw, gnarled, even unfinished. There were some who were repelled, among them such able composers as Spohr and Weber, but many more, despite or perhaps because of these qualities, found Beethoven's music to be warmer, more intense, and more fulfilling than any other they had known.

Beethoven proclaimed that art not only is personal confession but represents the divine itself, being a higher revelation than any wisdom. The boundaries of Haydn's beautifully closed real world gradually recede around him, clouding into metaphysics. At the same time, the revelation, the spirit which Beethoven so loved to emphasize, now gave a new nobility to the musician as artist — Beethoven called himself a *Tondichter* rather than a composer. Like Schiller, he fervently professed that the principal and highest repository of the dignity of humanity is the creative artist. It was this clear and courageous consciousness of his vocation and destiny, which he maintained under all conditions of life, that made him what the world sees in him: the epitome of the sovereign artist. Haydn, though always of a sunny disposition and respecter of the prevailing order of the world, once admitted that he found it a galling thing to be forever a servant, but he quickly added that Providence decreed it that way. Beethoven proudly declared that a man should never humble himself before his fellows. At the celebrated encounter with Goethe in Teplitz, the whole assembled royalty could see that Beethoven would elbow them aside if they should get in his way. To Beethoven, unlike Goethe and most of his contemporaries, this independence was a cardinal necessity. With this new type of artist the old solidarity and commonality of the eighteenth century ended, and the solitary, individual, responsible, and challenging man steps forward. He in whom this overwhelming tempest took its course appeared to be no other than a Titan, the representative of humanity itself, and it is so indeed that not only romantic historiography but all the world sees Beethoven.

Those who expected to find in him Mozart's and Haydn's successor were taken aback when the young musician, only recently settled in Vienna, began to show the pride of a plebeian who jealously guards his independence and is filled with ambitions going far beyond those associated with his profession and social standing. There was something arrogant, wildly gauche, even offensive, in his attitude, and his supreme creed seems to have been pride and power; he believed that he was not only the equal of the men with whom he dealt, but their superior. His contemporaries felt that in contrast to Mozart, a sun that illuminated and warmed without leaving its lawful orbit, Beethoven was a comet that followed uncharted paths without submitting to a systematic world order, giving rise by its very appearance to unsanctioned ideas. Then in our day the composer has been fair game for the psychoanalysts, with their explanations of guilt, remorse, and hostility, but Beethoven is a difficult subject and the analyses are disconcertingly contradictory. Life's flame burned in Beethoven so vehemently, his mental travails were so intense and strenuous, that the passions of a decade in anyone else's life seem compressed more nearly into one year in his life. He was never calm or objective, for he reacted violently to everything, both embracing and hating life, and he could not remain indifferent toward anyone, nor forbear expressing his strong feelings. Those who knew and related to him as composer became, under the impact of his personality, his fervent partisans. His enemies defended themselves against his inescapable influence by excessive malignance, their every attack and every insult still a reaction to his prestige. He himself received homage as his due, and he was accustomed to mobilize nearly everyone in his retinue for his purposes. He was a republican who also liked to work for royalty; he believed in the brotherhood of all men while priding himself on his German qualities and showing the old German prejudice toward Italian music and musicians; he preached the highest moral standards but could be less than fair in business matters and grossly abusive when inconvenienced. Much has been made of his yearning for the realization of the aims of the French Revolution, but these were only half-understood ideals with a romantic tinge. The younger Schlegel once held up *Wilhelm Meister* as the German counterpart of the French Revolution. Indeed, in Germany there could not be a real revolution at the turn of the century, no one would even think of it. The men born to action either were silenced or became mere utopians. It is in this sense that we must look at the *Eroica,* and even at the Ninth Symphony, for with the Germans in general and Beethoven in particular, every energetic impulse turned inward.

We have still not answered, however, the question of why Beethoven occupies such an exceptional position in the history of music, why he became the composer who more than any other speaks to all humanity beyond the German borders, the international composer in the best sense of the word. Different nations or cultural circles see and value works of art differently, and some works greatly esteemed in their homeland are rejected elsewhere. It may sound paradoxical, but an artist is none the less universal for being highly individual, and this particular universal individual who is everyone's hero had two qualities that no other musician possessed to such a degree: power, and the desire for communication. "Was nennt ihr brave Kerls?" asks Goethe's Wieland, "Einen der mitteilt, was er hat," answers Hercules. Indeed, the desire for sharing, for communication, is as strong in Beethoven as the expression itself, but he makes excessive demands on the listener, creating a sense of urgency, always unwilling to make concessions and refusing to soften his attitude. His listeners everywhere have felt that he strives to break into the processes of life itself, to reveal himself — not only himself but also the soul of humanity — with such courage, with such élan and passion as has no one before or after him. The sketchbooks show the flaring up of passions, the struggle with ideas as they change their shapes like drifting clouds, the mixture of elation and pain that is creation, and the incompatibility of the finished work with the imagined one. And all this struggle is in his music; he communicates it with unparalleled directness, and the listener is overwhelmed by the nearly incredible will power, the unexampled integrity of a creative artist who always strives for absolutes.

Bettina Brentano, reporting to Goethe, remarked that in no crowned ruler had she seen such consciousness of power. Goethe, for his part, could not fathom the composer and was intimidated by a man who could deduce: "Power is the morality of outstanding men, and it is my morality too." The boast may at first glance seem cynical, but we must remember that the relationship between genius and ideas is tortuous. The meaning of this statement becomes much clearer when we join to it the desperate resolution of the Heiligenstadt Testament, when his faith in power and human strength met a terrible trial. The realization that his growing deafness would deprive him of the voices of the outside world brought Beethoven to the brink of suicide; but then his characteristic courage gained the upper hand. "It seemed to me impossible," he said, "to quit before I had produced all that I felt myself called on to accomplish." Beethoven now realized this affliction to be the supreme test, and he lifted his head and accepted the challenge: "I will grab Fate by the throat." Popular tradition has it that Beethoven died during a storm with raised fist. Apocryphal or not, fist and storm both could be characteristic symbols of this man throughout most of his life, for he wanted to be a free man of power, a world conqueror. But this power, as well as his limitless will, he directed not to the purposes that animated the once admired Napoleon; his ambition was to conquer the more distant spheres of the spirit.

As the years went by, Beethoven broke with social conventions and accepted the unavoidable consequences: banishment and solitariness. He now knew that he must count on no one, need reckon with no one, and from this point onward he became increasingly ruthless, even in his composing, in the end trampling the instruments and violating the singing voice. It is idle speculation to attribute this solely to his physical affliction; deafness only liberated elemental and atavistic penchants, that ancient Germanic spirit which treasures the idea and has never bothered much with the means. In the last period of his creative activity, when the world saw in him an eccentric recluse, and Vienna greeted Rossini as the savior of music, his deafness seems almost to have been welcome; the material nature of music was less binding on him, he could advance into the realm of visions. There is in this music of Beethoven's last period something that was totally strange to nineteenth-century musicians: the delight in abstraction. The romantics were happy only when they could dress up the abstract, but works like Beethoven's *Grosse Fuge* are the great undressing act in art; the garments are thrown away, and only the naked ideas remain.

When in 1849 Millet arrived at the artists' colony in Barbizon, his colleagues, following their custom, tried to classify him according to "school." They could not agree, whereupon Millet exclaimed: "Well, if you are at a loss, place me in my own school." Beethoven could have said the same, for he too seems impossible to place in anyone else's category, yet to the romantics the man who was born in the same year as Hölderlin and Hegel, and who died two years after Weber and one year before Schubert, was seen as the father and patron saint of Romanticism. The new movement could not defend itself against Beethoven's invincible art; all its instincts of self-preservation ceased when confronted with him, for there was everything in this music that the romantics desired and valued. *"Terribile!"* exclaimed the enervated Pope Leo X at the sight of Michelangelo's murals; it is this *terribilità* that the romantics saw in the *Sonata appassionata* or the Fifth Symphony. But they saw only the means in this music, not its essence, they saw how Beethoven demolished the boundaries but did not see that he demolished only to force the unbounded into severe and logical unity. The secret longing of the romantics was for the no longer attainable classical ideal of form; the entire nineteenth century was a vast sigh of nostalgia for Bach and Beethoven. But Romanticism would have sawed the limb from under itself if it had admitted that its indulging in classicistic dreams was only a game, the equator dreaming of the poles. Berlioz saw himself as Beethoven's direct descendant, Brahms believed that he followed in Beethoven's footsteps, even Wagner incessantly declared that Beethoven — had he lived longer! — would have taken the path he himself took. The confusion has continued into our century because many still mistakenly see in Beethoven emotion dominating the intellect; many see only the Titan, the hero, the fighter.

We tend to think that in Beethoven it is exclusively the heart that speaks to us, for we know about his deep interest in freedom and brotherly love, and our predecessors have already proclaimed him the liberator of music, or, as a book popular a generation ago was entitled, "The man who freed music." Even much earlier he was regarded as the first great composer who in his music withheld nothing of himself, and so was the first true romantic. And yet the voice of the intellect is never absent in Beethoven, even when he is rebellious, because he immediately proceeds to rebuild what he demolishes; he does not deny, he only contradicts. It was romantic anti-intellectualism in the arts that created the fashion of banishing from music logic of construction and procedure as inimical to poetry, thus creating the greatest impediment to true appreciation of Beethoven. This view created havoc as able composers denied their own healthy talents to follow the imagined Beethovenian code, and may have been the principal reason for the subsequent decline of symphony, quartet, and sonata. Yet we must also beware of considering Beethoven a belated product of the Enlightenment, for he represents the triumph of a new synthesis: the crowning of the "Classic era" in music as Dante crowned the Middle Ages.

The question arises, how far behind did Beethoven leave his heritage? How shall we measure his relationship to Haydn, Mozart, Cherubini, and others? He did not turn away from them; he abandoned nothing that was noble, nothing that he could not develop with historical logic. To be sure, this heritage was modified, it moved forward, and it rose in him to new heights.

We have already mentioned the surprising fact that this archclassic was still alive and creating when such full-blooded romantics as Weber and Byron were already dead. Together with such masters of the late classic era as Clementi and Cherubini, Beethoven lived in an age when early Romanticism was in full bloom. This late Classicism endeavored to absorb and use the moods of the new movement without, however, abandoning the principles of construction focused on a center. This almost paradoxical reconciliation of styles tempted many a composer of the era, but it led to half-solutions, Beethoven being the only one who knowingly and deliberately mastered this formidable problem. He took the large dimensions that Clementi and Cherubini introduced, eliminated what was inessential or watery, condensed and concentrated the texture, on the one hand, while giving a new meaning to the large forms, on the other, stretching them to their maximal tensile strength. The equilibrium often teeters on pinpoints and can be maintained only by overwhelming force, but it never sags. His solution is unique in the millennial history of Western music, and it is once more Beethoven's coercive power that so deeply affects the listener, who feels it even if he does not understand it. Surrounded by the stream of Romanticism, with all bonds and restrictions changing into relativism, Beethoven permits the new elements to pour in and be salvaged from dissolution. For we must remember — Goethe is our witness — that the late classics considered Romanticism an abuse of true art. It was the very fact that Beethoven's particular genius could admit so many romantic elements into an essentially classical concept that gave him his unique and revered position, the entire nineteenth century claiming him as its lawful progenitor. The romantics, however, since they could not really follow him, remade him in their own image, presenting his whole life as the manifestation of the *Sturm und Drang,* a movement with which he had little in common.

When the theorists of the romantic age explain the harmonic practices of their movement, they cite Beethoven's great contributions to their art. They did notice in Beethoven's music the distant excursions from the tonal center; what they did not understand was that this is a modulatory maximum which still permits the work to be held within classical unity. Nor could they fathom the rate and complexity of the harmonic motion, the relationship of key centers to themes — in a word, they did not notice the brakes which Beethoven applied ceaselessly but which they had already abandoned. Beethoven does experiment a great deal, but his power of synthesis, of comprehensive summing up, was so strong that even in his early works we see a constant effort to strengthen cohesion. Though he received superbly developed forms from his predecessors, he had to conquer every bit of the territory upon which he built his music, and did so with unparalleled will power. The classical perfection of the Viennese school, erroneously equated with formalism, does not signify merely faultless form; this is but the external expression of inner clarity. Man speaks in perfect sentences only if wholly conscious of self. What puzzled and misled the romantics was that within the barriers of this great self-control, Beethoven at times cannot carry his burden, and, as if from a burning house, runs wildly outside. But this does not change the fact that in him the spirit of the new age reconquers what in the first flush of excitement it had been ready to cast away: the disciplined métier and classical tradition.

Looking at the famous sketchbooks, one's first impression is that they are haphazard and sporadic; we also see that while Beethoven's imagination and inventiveness are inexhaustible, he often struggles with his material, notably with his themes, and there is a constant and ever-growing need to set things right, "order from disorder sprung." The approach is always analytical and synthetic, he raises questions and then answers them, often years later. He neither gives way to the impatience that characterizes the romantic, nor allows his expression to fail for want of craftsmanship. It seems as if the germ of every idea has been there in his soul from the beginning, growing slowly as Beethoven returns again and again, attempting to prune it down or extend it to the shape he desired. Indeed, the sketchbooks disclose the triumph of the *ars combinatoria* of old, or, as Lenz so engagingly says about the "Waldstein" Sonata: "In the development section Beethoven makes a nest from torn feathers."

These ideas and the problems of shaping they caused were purely musical and had little to do with the *Weltanschauung* music the romantics hung on Beethoven. Indeed, the romantics not only evinced a tendency to endow the notes with symbolical meanings, but turned this sincere and ardent lover of nature into a category: Beethoven, the father of romantic program music. Nature pictures have, of course, always attracted painters, poets, and musicians, but what did the word "Nature" signify? The painter's and poet's representation of nature was background or lyricism, for nature provides man's surroundings, perhaps his dream world. That nature is a great truth independent of man, of which man is only part but which makes possible and explains his life, was an altogether modern thought. Beethoven, who always found beauty in the simplest phenomena of nature, now discovers the greater truth, deriving from his discovery depth of feeling and a musical lesson whose motto, "More an expression of feeling than painting," he placed at the head of his Sixth Symphony. It was mainly this symphony that composers and writers from Berlioz onward used as the principal document to support their argument, but few stopped to ponder the significance of the motto.

Beethoven found in nature a liberating force; not in nature's individual manifestations, but in their effect on the beholder. Programmatic titles and superscriptions he did use in order to enhance a certain mood, but except for the few spots in the *Pastoral Symphony,* his so-called program music has little of the descriptive in it; as a rule he induces a mood not with experience described but with the musical association evoked. This is a purely poetic art, for programmatic interpretation can be justified only when the possibility for purely musical apprehension is not present, when music abandons its very own conditions of existence and depends on extramusical glosses. The mystery of poetic imagination defies scientific analysis, and it is easier to grasp Einstein's theory than to explain the essence of this supposed program music to one who is looking for pictorial verisimilitude in it. The deaf composer could not hear the sounds of nature, he could hear nothing but his own music. It is even immaterial in whose memory the funeral march in the *Eroica* was composed; it is not different from the one in the A-flat Sonata, which has no story attached to it. In the end, both are "absolute" music, conceived and executed along purely musical principles altogether free of extramusical, conceptual connotations. Even the overt and announced program can be very deceptive: the little concert of the birds in the *Pastoral Symphony* comes *after* the movement's musical construction is fully achieved. Beethoven, like most other great masters, created so many moods that any additional program is only a superfluous burden, as is well demonstrated in the sad aberrations with which Schering ended a distinguished career.

One would think that this universally admired and most performed composer, who gave a new heart and a new pulse to the world (to quote Tennyson's words about Shelley), is firmly ensconced on his throne, but there was no dearth of criticism even after Beethoven was beatified. The men of letters, with such notable exceptions as E. T. A. Hoffmann, seem to have been particularly at odds with him. Goethe never really understood Beethoven, remaining cool and reserved toward the composer whose power alarmed him. Grillparzer, who wrote a great deal about music with indifferent results, could not help recognizing Beethoven's greatness — we are in the 1830s and '40s — but he too was frightened, denouncing the composer as the destroyer of form and too much devoted to power. We must jump over a large literature devoted to the master to consider the curious ambivalence of attitudes toward Beethoven in more recent times.

Spengler, who saw in the culture of a democratic society nothing but a spiritless material civilization, considered Beethoven the most typical agent of the transition from the perfection of eighteenth-century Classicism to the dullness and decadence of the middle-class world. To Spengler, and others as well, the last sonatas and quartets seemed to sunder classic construction. Is this not dissolution, the beginning of the abandonment of form, is this not the beginning of decline, the autumn of Western music? These sonatas and quartets, and that vast choral symphony called a Mass, are they not the harbingers of the fall that begins as the zenith is reached? We must deny all of it. The freeing of the individual from convention is always infinitely baffling and ambiguous, but the miracle of Beethoven's music is that in its liberty and individuality it is also finitely organic and compelling. In its caprice there lives the passionate logic of dissection and synthesis, in its dissolubility there is no looseness, for despite all its arbitrariness and its many crises, this music reaches final harmony.

Today some young and impatient musicians find Beethoven objectionable; they are alienated by his security, by his imperious determination, they deride his majestic egotism, they resent his timelessness which still gives us lessons, but above all, they are dismayed by the eternal presence of the hero who cannot be undone. As each new generation comes along, it sees its own place in the sun as requiring the downfall of its predecessors and of their idols and heroes, so that rebirth can follow. The world needs rebels in order to be able to move and preserve its rhythm. Beethoven does represent the highest heroism precisely because the revolutionary character of his music is kept powerfully within bounds, the mind of the classically schooled craftsman is always in command, ordering and organizing. Bartók and Stravinsky were still full of admiration for Beethoven, but many of today's musicians are completely estranged from him; they misjudge Beethoven's heroism, its humanity, its intensity of expression and communication. It is this passion that gives Beethoven's music its heroic clangor, its rhetorical force.

In the end, the grandeur and the heroism are Beethoven himself, the creative man who cannot be fulfilled, and it is this lack of complete creative fulfillment that paradoxically shows the richness of his soul. For he realized that he would never find the old Haydn's absolute peace, only relative calms in the struggle. This is what eternally drove him, from masterpiece to masterpiece, toward the unattainable fulfillment, and this is what creates in his music the great tensions that enthrall people all over the world.

BEETHOVEN'S EARLY SKETCHES

By JOSEPH KERMAN

B EETHOVEN'S sketches are still known largely through the studies of Gustav Nottebohm, studies that are already a hundred years old, give or take a few years on either side. Nottebohm issued short monographs on two single sketchbooks, dating from 1801-1802 and 1803, and even shorter accounts of dozens of other sketchbooks and sketches, under the general title "Beethoveniana." That all this material was reprinted verbatim in 1924 and then again in 1970 — an *Erfolg* that has not been enjoyed by many of the monuments of nineteenth-century musicology — is a tribute both to the fascination of the sketches and to the solidity and intelligence of Nottebohm's work. But musicians who have tried to look into the subject more closely, and I believe they have amounted over the years to a considerable number, have found themselves up against a blank wall. Although the "Beethoveniana" are presented as a series of separate articles, one comes to the realization that Nottebohm was surveying all the sketch material available to him. Yet he plainly withheld much information, he printed for the most part curtailed transcriptions which happened to make his own particular points, and he indulged his famous laconic manner to the point of shunning exact manuscript references, among other things, with exasperating regularity. As a consequence it is extremely hard to check back on his work for purposes of amplification; and neither the later monographic literature nor the very variable published inventories of the main Beethoven archives has made up for the lack of a down-to-earth catalogue of existing Beethoven sketches. A catalogue can be a dry thing, but what Nottebohm produced — a sort of tantalizing anticatalogue — can be a very frustrating one.

Therefore the *Verzeichnis der Skizzen Beethovens* recently issued by the Beethovenhaus at Bonn under the editorship of Hans Schmidt is greatly to be welcomed.[1] This is a preliminary list, expressly presented as a work of compilation rather than of systematic research, and as such it

---

[1] *Beethoven-Jahrbuch*, VI, Jahrgang 1965/68 (1969), 7-128. In the present article, sketch sources are identified by S. numbers as assigned in the Schmidt *Verzeichnis*.

admittedly has some entries that are much less complete and accurate than others. But since Dr. Schmidt tells us that only about half of the thousands of surviving sketch pages have yet been studied, it is hard to know how else the Beethovenhaus could have proceeded, unless they determined to wait upon the investigation of the remainder — which may well take until the tercentennial, given the currently received schedule of musicological priorities. Fortunately this course has not been followed. Broader sketch studies, such as the present one, will need to go beyond the Schmidt *Verzeichnis,* but the *Verzeichnis* provides an invaluable starting point for investigations which up to now have seemed forbiddingly difficult. For example, it is now a fairly direct matter to identify all or almost all the surviving compositional materials for a single work. More comprehensive questions can also be broached, concerning Beethoven's compositional practice in general as manifested by the total preserved corpus of sketches. The present article addresses one such general question, the question of Beethoven's sketching procedures in his earliest years as a composer.[2]

I

Of the 394 entries in the Schmidt sketch list, approximately fifty refer to sketchbooks of various shapes and sizes. (The exact number of traceable sketchbooks remains to be determined. There are items described as "Skizzen" which may turn out to be extracts from known sketchbooks, or which may be brought into conjunction with other such items to reveal the torsos of unknown ones.) The other 350-odd sketch sources are single sheets or bifolia, small gatherings, snippets of sheets, entries on autographs, etc., and bound books and portfolios which bring together more or less arbitrary collections of papers. These we may call sketch miscellanies, to distinguish them from true sketchbooks in which

[2] This article is an outcome of work on an edition under the auspices of the British Museum and the Royal Musical Association: *Beethoven. Autograph Miscellany from c. 1786-99, B. Mus. Add. Ms. 29801, ff. 39-162 (the 'Kafka Sketchbook'),* 2 vols. (facsimile and transcription), ed. Joseph Kerman (London, 1970). A few of the paragraphs below are repeated from the introduction to this edition. I wish to thank the Keeper of Manuscripts at the British Museum for permission to print the transcriptions and a facsimile from the London source, and Dr. Hans Schmidt (Beethoven-Archiv, Bonn), Mr. Thomas T. Watkins (Columbia University Library), and Dr. Wilhelm Virneisel (Stiftung Preussischer Kulturbesitz, latterly at Tübingen) for providing me with access to and photocopies of other materials. I am indebted to Dr. Dagmar von Busch-Weise for assistance in reading many words and inscriptions in Beethoven's hand. Mr. Douglas Johnson, who is engaged in a study of the early Beethoven miscellany Berlin Aut. 28, has kindly allowed me to make prior use of his transcriptions and findings.

pages were actually used together. The earliest true sketchbooks that are known (or known about) are listed below, with an enumeration of the main works treated. Works that appear only briefly are enclosed in parenthesis, and those that appear in more than one book are indicated in boldface type. The dates are Nottebohm's.

Deutsche Staatsbibliothek, Berlin: Grasnick 1. 39 fols. Mid-1798 to 1799. (S. 45)

(Piano Sonata in C' minor, Opus 10, No. 1); Piano Concerto No. 2, Opus 19 (revision); Variations on "La stessa, la stessissima"; String Quartets in D, Opus 18, No. 3, and **in F, Opus 18, No. 1.**

Stiftung Preussischer Kulturbesitz, Dahlem: Grasnick 2. 42 fols. Mid-1799 to December, 1799. (S. 46)

Quartets in F, Opus 18, No. 1, in G, Opus 18, No. 2, and in A, Opus 18, No. 5; **Piano Sonata in B-flat, Opus 22;** Variations on "Ich denke dein" and on "Kind, willst du ruhig schlafen"; (Septet, Opus 20).

Stiftung Preussischer Kulturbesitz: Aut. 19e, fols. 75-94. ("Petter"; S. 29)

Piano Sonata in B-flat, Opus 22; Quartets in F, G, and B-flat, Opus 18, No. 6; **Violin Sonata in A minor, Opus 23;** (Horn Sonata, Opus 17; **Variations in F, Opus 34).**

Stiftung Preussischer Kulturbesitz: Landsberg 7. 93 fols. January to December, 1800. (S. 61)

(Quartet in F, Opus 18, No. 1); **Violin Sonatas in A minor, Opus 23,** and F, Opus 24; Piano Sonatas in A-flat, Opus 26, and E-flat, Opus 27, No. 1; *Prometheus;* **Symphony No. 2 in D; (Bagatelles, Opus 33).**

A dismembered sketchbook, identified by Wilhelm Virneisel (see *footnote 3*) (S. 33, S. 55, 113, 115, 163, 261, 262, 309, 314, 325, 370, 380, 394 *inter alia*)

Piano Sonatas in C-sharp minor, Opus 27, No. 2 ("Moonlight"), and D, Opus 28; String Quintet in C, Opus 29; **(Bagatelles, Opus 33;** ?Serenade in D, Opus 25).

Gesellschaft der Musikfreunde, Vienna: A 34. 96 fols. October, 1801, to May, 1802. ("Kessler"; S. 263)

Symphony No. 2; Violin Sonatas Opus 30, Nos. 1, 2, and 3; "Kreutzer" Sonata; **(Bagatelles, Opus 33);** Piano Sonatas in G and D minor, Opus 31, Nos. 1 and 2; **Variations in F, Opus 34, and** E♭ **("Eroica"), Opus 35;** "No, non turbati"; **"Tremate, empi."**

Glinka Museum, Moscow. 87 fols. April, 1802, to March, 1803. ("Wielhorsky"; S. 343)

Piano Sonata in E-flat, Opus 31, No. 3; **Variations Opus 34 and Opus 35;** *Christus am Oelberge;* "Kreutzer" Sonata; **("Tremate, empi");** Duet "Nei giorni tuoi felici"; **(Bagatelles, Opus 33).**

Although these early sketchbooks have been treated very well by Beethoven scholarship,[3] at least as compared with most others, many questions about their interrelations, their completeness, and the order of their pages have not yet been answered. Still, the extent of their coverage is impressive, even if we look no further than the summaries of their contents. With very few exceptions — the First Symphony, the String Quartet in C minor, Opus 18, No. 4 — all the important works are present, some of them (though not all) sketched at considerable length. And the large number of works treated in more than one book shows that the books were used shortly after one another, some of them surely in direct sequence, or at overlapping times. It is clear that from the five-year period 1798-1803 a very respectable proportion of Beethoven's sketches has been preserved.

Prior to mid-1798 no sketchbooks are known, but there exist upwards of two hundred loose sheets of sketches, dating back to Beethoven's days in Bonn, to 1790 or even earlier. The majority of these sheets have been assembled from early times in two large miscellanies, in which the distribution of material appears to be quite arbitrary, apart from the fact that it is all early (with minor exceptions). The larger miscellany, British Museum Additional Manuscript 29801, Part 2, is well known in the Beethoven literature thanks to a detailed article in *The Musical Times* of 1892 by J. S. Shedlock.[4] This is the "Kafka Sketchbook," so named (or

[3] Grasnick 1 and 2: Gustav Nottebohm, *Zweite Beethoveniana* (Leipzig, 1887), pp. 476-94, and Erna Szabo, "Ein Skizzenbuch Beethovens aus den Jahren 1798-99," (diss., Bonn, 1951). Petter: Wilhelm Virneisel, "Aus Beethovens Skizzenbüchern," *Colloquium Amicorum Joseph Schmidt-Görg zum 70. Geburtstag,* ed. Siegfried Kross and Hans Schmidt (Bonn, 1967), pp. 428-31. Landsberg 7: Karl Lothar Mikulicz, *Ein Notierungsbuch von Beethoven,* complete transcription (Leipzig, 1927). The dismembered sketchbook: Wilhelm Virneisel, "Aus Beethovens Skizzenbuch zum Streichquartett op. 29," *Zeitschrift für Musik,* CXIII (1952), 142-46. Kessler: Gustav Nottebohm, *Ein Skizzenbuch von Beethoven* (Leipzig, 1865). Wielhorsky: N. L. Fishman, *Kniga eskizov Beethovena za 1802-1803 gody,* 3 vols., complete facsim., transcription, commentary (Moscow, 1962). In the *Zeitschrift* article, Virneisel pointed out that the Viennese dealer Ignaz Sauer, who was one of the treasurers at the *Nachlass* auction in 1827, purchased a sketchbook for Opus 29, etc., as lot 17 and then dismantled it and dispersed it sheet by sheet. Sauer says as much in affadavits accompanying many of the sheets, over a dozen of which can still be located. Incidentally, Virneisel's discovery was anticipated by Edward Speyer, who had one of the sheets in his collection, S. 314. When he donated this to the Fitzwilliam Museum, Cambridge, in 1903, he sent the librarian a letter saying that he meant to try to track down other sheets from the sketchbook and write about them for *Die Musik.*

[4] J. S. Shedlock, "Beethoven's Sketch Books," *Musical Times,* XXXIII (1892), 331, 394, 461, 523, 589, 649 et seq. The detailed inventory in the British Museum catalogue (1909) was made with the assistance of this and other information from

misnamed) after the former owner, Johann Nepomuk Kafka (1819-
1886), a Viennese pianist and salon composer who was a collector and
something of an amateur dealer in autographs. By rights Kafka does not
deserve to have his name attached to the manuscript, which he owned
along with others for but a few years, obtaining it from Artaria and Co.
in Vienna after 1870 and selling it to the British Museum in 1875.[5]
Beethoven's old publisher Domenico Artaria must have bought up the
material at the auction of the *Nachlass* in 1827, an occasion which he
and his fellow publisher Tobias Haslinger largely manipulated.[6] In contents the London miscellany is very various, not to say confused. Besides
sketches, it includes one sheet in a foreign hand, copies by Beethoven of
music by Handel and Mozart, and several complete or fragmentary autographs of finished compositions — some of which were later used over
again for sketching; and then the whole collection was bound up with a
36-folio sketchbook for *Die Ruinen von Athen* (1811). Of the total of
124 early folios, some 113 may be counted as sketch sheets.

The other miscellany, Beethoven Autograph 28 of the Stiftung
Preussischer Kulturbesitz, now at Dahlem, West Berlin, is less well-
known, because its very nature was camouflaged by a singularly uninfor-
mative entry in Kalischer's inventory of Berlin Beethoven manuscripts.[7]
The Schmidt sketch list makes public for the first time a clear picture of
its contents. It was purchased by the former Königliche Bibliothek as
early as 1859, after the death of the prior owner Joseph Fischhof (1804-
1857), who was another Viennese pianist-collector. When and from
whom Fischhof obtained the collection is not known; but it is known that
in 1837 and again in 1848 he made presents of Beethoven autograph
sheets dating from the same period as his miscellany,[8] which suggests that

---

Shedlock. Schmidt follows the British Museum catalogue, with some additions (S.
185). A fuller inventory appears in my edition (see note 2, above).

[5] This is discussed in the introduction to *Beethoven. Autograph Miscellany from
c. 1786-99* (see note 2, above).

[6] See Georg Kinsky, "Zur Versteigerung von Beethovens musikalischem Nachlass," *Neues Beethoven-Jahrbuch,* VI (1936), 66-86.

[7] S. 31; see Alfred Christlieb Kalischer, "Die Beethoven-Autographe der Königl.
Bibliothek zu Berlin," *Monatshefte für Musikgeschichte,* XXVIII (1896), 1. Nottebohm, of course, drew extensively on this manuscript for the *Beethoveniana* essays,
without ever once identifying it.

[8] He gave a sheet containing a second trio for the scherzo of the String Trio in
G, Opus 9, No. 1 (1797-98), to Clara Wieck in 1837 (see Arnold Schmitz, *Beethoven. Unbekannte Skizzen und Entwürfe, Veröffentlichungen des Beethovenhauses
in Bonn,* III [1924], p. 12) and the sketch sheet S. 110 (1796) to the pianist and

he owned it all this time and periodically separated sheets from it. There remain fifty-three sheets with early sketches (plus two later sheets, and one sheet devoted exclusively to counterpoint exercises done for Albrechtsberger).

Half of the sketched works that have been identified are also found sketched in London, and indeed certain pages are demonstrably contiguous between the two collections: music beginning on folio 48^v of the Berlin miscellany continues directly on folio 141^v of the London, and music beginning on London folio 117^r continues directly on Berlin folio 20^r. Evidently the two miscellanies once belonged together as a single large portfolio.

More than two dozen loose sheets from the early period may be identified, scattered among libraries and private collections from Moscow to Providence, Rhode Island.[9] For some of these, too, there are indications that they once figured in the large portfolio. A few were previously in the possession of Fischhof or Kafka; others — large Bonn sheets — have been water-damaged at the sides like similar miscellany sheets; and besides many parallels in physical appearance and general contents, some sheets have very close concordances with music in the miscellanies.[10]

The music sketched in these sources, considered all together, is distributed over Beethoven's early output in a rather surprisingly even way. This holds true at least for the Vienna sheets, dating from late 1792 to mid-1798; with the even earlier Bonn sheets, the surprising thing is that

---

future publisher Henry Litolff in 1848 (see B. Szabolcsi, "Ein Skizzenblatt Beethovens aus den Jahren 1796/97," *Zeitschrift für Musikwissenschaft*, XVII [1935], 545).

[9] S. 3, 51, 74, 88, 91, 95, 109, 110, 172, 181, 193, 214, 223, 231, 235, 241, 259, 260, 264, 291, 292, 294, 295, 296, 297, 299, 306, 329, 344, 366, 367, 375, 392, and surely others among the unspecified items in the Schmidt *Verzeichnis*.

[10] For Fischhof's two presents see note 8, above. He also owned Paris Conservatoire 61, an early autograph sheet (1795) similar to others in the London miscellany. Kafka owned S. 88 (ca. 1793-95) and the autographs of the Bagatelle in C minor, WoO 52 (1797), and *Zärtliche Liebe*, WoO 123 (1797). Water damage was suffered by S. 91 and 291 — cf. London fols. 96, 125, 129 and Berlin fols. 1, 2, 10, 15, 18, 19 — and by the autograph of the Bonn song *An Laura*, WoO 112, which was reproduced in facsimile in Ludwig Schiedermair, *Der junge Beethoven* (Bonn, 1925; 3rd ed., 1951), opp. p. 272, before being destroyed by fire. Some concordances: (1) S. 296: Schmidt's "Sequenzen (F-Dur) für Klavier" and "Vierstimmiger Chorsatz (B-Dur) mit Klavier" also appear in London fol. 141, and in London fol. 100 and Berlin fol. 1, respectively; (2) S. 91: a distinctive referral mark relates this sheet to London fol. 130; (3) S. 260: music continues from London fol. 161^v; (4) S. 264: an imitative fragment in A major recurs in London fol. 51 (5) S. 375 (facsimile in *Svensk Tidskrift f. Musikforskning*, III [1921], 85): sketches for Opus 14, No. 1, are almost identical to some in London fols. 121-22.

any survive at all (but around twenty have indeed been preserved; we shall return to them presently). The Vienna sheets contain sketches for most of the works that Beethoven deemed important enough to publish with opus numbers. Of the twenty-five separate pieces that make up the works from Opus 1 to Opus 16, only three are missing, the String Trio, Opus 3, the Violin Sonata in D, Opus 12, No. 1, and the Piano Sonata in G, Opus 14, No. 2.[11] (Does some of this music stem from Bonn?) The other early Vienna compositions — a ragtag assortment which is not easy to tally — are also well represented. However, there is a marked difference in sketch density, by comparison with the actual sketchbooks. Some of the works are "covered" by only a few sketches, and none is sketched as fully as, for example, the String Quartet in D, Opus 18, No. 3, for which eighteen sheets of sketches appear at the very beginning of the Grasnick 1 sketchbook. A maximum of seven is found for any earlier known work.[12] The total number of preserved sheets from the five-year period 1793-98 is less than half the number contained in the sketchbooks of the next five-year period, 1798-1803.

Nevertheless, after making all due allowances, we can at the very least affirm that Beethoven's early sketches and sketchbooks have not been preserved in a notably haphazard way. We may therefore be en- titled to take this material as evidence of changing compositional pro- cedures during the years in question. The following picture emerges. Even in Bonn, Beethoven sketched, and he appears to have thought highly enough of his sketch sheets to bring some of them along with him when he moved to Vienna, in November, 1792. In Vienna he continued to work on loose sheets and bifolia, and he began to keep these papers more systematically. Then in 1798 he started using sketchbooks rather than (or possibly in addition to) loose sheets; among other advantages accruing to bound books, they would have been easier to keep and easier to consult. The older material was swept into a large portfolio, which Beethoven stopped adding to after 1798, but which he occasion- ally consulted over the years, and occasionally marked,[13] and which re-

---

[11] Not all the sketches for Opera 1-16 are identified in the Schmidt *Verzeichnis.* Sketches for Opus 5, Nos. 1 and 2, Opus 6, Opus 8, and Opus 10, No. 2, appear in London, fol. 83, 119, and 142; 83 and 119; 110; 103; and 101 respectively. Sketches for Opus 1, No. 1, Opus 2, Nos. 2 and 3, and Opus 5, Nos. 1 and 2, appear in Berlin, fols. 38, 25, 21, 13, and 13, respectively. Sketches for the three trios Opus 9 appear in S. 367.

[12] But (exceptionally) there are at least thirteen sheets with sketches for the un- finished Symphony in C of 1795-96 (see note 22, below).

[13] On two sheets in the London miscellany bearing song sketches, fols. 51 and 100, Beethoven tried to identify the poems by means of inscriptions penciled in a

mained to be auctioned off in his estate. Much of this material is still found together in the London and Berlin miscellanies.

The Grasnick 1 sketchbook, of 1798-99, seems to have been the first; the evidence does not support the alternative proposition that earlier sketchbooks existed and were then lost. For if sketchbooks were lost, either this happened by accident or Beethoven destroyed them. The first possibility is unlikely — at least, it is unlikely that many have been lost — in view of the remarkably full array of sketchbooks that suddenly appears in 1798-1803. That Beethoven had been using sketchbooks all along and then suddenly started saving them is also unlikely, for if he saved loose sheets with some care in the years before 1798, as we have seen, it is hard to imagine him throwing away sketchbooks at the same time. A further piece of negative evidence can be read in the sketch situation for the Piano Sonata in D, Opus 10, No. 3, which was one of the last pieces written before the 1798 sketchbook. Sketches for the sonata are to be found on seven sheets of four different types of paper,[14] which shows that they were not written in a single uniform book. Generally speaking, analysis of the make-up of the London and Berlin miscellanies fails to support any hypothesis that they include the torsos of actual sketchbooks.

The use of sketchbooks instead of loose sheets enabled Beethoven to sketch more systematically and more extensively. He was gradually becoming more serious and more self-conscious about composition, and at some point this had to force a change in his composing routine. That the change apparently took place in connection with the string quartets Opus 18 suggests that these works held a particular importance for Beethoven's career, a fact that is already rather clear from other signs. They are discussed in my recent study *The Beethoven Quartets*.[15] To summarize briefly: the string quartet was the first genre, excepting piano music for his own use, in which Beethoven really met Haydn and Mozart on their own ground. His circumspection about this meeting is evidenced earlier by his refusal of a generous commission for quartets — to the

---

large, manifestly later handwriting. Furthermore, fol. 62, an autograph of *Der freie Mann*, WoO 117, is numbered "No 4," referring to the position we know the song was to have occupied in a set that Beethoven planned, but failed, to publish in 1804 (see Kinsky-Halm, p. 122).

[14] London fol. 102 (12-staff paper: watermark three crescent moons), fols. 156-57 (12-staff: central fleur de lys), Berlin fols. 44-45 (16-staff: three crescent moons and eagle over CFA), fol. 30 (16-staff: REAL).

[15] Joseph Kerman, *The Beethoven Quartets* (New York and London, 1967), pp. 7-12, 54-55, 82-86.

surprise of his friend Wegeler — and later by his careful retouching of
the F major Quartet even after having it professionally copied and dis-
patched as a gift to another friend, Amenda. Early in the project, several of the movements evolved into more impressive pieces than any
the young composer had yet achieved: the first and second movements of
the F major Quartet, perhaps also the finale of the D major. I have also
suggested that a little later, as Beethoven doggedly pursued his plan to
produce six pieces, he experienced what was perhaps the first — and
surely not the last — of those periods of uncertainty and crisis during
which he threw received ideas about composition in doubt. Incidentally,
this would have occurred at about the time he first noticed his deafness.
Among the signs of uncertainty are the close modeling on Mozart in the
A major Quartet; the presumptive borrowing of older materials in the
C minor; prevarication about the form of the adagio in the G major;
and in the A major and B-flat major, a radical revision of the accepted
weight of the various movements within a cyclic work, resulting in "ex-
perimental" movements such as *La Malinconia* and its associated dance-
finale. Doubtless this whole matter could be further illuminated by a
study of the early sketchbooks.

II

But let us return instead to the even earlier sketch sheets. Perhaps the
first thing that emerges from an examination of any considerable number
of them is a paradox: a high proportion of their contents is not devoted
to sketches at all. For while the early sheets include sketches for known
works, and notations which give every indication of being sketches for
unknown works, they also include notations which give no such immediate indication. These notations are of several kinds, and their function is far from clear. One's first instinct is to regard them all as sketches,
but on further study it becomes apparent that they should, in fact, be
sharply distinguished from sketches proper.

The most characteristic of the various kinds is the small fragment
consisting of a few bars in piano score. Some examples, taken from the
London miscellany, are given in Ex. 1. Whereas in general sketches are
written roughly and hastily on one line, with many elisions and omissions, these fragments in piano score are often surprisingly neat and
complete — down to the clefs, key and time signatures, even sometimes
tempo indications and dynamics. In contrast to sketches, they are concerned not with linear or thematic development but with piano figura-

Joseph Kerman

Ex. 1

tion or texture; they may be founded on a single alternation of two harmonies, such as tonic and dominant, or on a rigid sequential pattern, diatonic or chromatic. Again in contrast to sketches, which for obvious reasons tend to come in groups, they almost invariably appear in isolation; they are not developed.[16] Sketches record an idea taking shape in the composer's mind, a fleeting moment in a process. But these notations appear to have been written down in relative tranquillity after they were fully formed in Beethoven's mind, or under his fingers. They record something at least temporarily fixed and final.

The function of these notations in piano score is not clear, as has already been said. Many of them look as though they might be imported bodily into piano sonatas or variations; but in point of fact not a single one of them has been found to reach such a destination. They might have been designed as basic cells for piano exercises, either for the composer or his students — a function certainly fulfilled by another smaller category of notations which are provided with remarks about the technical problems addressed. (Nottebohm reprinted some examples of the latter category in the article "Clavierspiel" in *Zweite Beethoveniana,* pp. 356-63.) The notations of the main kind we are discussing may have been designed as memoranda for improvisations. It seems most likely, however, that they were rather "improvisations on paper," random ideas about figurative or modulatory patterns which seem to have come frequently to Beethoven's restless imagination. They may be admitted under the general rubric of compositional studies, but at best they can only be considered as studies in the abstract, to be distinguished from sketches in a concrete situation where a particular work was being composed.

The same must be said for another major category of notations, the minuets, trios, contredanses, *teutschen* or allemandes, and other little tunes that abound in the early sketch sources. Some are complete, some incomplete, some have accompaniments, some do not. Once again, the first instinct is to regard these as sketches for actual ballroom dances to be played at the Vienna Redoutensaal or for sonata minuets and rondos. But significantly few turn up in the expected places; and once again the suspicion grows that they must have been studies in the abstract, without any specific destination. Here, as with the notations in piano score, one has the impression that, when he was not sketching actual works in progress, Beethoven liked to keep his hand in, as it were, by jotting down whole sets of melodies and pianistic patterns.

---

[16] On a very few occasions they are copied exactly (or transposed into other keys!) from one sheet to another.

That young Beethoven worked in this way does not appear to have been pointed out specifically, though a number of such notations were published as early as 1924 in *Beethoven: Unbekannte Skizzen und Entwürfe,* by Arnold Schmitz. This very valuable study includes a facsimile and transcription of Beethovenhaus MS 114, a bifolium from ca. 1793-95 which was once owned by Kafka (S. 88). Sketches for the *Flohlied* from *Faust,* Opus 75, No. 3, appear on the inner pages, with all the remaining space filled with miscellaneous notations, nineteen in all. Although only a few look like actual sketches, Schmitz interpreted them all as "sketches [which] remained uncompleted projects," and he could therefore entertain the hope that one day they might be related to other sketches or even finished compositions. This hope is bound to be unfulfilled, both for the Bonn items and the several hundred similar ones in the London and Berlin miscellanies.

Incidentally, Nottebohm copied out a little allemande in A from this Bonn bifolium, and after his death Mandyczewski printed it from his copy in the 1888 supplement to the *Gesamtausgabe.* The piece should surely not be regarded as an actual "work" and awarded a regular Kinsky-Halm number (WoO 81); at all events, one could dig out many more such items from the early sketch sheets, as Nottebohm certainly knew. He copied this particular one, I imagine, mainly on account of its curious forecast of a passage written thirty years later in the Quartet in A minor, Opus 132 — though characteristically Nottebohm says nothing about this. (Neither does Schmitz.) The allemande draft provided material not only for the late quartet but also for one of Beethoven's ballroom dances, much earlier: WoO 13, No. 11.

It is natural to assume that the method of compositional study described here, namely, the recording of abstract melodic and figurative ideas, was more common early in Beethoven's career than later. Indeed there are only a few such notations — though there are some — in the first sketchbooks. Most of the Bonn sheets contain such notations, and so do many sheets from the earliest Vienna period, 1793-95. Appreciably fewer appear on the sheets dating from 1796 and 1797, the years of Beethoven's extensive concert tours and his somewhat mysterious, but reportedly serious, illness.

III

The sheets dating back to Bonn are especially intriguing. By Beethoven's later standards, they are almost unbelievably neat and legible;

they look less like working notes which happen to have been preserved than memorandum sheets designed for preservation. Many of the items are written in piano score, and may seem to promise glimpses of mysterious lost compositions. But the fact to keep firmly in mind is that by contrast with true sketches, none of them (or next to none) is repeated or developed. They much more likely represent notations of the kind described above — in great profusion.

However, the Bonn sheets do contain some sketches, sketches which fall into certain of the types known from later sources. One sheet, for example, has rapid drafts of dozens of contredanses and allemandes, all sixteen or eight measures long, written rapidly on one line with little correcting.[17] References to a coda and to some instruments indicate that they were planned for a ballet or dance set (or sets); the project was probably abandoned, although one piece was salvaged around 1800 for the Twelve Allemandes for Orchestra, WoO 13 — curiously, the single one that was sketched in piano score (No. 10, trio). Another page is filled with advanced sketches for the Variations on a Theme by Count Waldstein, for Piano, Four Hands (1792). There is a moderate amount of revising here; the theme itself is sketched twice, at times on four, two, or single staffs, which shows that Beethoven was not willing to buy a ready-made theme even from Waldstein. Variations 1-4 and 6 are drafted at approximately full length, mostly on one line, and a few shorter sketches occur, including a thirteen-measure study for the rather Schubertian "capriccio" after Variation 8. A third page shows preliminary planning for the Twenty-four Variations on "Venni Amore" by Righini, for Piano (1790). Figurative "cues," one to ten measures in length, are set down for ten separate variations, of which only two or three were ultimately used. Much the same technique is observed with later variation sketches,[18] except that in 1790 the ideas for variations are all written out in piano score, rather than on a single line. A set of sketches for the bass aria from Goethe's *Claudine von Villa Bella*, "Mit

[17] These sketches, and the others mentioned below in this paragraph, are found in the London miscellany fols. 124ʳ and 124ᵛ, 100ᵛ, 123ʳ, and 130ᵛ (transcribed in Kerman, *Beethoven. Autograph Miscellany*, II, 98-99, 87-88, 86, 90-91).

[18] See, for example, sketches for the Piano Variations in F, Op. 34, and the variations of the Sonata in A-flat, Opus 26, in the editions cited in note 3, above: Fishman, II, 19, and Mikulicz, p. 166. Working at the British Museum, I saw similar planning sketches for the variations Opus 66 (Add. 29801, fol. 71), WoO 44¹ (*ibid.*, fol. 73), WoO 75 (Add. 29997, fol. 8), and Opera 105-107 (*ibid.*, fol. 28, and Egerton 2327). See *Autograph Miscellany*, II, 66-67 and 83-84.

Mädeln sich vertragen" (ca. 1790-92), runs through about a dozen melodic segments of four to sixteen measures, showing occasional variants and corrections, and branching into piano score only when the orchestral part is treated along with the voice line.

It is interesting to see these types of sketching manifested so early. But it is also noteworthy that the examples are relatively few. Adding them all up, one would accumulate a much smaller total number of measures than is provided by miscellaneous notations of the kinds described above. In short, the Bonn sheets are only secondarily sketch sheets. Furthermore, they do not appear to provide any example of really long drafts, encompassing segments of the size of an entire sonata exposition or even an entire movement. The famous drafts of the *Eroica* first movement are of this type, which probably counts as Beethoven's most characteristic and interesting; Lewis Lockwood has recently suggested calling them "continuity drafts" — for continuity is their chief end, the shape or progress of the piece as a whole, in terms of phrases and sections and in terms of harmonic goals.[19] Melodic detail is often indicated roughly and incompletely. It may indeed be significant that the earliest known "continuity drafts" refer to the first major works that Beethoven prepared in Vienna under the shadow of Joseph Haydn, the piano trios Opus 1 and piano sonatas Opus 2, published in 1795 and 1796. Good-sized drafts for the F minor Sonata have been discussed by Nottebohm and Fishman,[20] and some of Nottebohm's sketch transcriptions for the G major Trio are excerpted from much longer items: for the allegro vivace and the presto of this trio, there exist three drafts of from 80 to 120 measures running from points in the development sections well into the recapitulations.[21] Even longer drafts are known for the Piano Concerto in B-flat, Opus 19, and the unfinished Symphony in C of 1795-96 which has been noticed

[19] See the recent study by Lewis Lockwood, "On Beethoven's Sketches and Autographs: Some Problems of Definition and Interpretation," *Acta musicologica,* XLII (1970), 42. The term "continuity draft" is due to Mr. Joshua Rifkin. Especially for the present discussion, I have profited from Lockwood's revealing analysis of the relation and overlapping functions of Beethoven sketches and autographs. For some analyses of continuity drafts (for the *Pastoral Symphony*), see Joseph Kerman, "Beethoven Sketchbooks at the British Museum," *Proceedings of the Royal Musical Association,* XCIII (1967), 85-94.

[20] *Zweite Beethoveniana,* pp. 564-67, and N. I. Fischman, "Beiträge zur Beethoveniana," *Beiträge zur Musikwissenschaft,* IX (1967), 317-20 and plate VII.

[21] London, fols. 69ʳ, 86ʳ, 116ᵛ (*Autograph Miscellany,* II, 1-3, 5). The sketches for this trio given by Nottebohm in *Zweite Beethoveniana,* pp. 21-25, are taken from Berlin, fol. 40ʳ, London fol. 69ʳ, Berlin fol. 49ʳ (two sketches), 40ᵛ, and 47ᵛ respectively.

several times in the Beethoven literature.[22] After 1795, in fact, "continuity drafts" are generally to be found in all sketch sources.

On the Bonn pages, the closest thing I have seen to a "continuity draft" is a thirty-seven-measure draft for the not uninteresting soprano aria "Fliesse, Wonnezähre, fliesse!" in the Cantata for the Elevation of Leopold II, composed October, 1790.[23] This is roughly written in piano score, though the lower staff is used only occasionally, and one measure is left completely blank. The passage seems to refer to the second (tonic) section of the aria, but apart from the ritornello theme it is still far from the final version — one cannot even be absolutely sure that all thirty-seven measures go together.

Had Beethoven not yet begun to think seriously about large-scale problems of continuity or construction? The evidence of the sketches is perhaps too spotty to affirm, but does not contradict, this likely hypothesis. For some long drafts do exist from the Bonn years, and these drafts differ considerably from "continuity drafts." The most interesting of them is a 112-measure "Sinfonia" in C minor which was first noticed by Nottebohm (who missed very little) and then printed in full by Fritz Stein in 1912, when he was hot in pursuit of the "Jena" Symphony.[24] Written swiftly but very neatly on two staffs, with next to no corrections, omissions, or irregularities of spacing, this draft completely fills its page and probably ran directly on to another lost one; overleaf, small one-line sketches refer to passages that are not present in the surviving section. The contrast between a draft of this description and the usual "continuity draft" is striking. Obviously the symphony draft was copied, not composed or developed on the spot. Yet it is not the final copy of a finished composition — not a symphony autograph — nor the piano reduction of one; it is quite unpianistic, consisting almost throughout of treble and bass lines only.

From Beethoven's early years, then, we have carefully worked-out,

[22] *Ibid.*, pp. 228-29; Erich Hertzmann, "The Newly Discovered Autograph of Beethoven's *Rondo a Capriccio*, Op. 129," *The Musical Quarterly*, XXXII (1946), 174-78; also Kerman, *Autograph Miscellany*, II, 166-74, etc.

[23] London, fol. 88ᵛ (*ibid.*, II, 89-90). There is a facsimile of this page in *Composers' Autographs [Musikerhandschriften]*, compiled by Georg Schünemann, tr. Ernst Roth (London, 1968), Vol. 1, ed. Walter Gerstenberg, plate 145, but the various editors did not identify the work sketched. For another facsimile of a characteristic Bonn sheet, see Stephan Ley, *Beethoven als Freund der Familie Wegeler-v. Breuning* (Bonn, 1927), opp. p. 128 (S. 329).

[24] London, fol. 70 (*Autograph Miscellany*, II, 175-76); *Zweite Beethoveniana*, p. 567; Fritz Stein, "Eine unbekannte Jugendsymphonie Beethovens?" *Sammelbände der internationalen Musikgesellschaft*, XIII (1912), 131-32.

carefully written drafts in a sort of preliminary or pre-autograph stage. Elsewhere in this issue Lockwood draws attention to manuscripts of another kind from later years, three-line drafts prepared as a step between advanced "continuity drafts" and actual autographs. The Sinfonia is a parallel and a precedent for these, but of course with a difference: in Bonn Beethoven copied out his intermediate drafts proudly like preliminary autographs, whereas later he dashed through them like expanded sketches. Other Bonn items seem to fall into the same class, even though they look rather different from the Sinfonia. One is the Adagio in D, for a piano concerto in A, which was transcribed in full from the London miscellany by Shedlock; the entire movement is mapped out, with some sections filled in in piano score and others "explained" by careful verbal inscriptions.[25] Among sketches of various kinds for the Variations on Righini's "Venni Amore" and on Mozart's "Se vuol ballare" there exist three variations for each set written out in piano score, complete or almost complete down to an ordinal number for the variations.[26] Some Bonn song drafts, too, are halfway or more to the autograph state.

These pieces may not all have been fully completed. They may have been student essays which Beethoven conscientiously pursued a good way without actually intending to finish at the time. (In Bonn, was a symphony really within his practical range of possibilities?) It is therefore not so surprising after all that he took his "sketch" sheets along with him from Bonn to Vienna. If these papers included not only brief studies for figuration patterns, modulatory schemes, minuet tunes, and so on, but also outlines of likely compositions which were deliberately left in an advanced sketch or preliminary autograph stage, of course they would have been useful to the young composer launching his career in the capital. Some of these drafts were in fact turned into finished compositions during the early Vienna years. We happen to be informed of two, the Variations for Violin and Piano on "Se vuol ballare" and the little Piano Sonata in C, WoO 51, thanks to Beethoven's bad conscience vis-à-vis Eleonore von Breuning, to whom they were dedicated. He writes to her in 1794 about the sonata: "I have a great deal to do, otherwise I would have copied out for you the sonata I promised you a long time ago. In my manuscript it is practically only a sketch and even Paraquin, who in other respects is so very clever, would have found it difficult to

[25] London, fol. 154 (*Autograph Miscellany*, II, 127-28); *Musical Times*, XXXIII (1892), 333-34.

[26] Righini: London, fol. 123ᵛ (*Autograph Miscellany*, II, 85-86); Mozart: S. 291.

Plate I

Beethoven's sketches for an unknown song in C, ca. 1793-95.
(London Miscellany, British Museum Add. 29801, part of folio 46ᵛ.)

copy." [27] From the correspondence a similar history has been inferred for the Mozart variations, and this can be confirmed by the sketches. A Bonn sheet, S. 291, contains sketches and drafts (mentioned above) which do not yet correspond with the final version, whereas an early Vienna sheet, Berlin folio 6ᵛ, contains a coda sketch which is almost identical.

Thayer had a favorite theory that when Beethoven came to Vienna in 1792 he brought a sizable portfolio of music which he dipped into and published — perhaps after some revision — during the next decade. The theory has received some setbacks over the years, and the process that Thayer postulated has always been hard to substantiate. We have at least drawn attention to another mechanism by which the process operated. Some early Vienna works might have been revised from fully completed, but lost, Bonn autographs. They might also have been written up from intermediate, semifinal Bonn drafts of the kind we have been discussing. It is less likely that they were worked up from shelved sketches. [28]

IV

To analyze Beethoven's early sketches in as thorough a way as they deserve would take us far beyond the limits of a single essay. This essay must not conclude, however, without at least a few examples. The first is put together from the sketches and drafts for the impressive Variations on "Venni Amore" by Righini, 1790 (Ex. 2). These sketches, among the earliest that have been discovered, exhibit a characteristic well known from later sources. Beethoven does not start with loose, free, improvisational ideas which are then molded into something more tightly organized. He starts with rigid and even mechanical ideas which are only later smoothed into something more imaginative and fluid. [29] To be sure,

[27] Emily Anderson, ed. and trans., *The Letters of Beethoven* (London, 1961), I, 13-14 (Letter 9).

[28] A footnote to this section suggests itself in reference to Beethoven's extraordinary devotion to his sketchbooks, which he kept and carried with him through all his endless changes of residence. It is sometimes said that the reason he kept them was in order to go back and pick up unused ideas. A number of cases have been pointed out in the literature when he actually did so, but they are really very few, given the great mass of preserved sketches. It seems to me quite understandable that he might have kept hoping to find promising material in his old papers, and understandable, too, that he would usually have been disappointed. Things were different in the early years, and Beethoven's later devotion to, and overestimation of, his used sketchbooks may perhaps be traced back to his success with the more practical Bonn sheets.

[29] These sketches were first identified by John V. Cockshoot, *The Fugue in Beethoven's Piano Music* (London, 1959), p. 146. Cockshoot printed a draft for Variation 7, which illustrates the same point as the others.

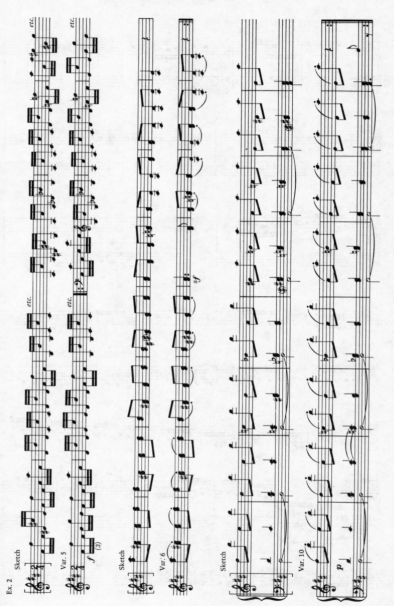

Ex. 3   *British Museum Additional MS 29801, fol. 116ᵛ*

scholars have speculated that the Righini Variations were thoroughly revised in 1802, the date of the earliest surviving edition. Might not the schematic, crude passages of the sketches have existed in the actual first edition of 1791 — no copy of which is known? Even if we imagined that Beethoven at twenty would have let them stand, the sketches would disabuse us, for in them Beethoven corrects the draft of Variation 6 to agree with the 1802 reading, and he is already seen to be altering the auxiliary-note figure of Variation 5.

Schematic sketches of the sort illustrated here — and there are many cruder examples — have often astonished students of Beethoven's work. Mighty oaks appear to have grown from such decidedly unmusical acorns. Perhaps it would be better to regard such sketches less as preliminary music than as notations for "precompositional assumptions" — less as seeds, that is to say, than as blueprints.

As an example of a longer draft, we may again select one of the earliest known, a draft for the first movement of the Piano Trio in G, Opus 1, No. 2, composed in 1794-95 (Ex. 3). Here large-scale planning is under way for the development section and much of the recapitulation (not shown). Once again, the draft is more mechanical than the final version, in which the opening circle-of-fifths sequence is held to four steps, rather than five as in the draft (or even six, if perhaps Beethoven has elided a step in E-flat. Notice that in both draft and final version, he escapes from the sequence by breaking the four-measure pattern.) Moreover, whereas the draft begins with a double counterpoint consisting of a new [30] cantus-firmus figure and a stiff little sequence on the main motif, the final development section begins with a triple counterpoint using the same cantus firmus but a different upper line, much more shapely and dynamic — derived from the original sequence, no doubt, but also paying respects to the thematic form of measures 2 and 32:

Ex. 4

---

[30] New to this movement — not new to Beethoven.

(This thematic form had not yet evolved at the time of the sketches, which include a different idea at measures 32-35 — the idea ultimately used at measures 55-59.) A few measures later the triple counterpoint evolves into this effective continuation, prolonging the last step of the main sequence:

Ex. 5

This idea is also introduced into the coda. Nottebohm, discovering sketches for the G major Trio among Beethoven's counterpoint exercises for Albrechtsberger in 1794-95, was able to contradict Ries's report that the trios Opus 1 had already been played before January, 1794.[31] We might well suppose that the above passage had profited from Albrechtsberger's instruction.

For the total plan of the development section, the following diagram may clarify the relation of the draft to the final version:

DRAFT: g ⌠ c ⌠ f ⌠ bb ⌠ ab Ab*   Dominant Harmony
        4 ⌡ 4 ⌡ 4 ⌡ 4 ⌡ 3 ‖:4:‖   1   "u.s.w."   4 ⌠ 4 4   12 "u. s. w." *recap.*
                                                      ⌡

TRIO: g ⌠ c ⌠ f ⌠ bb ab Bb*   Dominant Harmony
        4 ⌡ 4 ⌡ 4 ⌡ 15·····➤ ‖:4:‖ + 4 ⌠   c   ⌠ g   18 ·········➤ *recap.*
                                       ⌡ ‖:4:‖ + 4 ⌡ 4 + 4   8

The elongated *s* is used to denote a sequence. At the point marked with the asterisk, the draft shows a repeated four-measure phrase moving from I to V (in A-flat), articulated by a turn motif fragmented from the main theme. In the trio itself, this idea has grown and become the heart of the development section (though Beethoven thought better of the A-flat). Starting at the asterisk (measure 194), a twelve-measure passage is treated twice in free sequence, carrying an eight-measure tune which is more or less new to the piece — the second new idea in this development — and which is built harmonically on the same repeated four measures moving from I to V (Ex. 6).

[31] Gustav Nottebohm, *Beethoven's Studien* (Leipzig, 1873), pp. 202-3.

Ex. 6

But when Beethoven wrote the draft, either he had not yet thought of the tune, or else — what would be even more interesting — he had, and nevertheless considered it less important than the motif underpinning it. In the final version, the motif is handled in a more sophisticated way, coming on the weak rather than on the strong beats; the draft idea turns up verbatim only under the second four-measure phrase, in which the tune itself moves to the cello. Beethoven seems to have discovered that the motif on the strong beat sounds especially jolly underneath the cello. It also sounds like a witty afterthought; one would never guess that in fact it was the original driving force of the whole passage.

The first "u. s. w." in the draft (line 7) possibly elides further appearances of the repeated four-measure phrase. Thereafter the progress is much closer to the final version, with similar upward and downward scale passages (in double counterpoint, again). The augmentation idea of measures 244-50 is not yet present, but a sketch on another page makes it clear that the second "u. s. w." (line 12) stands for the upward chromatic run of measures 250-51 (cf. also measure 27). At this stage, then, the retransition was more clearly formed than the development section itself. Evidently Beethoven's first concern was to prepare the recapitulation — a special little problem in this piece, since the main theme begins off the tonic. He had never used such a theme before, though of course Haydn had done so, notably in G major compositions.

Plate I (p. 531) illustrates a kind of sketching that exists at the opposite pole from the long "continuity drafts." In question are the jottings at the right of the page; the beginnings of lines 2-4 are occupied by fragments of longer drafts. Beethoven is turning the first two phrases of a song this way and that, shuffling their rhythmic and melodic elements, recombining them with "oder" or cross or accent marks, trying them over and over again until they come out right. Detailed, close sketching of this kind is familiar from the later sketchbooks and very rare among the early sheets. But this example from ca. 1793-95 shows that the mental process, and even occasionally the written record of this process, goes back far in his career. Plate I, which is reproduced at very nearly the original size, also illustrates the characteristically small, neat hand used in these years for both music and words. The notes are seldom in doubt, and the inscription can be fairly easily made out as "da das lied nur allejahr einmal gemach[t] wird, so darf es schon etwas schwehr sein." [32] (The song is unknown — scarcely any words appear, beyond an occasional "Heil.") Certainly this page is a great deal easier to read than some of those horrifying facsimiles that are circulating of sketches from Beethoven's late years. But perhaps even *their* difficulties have been somewhat superstitiously exaggerated.

In conclusion, Plate I may serve to make a simple point and make it vividly. These sketches are really very strange. The work they record is work that anyone else would have done at the piano, not at the writing desk. Yet even at the height of his fame as a pianist, when deafness was an as yet unsuspected nightmare, Beethoven seems to have experienced a compulsion to get things down on paper — not only musical autographs, but also drafts of all kinds, sketches of all kinds, notions, memoranda, and the most picayune of compositional tinkerings. He had a veritable commitment to the graphic act, which by the way is a reassuring fact to those of us who try to understand his music at the desk, rather than at the piano. The simple point is that habits of writing run deep and form themselves very early in life, perhaps as far back as we are able to trace with any confidence. The same is true of Beethoven's other personality traits, and the same is true of the basic quality of his musical thought. For this reason, of course, the music and the documents of Beethoven's so-called formative period have attracted attention over the years, and continue to merit our interest.

[32] London, fol. 46^v (*Autograph Miscellany*, II, 157); see *Zweite Beethoveniana*, pp. 65-66.

A LITTLE-KNOWN
BEETHOVEN SKETCH IN MOSCOW

By BORIS SCHWARZ

SOVIET museums, libraries, and archives possess many Beethoven memorabilia — letters, musical manuscripts, and complete sketchbooks.[1] Beethoven's circle of admirers and patrons included members of the Russian aristocracy — Razumovsky, Galitzin, Browne, Wielhorsky, and even the imperial couple, Czar Alexander I and Czarina Elizabeth. It is a curious fact, however, that none of the letters and manuscripts sent by Beethoven to Russia has remained in Russian hands; these materials have been sold or given away and are now in Western collections. The present Soviet holdings of Beethoveniana consist mainly of materials acquired after the composer's death by Russian collectors and were either held in private libraries or presented to public institutions. The first to report such holdings was Vladimir Stasov, the distinguished scholar and librarian, in his catalogue of 1856, "Musical Autographs in the Imperial Public Library in St. Petersburg." After the 1917 Revolution all important private collections were nationalized, and their holdings were transferred to museums, libraries, and state archives. During the transitional years some materials were misplaced and reappeared years later, almost by accident. Thus, the so-called "Moscow" sketchbook was discovered in the early 1920s among property left behind by Russian émigrés; its previous owner is unknown. The so-called "Wielhorsky" sketchbook was acquired by Count Mikhail Wielhorsky (Vielgorsky) about 1853-56 for his private library and remained in the hands of his heirs until the early twentieth century. Its last known owner, M. A. Venevitinov (Wielhorsky's grandson), died in 1901, and the sketchbook disappeared from public eye, only to be rediscovered in 1939 in a Moscow archive. At present,

---

[1] For a complete listing, see Boris Schwarz, "Beethoveniana in Soviet Russia," *The Musical Quarterly,* XLVII (1961), 4-21.

both sketchbooks are in the Glinka Museum in Moscow.[2] It is entirely possible that further searches in Russian archives (particularly those of the former imperial court) might yield additional Beethoven materials.

As early as 1803, Beethoven established contact with the czarist court when he dedicated his violin sonatas Opus 30 to Czar Alexander I; the dedication copy (presumably sent to St. Petersburg) has not been found. Buried in the czarist archives may also be the musical manuscripts sent by Beethoven in 1805 to Maria Feodorovna, the widow of Czar Paul I. Missing is the dedication copy of the polonaise Opus 89 which Beethoven presented in person to Czarina Elizabeth in 1815 during her visit to Vienna. On this occasion Beethoven received not only a monetary gift for the polonaise, but also a belated remuneration for the violin sonatas Opus 30 that had remained unrewarded.

Among other missing items that might be located in Russia is Beethoven's letter to the St. Petersburg Philharmonic Society, dated June 21, 1823, offering the *Missa Solemnis* for subscription.[3] Similarly unavailable is Prince Galitzin's subscription copy of this work (written by a copyist under the composer's supervision) which he presented to the Philharmonic Society in connection with the historic St. Petersburg première of the *Missa Solemnis* on March 26/April 7, 1824. Prince Galitzin was the driving force behind that memorable performance.[4]

A generous gesture of Galitzin's son, Prince Yuri Galitzin, deprived Russia of the handwritten copies of the string quartets Opus 130 and Opus 132, dedicated by Beethoven to the older Galitzin. After hearing the Joachim Quartet give a superb performance of Opus 132 in London in 1862, the younger Galitzin presented the handwritten copies of both quartets to Joseph Joachim. The gift was accompanied by an admiring letter. Joachim, in turn, presented the manuscripts to the Beethovenhaus in Bonn in 1889. We may add that these were not Beethoven's autographs but copies of the parts (not score) made by nephew Karl under the composer's supervision.[5] It is not known what happened to the dedi-

---

[2] The "Moscow" sketchbook was published in facsimile in *Muzykalnoye Obrazovanie,* Moscow, 1927, Nos. 1/2, with comments by M. Ivanov-Boretzky; the "Wielhorsky" sketchbook was published under the title *Kniga eskizov Beethovena za 1802-1803 gody* (Moscow, 1962) in facsimile and transcription by Nathan L. Fishman.

[3] E. Kastner, ed., *Beethovens Sämtliche Briefe,* No.1112 (Leipzig, ca. 1910). Not included in the translated collection of Emily Anderson.

[4] See Boris Schwarz, "More Beethoveniana in Soviet Russia," *The Musical Quarterly,* XLIX (1963), 147-49.

[5] Johannes Joachim und Andreas Moser, eds., *Briefe von und an Joseph Joachim* (Berlin, 1912), II, 186. The editors were in the mistaken belief that Joachim had been presented with Beethoven's original manuscripts.

cation copy of Opus 127, the first of the three "Galitzin" Quartets, which Beethoven sent to the prince in March, 1825. Of Beethoven's letters to the older Galitzin, two found their way into the collection of the Polish pianist Maria Szymanowska (1789-1831), who was a close friend of the Galitzin family; they are now in Paris in the Musée Adam Mickiewicz.

At one time, the (now famous) first manuscript version of the string quartet Opus 18, No. 1, was within Russia's borders. Beethoven gave the manuscript as a farewell present to his friend Karl Amenda who had to return to his native Courland (Latvia) in 1799. But on July 1, 1801, the composer wrote to Amenda, "Be sure not to hand on to anybody your quartet, in which I have made some drastic alterations. . . ." [6] Amenda kept his friend's trust: the autograph remained in the possession of the Amenda family until the early twentieth century; it was sold in Berlin in 1913, and is now in the Beethovenhaus in Bonn.

Despite these "losses," the Soviet holdings of Beethoveniana are quite impressive, and Russian musicologists continue to explore them with great thoroughness. Among the materials in the Glinka Museum is a single oblong sheet in Beethoven's hand: on the recto page is a sketch for the first movement of his Piano Sonata in F minor, Opus 2, No. 1 (with the name "Beethoven" penciled in the upper left corner by an unknown hand); the reverse side contains a number of disconnected miscellaneous sketches and jottings. [7]

The Moscow sketch for the sonata Opus 2, No. 1, is of particular interest. Although it had been in Russian hands since the nineteenth century (it once belonged to the Museum Nikolai Rubinstein as can be seen by the rubber stamp in the lower right corner of the verso page), [8] the sketch escaped the attention of scholars until 1961, when it was made public in Moscow. [9] Prior to that, the only known sketch for the sonata Opus 2, No. 1, was a rather rudimentary fragment discussed by Notte-bohm. [10] The Moscow sketch shows the movement at a far more ad-

[6] Emily Anderson, ed. and trans., *The Letters of Beethoven* (London, 1961), I, 65 (Letter 53).

[7] See Plates I and II. The facsimiles are a gift to the author by the Glinka Museum which is hereby acknowledged with thanks.

[8] See Plate II. The Rubinstein Museum was absorbed by the Glinka Museum in 1943.

[9] In the journal *Sovietskaya Muzyka*, 1961, No. 8, pp. 67-71, with comments by N. L. Fishman. Translated in *Beiträge zur Musikwissenschaft* (East Berlin), 1967, Nos. 3/4, pp. 317-20.

[10] Gustav Nottebohm, *Zweite Beethoveniana* (Leipzig, 1887), p. 564-67.

vanced stage, revealing the creative process with unusual clarity. No precise dating of these sketches is possible. The Nottebohm sketch could date back to 1790, while Beethoven was still in Bonn, or — more probably — it was jotted down late in 1792 after he began his studies with Haydn in Vienna.[11] The Moscow sketch could be assigned to the year 1793. The sonata was completed by 1795 (handwritten copies circulated in March of that year), and Artaria published it in March, 1796, with a dedication to Haydn.

The Nottebohm sketch must be considered as an initial stage. It comprises the exposition of the first movement — forty-two measures of which Beethoven retained only fifteen. Nottebohm called this sketch a "curiosity," perhaps because it is so remote from the final version, yet contains the germs of several significant ideas. Sketched and retained, though with changes, were two themes: the opening subject (first eight measures) with its rocketlike rise, but as yet without upbeat, and the closing theme (last seven measures of the exposition). Discarded was the intervening material — an abortive second theme in A-flat major and some passages. However, the latter have an implied harmonic framework that is similar to the final version. This obscure relationship was noted by Nottebohm and confirmed by Paul Mies.[12] Nonetheless, the Nottebohm sketch is hardly more than a rudimentary outline.

In comparison, the Moscow sketch (Ex. 1) represents a decisive step toward the ultimate realization of the movement. It goes beyond the Nottebohm sketch by including not only the exposition but also the development and a few bars of the recapitulation. The handwriting is more careful than usual, particularly if compared to the almost illegible scrawls of the later years.

In the Moscow sketch, the exposition has all the characteristic components of the final version. The first theme has acquired an upbeat, a device favored by Beethoven.[13] In the ensuing bridge passage, the distribution of the thematic material between left and right is clearly defined. A most important addition is the subsidiary theme, derived from the first theme in a mirrorlike fashion. The subsequent passage has the characteristic "breathless" pulse by skipping the first and third beats, but the sequential pattern (measures 20-23) is as yet dry and shortwinded. These four measures are expanded to seven in the final version. The

[11] See J. G. Prod'homme, *Les Sonates pour piano de Beethoven* (Paris, 1938), pp. 36-38, where the Nottebohm sketch is reprinted.

[12] Paul Mies, *Beethoven's Sketches*, trans. D. Mackinnon (London, 1929), p. 139.

[13] *Ibid.*, pp. 5ff.

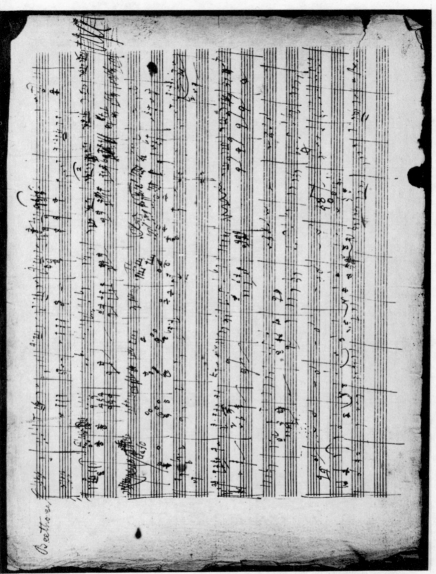

Plate I
Sketch for the Piano Sonata, Opus 2, No. 1, first movement.

Ex. 1
Beethoven

All editorial additions are in [ ].

*Composer's correction in left hand:

**The Roman numerals indicate the beginning bar of the systems of the Beethoven original.

*usw. *und so weiter* (German abbreviation for *etc.*)

descending scale passages that follow are outlined in the sketch, but the significant bass line is still missing; only a chordal support is indicated which is later discarded. Once the closing theme is reached, Beethoven returns to the Nottebohm sketch but does not recopy the harmonies. Thus, at this point (measures 34-39), the Moscow sketch appears barren unless one realizes that the chords were jotted down in the earlier (Nottebohm) manuscript.

What distinguishes the Moscow exposition from the final version is its laconic nature; in sketching the transitions, Beethoven is terse, almost abrupt. He rushes forward impatiently, avoiding any repetitions of motives. For the printed version, he refines and expands the transitions, creates breathing spells, reiterates motives for greater emphasis. He introduces several threefold repetitions, a favorite device of his earlier style. In later years, Beethoven dispenses with such niceties: one need only think of another piece in F minor, the *Quartetto serioso,* Opus 95, with its angular transitions. Because of its "contracted" nature, the exposition in the Moscow sketch has only thirty-nine measures compared to forty-eight in the printed version. Here are some examples of contractions.

Ex. 2

The same terseness is evident in the development section of the Moscow sketch. It opens with four measures instead of six in the final version, and the ensuing subsidiary theme is repeated only twice, not three times. As the development unfolds, the Moscow sketch is close to the final version in the distribution of the thematic material between right and left hand; the harmonic progressions, too, are similar. However, a significant change occurs toward the end of the development, at the point where Beethoven begins to prepare the recapitulation (starting with measure 81 of the printed version). The Moscow sketch (Ex. 1) at measure 67 begins a conventional eight-bar transition which will be discarded entirely. It is replaced by a twenty-bar transition full of tension and suspense. Because of this expansion, the development section of the printed version grew to fifty-two measures, compared to only thirty-six in the Moscow sketch.

Once the recapitulation is reached, the Moscow conception breaks off after indicating briefly the re-entry of the first theme. The purpose of the sketch was achieved: the overall design of the movement was established, the basic themes were set down in their logical sequence, the harmonic structure was outlined. Despite its imperfections, the Moscow sketch is so close to the ultimate realization of the movement that it can be considered the final stage prior to the fair copy. Unfortunately, a comparison between sketch and final autograph is impossible since the latter is lost, as are so many of Beethoven's early manuscripts. In the early years of his career, Beethoven's autographs of completed works were sent to the engraver to serve as *Stichvorlage;* once the proof sheets were corrected, the composer's autograph became expendable and was handled carelessly.

Whenever Beethoven's sketches can be related to completed compositions, they gain in significance because they reveal the evolution of his creative thought. In comparing a sketch with the final version, one finds the divergencies often more interesting than the similarities. However, it is not always possible to connect a sketch to a completed work. Beethoven's sketchbooks abound in scattered musical ideas — themes that were abandoned, fragments that never matured. Such examples can be found on the reverse side of the Moscow sheet. Here, an entire page is filled with musical themes and fragments, none of which seems to bear any relationship to a finished composition (see Plate II). Sometimes one is tempted to speculate; for example, the following jolly tune (perhaps inspired by the rondo of Haydn's Symphony No. 88) could have fitted well into Beethoven's piano trio Opus 1, No. 2.

Ex. 3

The page includes three extended themes in keys with four flats — one in F minor (6/8 time), the other two in A-flat major. Despite the key relationship with the sonata sketch on the other side, none of the themes belongs to Opus 2, No. 1. The three themes are shown in Ex. 4 (p. 47).

One wonders why Beethoven abandoned these rather attractive themes. I have not been able to relate them to any of his completed compositions, though a perceptive reader might correct me on this point. Some of Beethoven's themes have gone "underground" for decades, only to reappear at the most unexpected places. The early roots of the Ninth Symphony are well-known. Another example is the reappearance of the

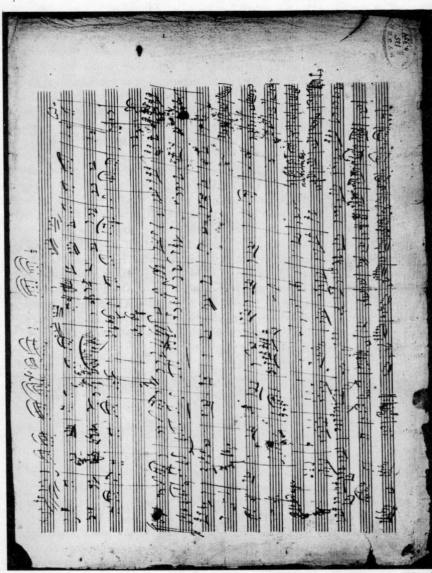

Plate II
Miscellaneous sketches by Beethoven.

Ex. 4a

Ex. 4b

[left hand line empty]

Ex. 4c

Adagio

Allemande in A major for Piano (ca. 1800, Kinsky-Halm WoO 81)
some twenty-five years later in the second movement of the string quartet Opus 132; the notes are virtually identical though the quartet version is more sophisticated by the shift in accentuation.

Ex. 5

WoO 81

Op. 132

The remaining jottings on the reverse side of the Moscow sketch sheet are of no particular interest — snatches of musical ideas that may have been meaningful to the composer at the time, but are of no consequence today. What is meaningful is the renewed realization of Beethoven's fanatical dedication to detail, his tireless quest for the perfect turn of a phrase, and his unerring intuition in always finding the best possible solution for a knotty problem. As Otto Jahn wrote in 1863, "Not infrequently the sketches convey the impression of uncertainty and hesitation. All the more we admire the truly inspired self-criticism: after everything is tested, only the best is retained with supreme assurance."[14]

[14] Otto Jahn, *Gesammelte Aufsätze über Musik* (Leipzig, 1866), p. 244.

THE 1803 VERSION OF BEETHOVEN'S
CHRISTUS AM OELBERGE

By ALAN TYSON

I

THE first performance of Beethoven's only oratorio, *Christus am Oelberge,* took place at the Theater an der Wien on April 5, 1803. The concert, which was devoted entirely to works by Beethoven and included first performances of the Second Symphony and Third Piano Concerto, as well as the First Symphony, was a financial success. Its reception was more mixed from the artistic point of view. Most of the comments were reserved for the oratorio, which marked Beethoven's first public appearance in Vienna as a dramatic vocal composer — a circumstance that had induced him to raise the prices of the seats. The *Freimüthige* reported that "the two symphonies and single passages in the oratorio were voted very beautiful, but the work in its entirety was too long, too artificial in structure, and inappropriate in expression, especially in the vocal parts. The text, by F. X. Huber, seemed to have been as carelessly written as the music." The *Zeitung für die Elegante Welt* was of the opinion that the music of *Christus* was on the whole good: "There are a few admirable passages; an air of the seraph with trombone accompaniment in particular makes an excellent effect." And although the critic of the *Allgemeine Musikalische Zeitung,* writing on the day after the concert, spoke of the "extraordinary approval" with which the oratorio was greeted, he was contradicted three months later by another correspondent: "In the interest of truth I am obliged to contradict a report in the *Musikalische Zeitung:* Beethoven's cantata did not please." Subsequent performances of the work in Vienna — one in the Augartensaal shortly before July 30 and another on August 4 — suggest that it had at any rate found its admirers.

Perhaps the most revealing indication that the composer, at least, had not been discouraged by the oratorio's reception comes from the last sentence of his letter to Breitkopf & Härtel of April 8, 1803 — three

49

days after the concert: "If you have a fine text for a cantata or any other vocal work, do let me see it." But that is not to say that he was altogether satisfied with the music; and in the course of the next year he revised it, as we learn from his letter to Breitkopf & Härtel of August 26, 1804:

The oratorio has not yet been published because I have added an entirely new chorus and have also made a few alterations, the reason being that I wrote the whole work in a few weeks and that naturally some passages did not altogether satisfy me later on. — That is why I have kept it back until now. These alterations were not made until after the date when my brother wrote to you about this work.[1]

In the years that followed we can detect two currents in Beethoven's attitude to his oratorio: a keen desire to have it published, and — after it had been accepted for publication — a somewhat apologetic attitude towards the merits of both words and music. Perhaps it was something of an embarrassment to him that, in contrast to the position with his instrumental works, no one in Vienna was interested in publishing a large choral score — and a religious one at that. The situation was even worse in the case of his first Mass (Opus 86), of which he thought highly. In Leipzig, too, Breitkopf & Härtel had told him, there was no demand for church works; and although in two letters of July, 1808, Beethoven defended the Mass and tried to make the offer of other works conditional on its acceptance, he was obliged in the end to make them a present of it in order to see it published. Only in 1809 did they finally agree to take the two works. Three further comments on the oratorio by Beethoven need to be examined in detail later, but may be quoted here:

1. To Breitkopf & Härtel, August 23, 1811, while revising the words:

I have just begun to revise the oratorio. . . . Here and there the text must remain in its original form. I know that the text is extremely bad. But once one has thought out a whole work which is based even on a bad text, it is difficult to prevent this whole from being destroyed if individual alterations are made here and there. And although it may only be the case of a single word to which sometimes great significance has been attached, well then, that word must stand. And he is a poor composer who is neither able nor anxious to extract as much good as possible even from an inferior text. And if he can't do this, alterations will certainly not improve the whole — I have accepted some alterations, because they really are improvements.

[1] In a letter of November 23, 1803, Caspar Carl Beethoven, who handled most of his brother's business matters at this period, had offered the oratorio to Breitkopf & Härtel for 1500 florins. Translations of Beethoven's letters are from Emily Anderson, ed., *The Letters of Beethoven,* 3 vols. (London, 1961).

2. To Breitkopf & Härtel, October 9, 1811, at the time that the oratorio was published:

> Arrange for the oratorio, and in general everything else, to be reviewed by whomever you like.... The only point to consider in connection with my oratorio is that it was my first work in that style and, moreover, an early work, and that it was written in a fortnight and during all kinds of disturbances and other unpleasant and distressing events in my life (my brother happened to be suffering from a mortal disease).... What is quite certain is that now I should compose an absolutely different oratorio from what I composed then.

3. To the Directors of the Gesellschaft der Musikfreunde, January 23, 1824, in criticizing the libretto of J. K. Bernard's *Der Sieg des Kreuzes,* which he had been asked to set:

> *Christus am Oelberge* was completed by myself and the *poet* in a fortnight. But the *poet* was musical and had already written several works to be set to music. And I could discuss our understanding with him at any moment.

It is clear, then, that the oratorio that was finally published by Breitkopf & Härtel in October, 1811, was somewhat different from the work performed in April, 1803: in the time that intervened both music and text had been changed. But how much, and in what ways, and to what end? In the present article I propose to see how far it is possible to reconstruct the version of the first performance, and to consider the subsequent changes in the light of Beethoven's deepening interest in dramatic vocal music, an interest which was to absorb him almost wholly for much of the next two years as he worked on his opera *Leonore*.

II

A necessary preliminary to a study such as the present one is a brief review of the primary sources. They are listed here in approximate chronological order; evidence in support of the suggested dates will generally be presented later.

1. (ca. March, 1803): Sketches for the original version, which received its first performance on April 5, 1803. Most of these are in the Wielhorsky sketchbook of 1802-1803, now in the Glinka Museum, Moscow. It has recently been reproduced in facsimile, together with a transcription and commentary by N. L. Fishman.[2] The sketches are

---

[2] N. L. Fishman, *Kniga eskizov Beethoven za 1802-1803 gody,* 3 vols. (Moscow, 1962). Cf. Boris Schwarz's extended review, *The Musical Quarterly,* XLIX (1963), 518.

to be found on most of the pages between 90 and 166, and also on
the last page (174). Other sketches, which will be discussed below,
are now located in the Beethovenhaus, Bonn (Bodmer Collection),
and in the Biblioteca Estense, Modena (Campori Collection). No
sketches have so far been traced of certain portions of the last number
of the oratorio.

2. (April, 1803): A set of parts said to have been used at the first performance (see Georg Kinsky and Hans Halm, *Das Werk Beethovens*
[Munich, 1955], p. 235); listed as No. 191 of the auction catalogue
to Beethoven's *Nachlass* and sold for 2 florins, 30 kreuzer. A set of
parts was returned to the composer by Breitkopf & Härtel (cf. the
firm's letter of June 21, 1805) together with the score of the work;
but this must have been the music of the revised (1804) form of the
oratorio. Such sets cannot now be traced and must be presumed lost.

3. (1803-1804 or possibly later): The autograph score, in the Staatsbibliothek, Berlin (Artaria 179), acquired as part of the Artaria Collection in 1901. For a general description see Kinsky-Halm, p. 235.
This score is in fact, as Kinsky-Halm has stated, "teils Autograph,
teils überprüfte und ergänzte Abschrift," only about a quarter of the
total number of pages being in Beethoven's hand. It will be argued
below that the parts of the work transcribed by the copyist reflect the
version performed in April, 1803, and that some (though not necessarily all) of the passages in autograph represent later revisions.

4. (1803-1811): A score in the hand of several copyists, with many
autograph corrections and minor revisions by Beethoven, now in the
British Museum, London (Egerton 2727). According to an inscription on a preliminary page, it was "purchased of Emanuel Nowotny
of Graz 9 Nov. 1889." [3] This score is not mentioned in Kinsky-Halm,
but is described, with only slight inaccuracies, in the British Museum's printed catalogue.[4] The final chorus is missing, the score ending
after VI: 259 with the words "attacca coro." Throughout most of the
work a second text has been added in red ink above or below the
original text (which corresponds with the text in the Berlin score),

---

[3] And Nowotny had bought it after the death of Julius Rietz (1812-1877), court
music director at Dresden. Presumably Rietz, who earlier had worked at Leipzig, acquired it from Breitkopf & Härtel. Cf. Pamela J. Willetts, *Beethoven and England* (London, 1970), p. 38.

[4] Augustus Hughes-Hughes, *Catalogue of Manuscript Music in the British Museum,* Vol. I, Sacred Vocal Music (London, 1906), p. 380.

and in a very few places a third line of words has been supplied. A number of marginalia in the score suggest, and comparison with the published version confirms, that it served as the *Stichvorlage* for the first edition (see sources 6 and 7, below); at that time it cannot yet have lost the final chorus.

5. (1804) : Sketches relating to a revision of 1804. These are to be found in the so-called *Eroica* sketchbook (Landsberg 6), and were first briefly described by Gustav Nottebohm in his monograph on the sketchbook.[5] They occur on pages 172-80, and appear to be confined to a passage in the middle, and another at the end, of the first aria, and to the second part of the second number, after the entry of the chorus at bar 122.

6. (1811) : The first edition of the full score, published as Opus 85 by Breitkopf & Härtel in October, 1811. As in the case of the first Mass, Opus 86, published by the same firm a year later, no orchestral or vocal parts were issued — a somewhat unusual omission at that date. A later issue of the score from the same plates had a slightly different title page, but the music was apparently unchanged. Details of both issues will be found in Kinsky-Halm, pp. 235-36. But unfortunately they have been confused: it is the earlier issue in which the words "ORATORIUM" and "PARTITUR" are in capital letters; in the later issue the words "IN MUSIK GESETZT" and "LEIPZIG" are in capitals.

7. (1811) : The first edition of the vocal score, likewise published by Breitkopf & Härtel in October 1811 (see Kinsky-Halm, p. 236).

No libretto appears to have survived which is not later than the published score.

III

Let us start our investigations by comparing the two main manuscript sources, the scores in Berlin and in London (sources 3 and 4, above), in their treatment of a particular passage, the aria of Jesus in the first number (I: 105-244).[6] In the Berlin score the majority of the

[5] *Ein Skizzenbuch von Beethoven aus dem Jahre 1803* (Leipzig, 1880), pp. 72-73. The sketchbook was formerly in the Preussische Staatsbibliothek (now Deutsche Staatsbibliothek), Berlin. It disappeared in 1945, but a microfilm has survived on which the present comments are based.

[6] In dividing the work into six numbers the *Gesamtausgabe* follows the first edition. Bar numberings are given here in accordance with the bar lines in the *Gesamtausgabe*. Some of the problems of the earlier part of the first number are discussed in Sections VI and X, below.

bars (99 out of 140) are in the hand of a copyist, here called Copyist A. Two substantial sections, however, amounting in all to forty-one bars, are in Beethoven's autograph: the whole of the end of the aria (I:219-44) and a passage in the middle of the aria where the same words are set (I:163-77). These two autograph passages are later insertions, since before and after the first passage, and before the second, the score contains deleted bars in the hand of Copyist A. The deleted bars — two before I:163, four after I:177, and six before I:219 — form no part of the oratorio in its published (1811) form and are evidently relics of an earlier version. Doubtless they owe their preservation to the fact that in each case the same page carries undeleted bars as well, which it would have been necessary to recopy if the page had been torn out. It is evident that other pages of the earlier version which lacked this safeguard have been lost.

In the London score there are no pages in Beethoven's autograph (though there are throughout numerous small revisions and corrections in his hand), and no deleted bars from a superseded version.[7] The aria we are now considering was transcribed by two copyists, here called Copyist B and Copyist C.[8] B's writing is very like that of Copyist A in the Berlin score — a point to be considered in a moment — but it is not in the least like that of Copyist C. Nor, apparently, was it intended to be: no effort, at any rate, was made to secure stylistic uniformity, and C even employed twelve-stave paper, whereas B used fourteen-stave paper. Two sections were copied by C (I:155-79 and I:216-44); and it is clear that they were copied at a later date than the parts copied by B, and that they were then inserted into the score to replace what had originally stood there. Occasionally the patchwork was clumsy; there are, for instance, one and a quarter blank sides after bar 169 (copied by C) before B's hand resumes at bar 170.

The relationship between the copyists in the aria can be shown more clearly in the table that follows at the top of the facing page. One can see that all the passages from this aria that are in autograph in Berlin appear in the London score in C's writing. The extra bars copied by C (155-62, 178-79, and 216-18) are explained easily enough: in incorpo-

---

[7] Except for one page of five bars after VI:119 which was not intended to be seen, as is explained in Section VI, below.

[8] Very close study indicates that the copyist here called B is in fact two copyists with almost identical hands, working together. B's part in the first number up to bar 136 is by B^1 (who habitually writes "cres" for crescendo); B^2 (who writes "cresc") starts at bar 137. B's parts in the second and third numbers are by B^1, and in the rest of the oratorio they are by B^2.

Berlin		London	
Copyist A	I: 105-162 ⎱ 2 deleted bars ⎰	Copyist B	I: 105-154
Autograph	I: 163-177	Copyist C	I: 155-179
Copyist A	4 deleted bars ⎱ I: 178-218 ⎬ 6 deleted bars ⎰	Copyist B	I: 180-215
Autograph	I: 219-244	Copyist C	I: 216-244

rating the revisions of the Berlin score into the London score, C's task was not merely to copy out the two autograph sections, but to eliminate all trace of any deleted bars by recopying the pages on which they occurred.

Slightly less, therefore, has survived of Copyist B's work in this aria than of Copyist A's. If one now compares the passages which they both copied (I: 105-54 and I: 180-215), one is immediately struck by the similarity in appearance of the pages in question. It is not merely that the two handwritings themselves are alike: there is the same spacing of notes, the same layout, the same abbreviations; and in each score the corresponding pages have exactly the same bars on them. Such small divergences as strike the eye are almost all due to changes and additions that were made by a later hand (often the composer's); since the London score became the *Stichvorlage,* it contains somewhat more alterations. There seems little doubt, in fact, that the two scores — or those parts at any rate which were written by Copyists A and B — were prepared at the same time by copyists well used to working together and to matching each other's style.[9]

The version which they copied was evidently not the final version of the oratorio. In the case of Copyist A we can see this, since it contained bars subsequently deleted; and in the case of Copyist B we can infer this, since Copyist C had to replace the pages on which the same deleted bars must have been found. Summarizing our conclusions so far (and confining them for the present to this single aria), we may say:

1. Two identical scores of the aria were prepared by Copyist A and Copyist B, doubtless working in collaboration. This was of an early, but apparently completed, version.

[9] I attempt to demonstrate elsewhere ("Notes on Five of Beethoven's Copyists," *Journal of the American Musicological Society,* XXIII [1970], Fall) that Copyist A was Wenzel Schlemmer (1760-1823), Beethoven's most reliable copyist. Presumably Copyist B was one — or, more accurately, two — of Schlemmer's assistants.

2. Two passages in the aria were subsequently rewritten — one in the
middle, one at the end. In the Berlin score, unwanted pages were
torn out, and bars were deleted on some pages that remained; for the
new version, the composer's autograph score was inserted. In the
London score, all the pages containing any part of the old version
were removed, and Copyist C supplied all the bars necessary to bring
this score into line with the revised Berlin score.

IV

Is it possible to assign approximate dates to the two versions? The
matter really turns on the dating of entries in two sketchbooks already
referred to. For sketches of the whole aria are in the Wielhorsky sketchbook; but it is precisely the two revised passages, in both of which the
words "Nimm den Leidenkelch von mir" occur, that are worked on near
the end of the *Eroica* sketchbook (Landsberg 6). Of the cadenza and of
the pathetic chromatic phrases that end the number there is scarcely a
trace in Wielhorsky. But these features are elaborated in Landsberg 6 —
and even in the Berlin score itself, where several bars are drafted and
then crossed out by Beethoven, and where a further sketch of the final
bars is scrawled on the blank lower staves under I:223-27.

That the main work of sketching for the oratorio is contained in the
Wielhorsky sketchbook cannot, I think, be doubted by anyone who has
studied it. As this portion of the sketchbook is examined in great detail
below, it will be enough at this stage to state that the preliminary and
tentative ideas for the separate numbers — the first things to be written
down — are worked on until in many instances they approximate their
final form. And since there seems no reason to doubt Beethoven's statements that the oratorio was written very rapidly in a matter of weeks,
this part of Wielhorsky must have been filled up by about March, 1803.[10]

[10] I cannot agree with Boris Schwarz (*op. cit.*, p. 523) that the sketches show
that "the oratorio must have been started in late summer or early fall of 1802, at
Heiligenstadt, and was continued through the crisis of the *Heiligenstadt Testament,*
dated October 6-10." But there is a story in Schindler suggesting that some sketching
for the work was done by Beethoven at Hetzendorf, in the summer of 1801 (A.
Schindler, *Biographie von Ludwig van Beethoven,* 3rd ed. [Münster, 1860], Part I, p. 90;
the date of "1800" in the first edition of the biography [Münster, 1840], p. 46, as
also given by Ries in F. G. Wegeler and Ferdinand Ries, *Biographische Notizen über
Ludwig van Beethoven* [Coblenz, 1838], p. 74, is obviously wrong and is linked with
other demonstrably false dates). Beethoven is said to have worked while sitting in a
natural saddle formed by a bifurcating oaktree in the grounds of the palace of
Schönbrunn. Sketches made under those conditions are likely to have been entered

Significantly enough, it includes sketches for the deleted bars in the Berlin score: staves 13 and 14 on page 96, for instance, contain a draft of the six deleted bars after I:218. The conclusion seems inescapable that the "first version" is the version of the first performance.[11] The date of the "revised version" must be inferred from the dates of the separate contents of the *Eroica* sketchbook: especially, perhaps, the work on two pieces for Schikaneder's opera *Vestas Feuer* on pages 96-120, a project subsequently abandoned, and the sketches for the first five numbers of *Leonore* on pages 146-71. The pages devoted to the revisions of the oratorio follow these last directly. The following dates are relevant here:

November 12, 1803   Georg August Griesinger to Breitkopf & Härtel: "At present he [Beethoven] is composing an opera by Schikaneder, but he told me himself that he is looking for reasonable [*vernünftige*] texts."[12]

November 23, 1803   Caspar Carl offers the oratorio (apparently unrevised: see above, p. 50) to Breitkopf & Härtel.

January 4, 1804   Griesinger to Breitkopf & Härtel: "Recently Beethoven has given Schikaneder his

---

in a portable or pocket sketchbook, not in a desk sketchbook (such as Wielhorsky), and to have been in pencil, not in ink; none has survived from this period.

[11] It is possible, indeed, that the main portions of the Berlin and London scores were copied out even before the first performance. The "air of the Seraph with trombone accompaniment" which the critic of the *Zeitung für die Elegante Welt* so much admired at the first performance can only have been the recitative of the third number, where in bars 7-13 the Seraph declaims Jehovah's words "Eh nicht erfüllet ist. . . ." In the Berlin score there is no sign of any trombones here (although Beethoven has added the indication "stark deklamirt und accentuirt" over the Seraph's words), and no provision has been made by A for trombone staves in the system at the beginning of the recitative. Exactly the same is true of the London score, written by B; but in III:7 Beethoven has written, in the empty staves of the first and second violins and viola, "trombone I," "trombone II," "trombone III"; and the trombone parts have been added, some (but not all) of the rests in these upper string parts being erased. All this suggests that the trombones here were a last-minute addition, as is implied also in Ries's account of how he was summoned to Beethoven at five in the morning on the day of the concert: "I found him in bed, writing on *single* sheets of paper. To my question what it was he answered: '*Trombones.*' In the actual performance the trombones played from these very sheets. — Had the copying of these parts been forgotten? Were they an afterthought? I was too young at the time to see anything of artistic interest in the incident; but probably the trombones were an afterthought." (Wegeler-Ries, *op. cit.*, p. 76.)

[12] Cf. Wilhelm Hitzig, "Aus den Briefen Griesingers an Breitkopf & Härtel entnommene Notizen über Beethoven," *Der Bär*, 1927, p. 28.

opera back because he feels that the text is too ungrateful." [13]

January 4, 1804   Beethoven to Rochlitz: "I have finally broken with Schikaneder. . . . Well, I have quickly had an old French libretto adapted [J. N. Bouilly's *Léonore ou l'amour conjugal*] and am now beginning to work on it."

March 27, 1804   Concert in Vienna by Sebastian Meyer which included Beethoven's Second Symphony and the oratorio.

August 26, 1804   Beethoven's letter to Breitkopf & Härtel, already quoted, describing alterations in the oratorio.

Thus it looks as though Beethoven continued to toy with Schikaneder's libretto till late in 1803, and did not begin to sketch *Leonore* till about the turn of the year. The sketches for the revision of *Christus am Oelberge* must accordingly be assigned to the early months of 1804. A performance of the oratorio in March, 1804, may well have provided Beethoven with the opportunity, or the impetus, to revise the work.

V

How far do these conclusions — drawn from an examination of only a part of the first number — stand up when applied to other parts of the oratorio? The second number appears at first to offer a bewildering series of puzzles; but it is in fact easier to find one's way — partly, no doubt, because no pages have been removed from the score. Most of the problems are confined to the latter part of the Seraph's aria. In the Berlin score the whole of an earlier version of the aria is preserved in the hand of Copyist A, and we can see that the original structure of the number was as follows:

II:1-23   Recitative: "Erzittre Erde" (here only twenty-one bars long)
II:24-49   Larghetto, 3/8: "Preist, preist," leading into —
II:50-197 (and nine bars later deleted) Allegro, common time: "O heil euch."

[13] *Ibid.,* p. 30.

The allegro itself is in the following form:

II:50-66	Orchestral ritornello
66-96	First vocal section, modulating from the tonic to the dominant
96-119	Second vocal section, passing through the dominant minor and ending in the mediant minor
120,121	Two orchestral bars modulating to the tonic and leading to —
122-138	Recapitulation of orchestral ritornello
138-166	Recapitulation of first vocal section, in the tonic
166-178	Approximate recapitulation of second vocal section, passing through the tonic minor, ending in the tonic major
178-197	(and nine bars later deleted) Coda

Thus the whole of the second number was given to the Seraph alone, and was scarcely more than two hundred bars long.

There is no difficulty, therefore, in identifying this as the place in the oratorio at which Beethoven, as he informed Breitkopf & Härtel in his letter of August 26, 1804, "added an entirely new chorus." Moreover, sketches for the additional and revised passages are in the *Eroica* sketchbook. It may be that Beethoven's original intention was simply to add the allegro molto, *alla breve* section (II:206 onwards), and that the difficulty of grafting this dramatic chorus onto a formal aria led him to revise the later sections of the aria as well. At any rate, the soprano in the revised version is accompanied by a chorus from the recapitulation onwards. To achieve this, Beethoven had to write some seventy-six bars of choral parts here; but he kept the Seraph's notes almost unchanged, and the orchestral parts entirely so. The only orchestral rewriting that was needed was at the very end of the aria, where a perfunctory cadential passage of nine bars was deleted (see Plates I and II) and eight somewhat more elevated ones were substituted, leading into the allegro molto (II:206).

All this can be seen in the Berlin score. The new coda to the aria and the whole of the allegro-molto section (II:198-205 and 206-97) are in Beethoven's autograph. And bound in at the very beginning of the volume are nine more autograph pages; these contain the five vocal parts (Seraph and four chorus parts) to the second half of the aria (II:122-97), and also some supplementary parts (corni, clarini, timpani) to the

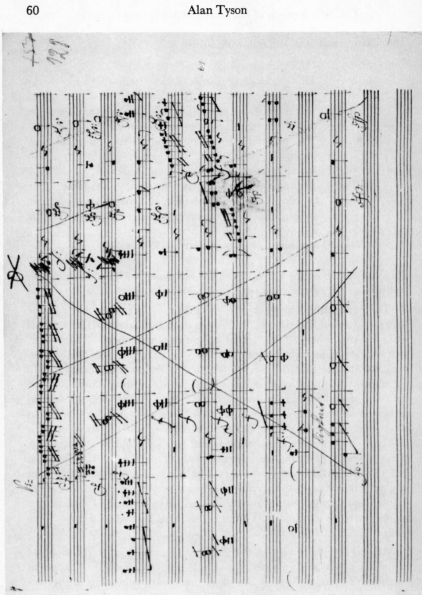

Plates I & II
From the Berlin score of *Christus am Oelberge* (Artaria 179). II: 197
and nine deleted measures of the 1803 version.

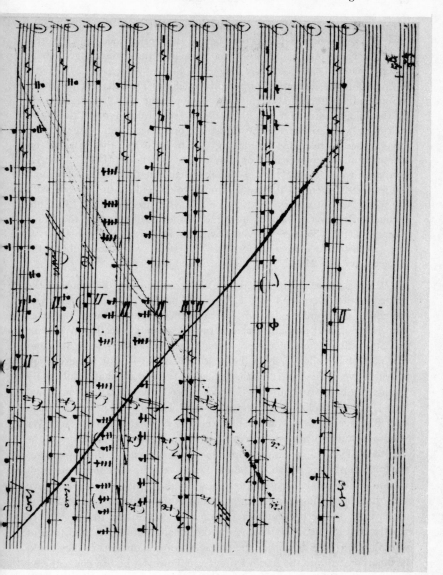

allegro-molto section (II:206-97) which could not be fitted onto Beethoven's sixteen-stave paper in the body of the work. Since the orchestral parts of the second half of the aria were to remain unchanged, there was no need to change any of the notes of Copyist A in II:122-97. Only at one point did Beethoven apparently vacillate. The aria begins with a seventeen-bar ritornello (II:50-66), the opening of which is repeated by the soloist; and later this ritornello is recapitulated (II:122-38) as well as its continuation by the soloist. At one stage Beethoven seems to have wished to telescope the design, and to have had the ritornello on its recapitulation represented only by its first two bars (II:122-23). Accordingly we find that II:124-38 are deleted in the Berlin score, and the Seraph is given, on the last quarter-note of II:123, the note d″ with the word "O"; it was evidently to be followed directly by II:139. Subsequently Beethoven changed his mind and decided to retain the whole passage; II:122-35 were provided with choral parts, and a bold wavy line (Beethoven's indication for "bleibt" [*stet*]) was added above the deleted bars II:124-38.

It will come as no surprise that in the London score the whole of the revised section is copied by C. C begins at bar II:122 and continues to the end of the number (II:297). Two further pages deal with the extra corni, clarini, and timpani parts for the allegro-molto section. With one exception all the rest of the second number (recitative, larghetto, and first part of the allegro) is in the hand of Copyist B. But the exception is instructive. After bar 18 of the recitative (copied till that point by B) a page has been stuck into the London score, in C's writing, containing bars II:19-23, and ending "Segue L'Aria." This page is obviously glued over B's page, of which only II:18 still shows. What is underneath? We need only turn to the Berlin score to find in A's writing, instead of the five bars II:19-23, a simpler three-bar ending. But on the lowest two staves of that score, which are blank, Beethoven has sketched in a rough version of the five-bar elaboration found in the London score. We have seen that, in revising parts of the aria of the first number and in adding a chorus to the second number, Beethoven went to the trouble first of working out the necessary changes in the *Eroica* sketchbook, and then of writing out a final version of the passages in question so that they could be incorporated into the Berlin score. Here, however, he has not bothered to bring the Berlin score up to date, and has contented himself with marginalia from which a scored-up version could subsequently be drafted and given to a copyist (see Plate III).

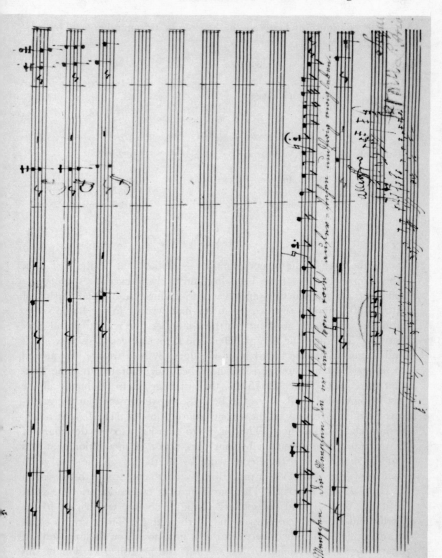

Plate III

From the Berlin score of *Christus am Oelberge* (Artaria 179). II:18 and
three measures of the 1803 version.

The relationships between the sources in this number can be tabulated as follows:

	Berlin		London
Copyist A	II:1-18	Copyist B	II:1-18
	3 bars corresponding to II:19-23	Copyist C	II:19-23
	II:24-197		
	9 deleted bars	Copyist B	II:24-121
Autograph	II:122-197, vocal parts only [14]	Copyist C	II:122-297
	II:198-297, full score		
	II:206-297, corni, clarini, timpani [14]		II:206-297 corni, clarini, timpani

VI

In the case of the second number — unlike that of the first aria, where some passages have been lost, probably forever — there is no difficulty in reconstructing, and even performing, the original version of April, 1803, since it is preserved in A's handwriting in the Berlin score. And the same holds good for the third number, the recitative and duet between Jesus and the Seraph. Here the later changes were very slight and involved only the final bars of the duet. By now we are accustomed to finding that the later revisions have been incorporated into the London score by C. Here III:75-83 (the last page) is in his hand, all the rest being copied by B. From the Berlin score we can see that the movement originally ended on the second quarter-note of III:79 with a fortissimo eighth-note chord. The più moto transition to the dominant of F, extending the movement by four bars, was a later addition that was crudely sketched into the Berlin score by Beethoven on the first violin staff only (See Plate IV), a procedure roughly comparable to the sketch of II:19-23 just discussed. The fourth number of the oratorio, the short recitative of Jesus and the soldiers' C major chorus, was copied in the Berlin and London scores by A and B, respectively. There are no significant musical differences between them, and no reason to suppose that, apart from some changes in the words,[15] the published version of this number differs from the version performed in April, 1803.

[14] Bound separately from the rest of the oratorio.

[15] The problem of the differences in the words here and elsewhere is discussed below (Section XI).

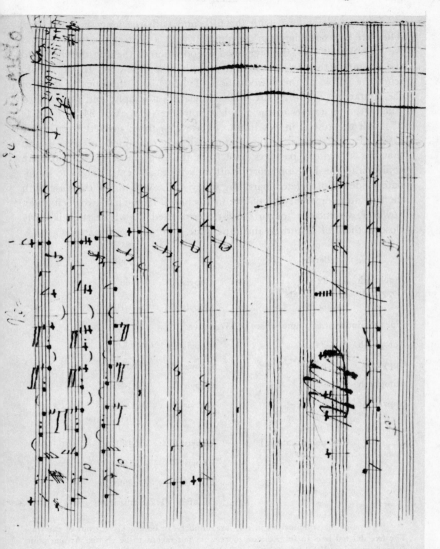

Plate IV

From the Berlin score of *Christus am Oelberge* (Artaria 179). III: 78-79
in the 1803 version.

New problems arise with the fifth and with the long sixth number. They are best considered in conjunction with a part of the oratorio that we have passed over, the orchestral introduction to the first number, and the recitative that follows it and precedes the first aria. In the Berlin score the whole of this introduction (I:1-54) and the opening bars of the recitative (I:55-62) are in Beethoven's autograph; and the same is true of the recitatives of the two last numbers (i. e., V:1-34 and VI:1-25). All the rest is in A's hand (as are also three deleted bars before I:63). In the sections of the oratorio already examined we have found that the autograph passages date from the revision of 1804, and were copied into the London score (with any necessary extra pages to eliminate evidence of deleted bars) by Copyist C. And this is the case with the first number here: I:1-66 are in C's hand. In the last two recitatives, however, we meet a fourth copyist, here called D, whose style is fairly close to those of A and B, and thus quite different from that of C.

	Berlin		London
Autograph	I:1-62	Copyist C	I:1-66
Copyist A	3 deleted bars ⎫		
	I:63-104 ⎭	Copyist B	I:67-104

[For remainder of first number see p. 557, above.]

	Berlin		London
Autograph	V:1-34	Copyist D	V:1-34
Copyist A	V:35-161	Copyist B	V:35-161
Autograph	VI:1-25	Copyist D	VI:1-25
Copyist A	VI:26-119 ⎫	Copyist B	VI:26-119
	5 deleted bars ⎬		5 deleted bars
	VI:126-432 ⎭		
	(= end of oratorio)	Copyist C	VI:120-125
		Copyist B	VI:126-255
		Copyist C	VI:256-259
		All after VI:259 missing [16]

[16] Some of the complexities in this last number can be quickly got out of the way. The five deleted bars in the London score were not meant to be visible. At one point (presumably in 1804) Beethoven decided to expand to six bars a five-bar cadential phrase following VI:119. In the Berlin score the page containing the five bars (in A's hand) was simply struck through; its replacement was evidently neglected. For the London score C copied out the new six-bar page, which was then superimposed on the earlier five-bar version (in B's hand) and secured to it by stitches and wax. The fastenings have since broken, and that is why a page with deleted bars is, in spite

The presence of three deleted bars, written by Copyist A, in the recitative of the first number of the Berlin score and the replacement of the autograph sections there by C in the London score suggest very strongly that the whole of the opening of the oratorio was revised by Beethoven in 1804. But what of the recitatives of V and VI — where there are no deleted bars, and where D, not C, copied the autograph? Are they, too, a bonus from the revisions of 1804? Before attempting to answer these questions, we must now consider the Wielhorsky sketchbook in greater detail.

VII

Sketches for the 1803 version of *Christus am Oelberge* occupy the major portions of pages 90-166 and also the last page (174) of this sketchbook: that is to say, rather less than half the book. The earlier pages are taken up with the piano sonata Opus 31, No. 3, the piano variations Opus 34 and Opus 35, and the duet for soprano and tenor with orchestra "Ne' giorni tuoi felici" (WoO 93). The work on the oratorio is followed by sketches for the first and for part of the second movement of the "Kreutzer" Sonata, Opus 47. The page numbering, very clear in the Moscow facsimile, is that of Ludwig Nohl, who nearly a century ago examined and discussed the sketchbook in detail after Lenz's somewhat earlier description.[17]

A table of pages devoted to each section of the oratorio is needed at this point.

I	Introduction	162, 163, 164, 165, 166
	Recitative: "Jehovah! du ..."	90, 91, 92, 104, 105, 108
	Aria: "Meine Seele ..."	90, 91, 92, 93, 94, 95, 96, 97, 104, 109, 132
II	Recitative: "Erzittre Erde ..."	111, 113
	Aria: "Preist, preist ..."	111, 112, 114, 115, 116, 118, 121, 122, 126, 142, 146, 149
	"O heil euch ..."	110, 111, 112, 114, 115, 116, 117, 118, 119, 120, 121, 122, 123, 124, 125, 126, 127, 128, 129, 130, 131

of C's care, visible today in the London score. C also copied what is now the last surviving page of this score. In the Berlin score VI:259 was heavily corrected by Beethoven after A had copied it, and C was evidently called upon to replace the corresponding bar (and therefore the page) in the London score.

[17] Wilhelm von Lenz, *Kritischer Katalog sämmtlicher Werke Ludwig van Beethovens mit Analysen derselben* (Hamburg, 1860), III, 221f.; Ludwig Nohl, *Beethoven, Wagner, Liszt* (Vienna, 1874), pp. 95-101.

III	Recitative: "Verkündet, Seraph"	132, 133
	Duet: "So ruhe denn . . ."	107, 132, 133, 134, 135, 136, 137, 138, 139, 140, 141, 142, 143
IV	Recitative: "Willkommen Tod!"	102, 103
	March: "Wir haben ihn gesehen"	133, 144, 145, 148, 150, 151, 152, 153
V	Recitative: "Die mich zu fangen"	145, 146, 154, 157
	Chorus: "Hier ist er . . ."	111, 145, 146, 147, 154, 155, 156, 157, 158
VI	Recitative: "Nicht ungestraft"	No trace
	Terzetto: "In meinen Adern"	133?, 147
	Chorus: "Auf, ergreifet . . ."	No trace
	Schlusschor: "Welten singen"	160, 161, 174

A few sketches for other works are found in these pages:

    105, staves 1-7 (piano figuration?)
    109, staves 1-5 (a piece in C major)
    113, lines 1-2 ("Rondo pour tous les instruments")
    166-173 ("Kreutzer" Sonata)

Pages 98, 99, 100, 101, 106, and 159 are blank.

From the above table we can see that the sketches are to be found in the sketchbook in approximately the same sequence as the numbers in the completed oratorio. It is true that the introduction to I is placed not first but last, and that the choruses of IV and V are intermingled; the recitative of IV, too, comes unexpectedly early. But nearly all of I is on pages 90-109; of II on 110-31; of III on 132-43; of IV and V on 144-58; and of VI (only the *Schlusschor*) on 161-62. The introduction to I comes on 162-66, where the "Kreutzer" Sonata then begins. This arrangement cannot, however, be taken as proof that Beethoven sketched or composed the various numbers in the order that they appear in the pages of the sketchbook. For he may simply have reserved certain pages for a particular number, and turned to another section whenever he wanted to work on another number. In that case chronologically disjunct sketches would be spatially adjacent.

The presence of blank pages is evidence that Beethoven sometimes skipped a few pages; and doubtless a few of those that remained blank for a while were later retrospectively filled up. Beethoven, in fact, seems to have employed both methods in the sketchbook: that is to say, in general he used the earlier pages first and the later pages later, so that the order of the pages is on the whole the order in which the sketches were made, but he sometimes leaped far ahead, leaving gaps which might or might not be filled in. At the top of several pages, for instance, there is the germ of an idea for a number: nothing detailed, only a suggestion for the scoring, or a brief hint as to the treatment. I shall call these, for brevity, "concept" sketches. Examples are to be found on pages 91 (stave 1), 110 (staves 1-4), 111 (staves 1-2) and 145 (staves 1-2); less clear instances are on pages 90 (stave 1, bars 1-2), 104 (stave 1, first half), 112 (staves 1-4). All these, it will be seen, are on the uppermost staves, and were probably written in this part of the sketch-book before anything else was there. The same is true of the short sketches in this part that have nothing to do with *Christus am Oelberge;* these too are on the uppermost staves only. In some instances one can see how they provided an obstacle to the sketches of the oratorio: thus the "vi-de" from stave 7 on page 104 had to pass to stave 9 on page 105 because of the passages of piano figuration already on the upper staves of that page.

But such slight dislocations are not enough to disturb the essentially logical progression of the sketches. It is possible to see, for instance, that the first section of the aria of II was originally drafted in 2/4 time, not 3/8 (pages 111f.); that the recitative of III once ended in E, not C (pages 132-33), and that the duet which followed was in A, not A-flat (page 134). Originally, too, the end of the recitative of V had to make its step-by-step climb from an A, not from a B (pages 146, 154, and 157).[18] Thus it makes sense to talk of the "logical" position at which a sketch with a particular content should appear — in spite of all the irregularities that can be observed.

VIII

The table also shows something else. Not all sections of the oratorio are equally represented in the sketchbook; in particular, there are very few sketches indeed for the last number, which in its present form is by far the longest of the work. We have therefore to ask ourselves whether in 1803 the oratorio had a different and much shorter ending, or whether it was much as it is today and we must simply look elsewhere for the remaining sketches — assuming that they have survived at all. It is obvious that the loose pages of sketches for the oratorio now in Bonn

[18] It is even possible to apply a crude sort of logic to "misplaced" sketches in the table given above. Pages 132 and 133, for instance, seem to have been used as a rag bag; they received not only a phrase from the aria of I (132, stave 1), but part of the march of IV (133, staves 7-10), a fragment apparently from VI (133, stave 6) and some of both the recitative and duet of III. And 98-103 were blank until the last two pages were used to accommodate the short recitative of IV; and 107, otherwise blank (like 106), was used for a comparatively late version of the duet's opening phrase which had been worked on earlier around page 138.

and Modena, referred to in the review of sources in Section II, above, have first claim on our attention.

I hope now to demonstrate that these sketches originally formed part of the Wielhorsky sketchbook.[19] Eight leaves have so far been located, all of similar appearance, whose *recto* and *verso* sides are easily identifiable. Two of the leaves are in the Biblioteca Estense at Modena.[20] It is for once fortunate that blotting paper was not available to Beethoven, since a line of notes that he wrote on the penultimate stave of the *verso* of one sheet, which I call "Mod 1," has produced an offset while the ink was still wet on the *recto* of the other leaf ("Mod 2"). From this we discover that the two pages were adjacent ones, and the sequence of the four sides is assured. The remaining leaves are in the Beethovenhaus at Bonn and are briefly described in Unger's catalogue of the Bodmer Collection,[21] where they are listed as Mh [= Musikhandschrift] 69 and Mh 70 — each a single leaf — and Mh 71, a sequence of four leaves whose eight sides I number here as Mh 71(1) to (8).

These eight leaves have much in common both with each other and with Wielhorsky. Mh 69 and Mh 70 evidently have the same provenance; Mh 70[v] is inscribed: "Beethovens Original Manusscript schenkt mir Calliste Rzewuska am 29 februar 1832," and a similar though undated inscription on Mh 69[v] indicates that she was a countess. It is notable not merely that all eight pages are on sixteen-stave paper, but that they exhibit the same irregularities in the beginnings of the staves as the pages in Wielhorsky.[22] Most important of all, the sketches on these pages are entirely analogous in handwriting and stage of development to the sketches in the Wielhorsky sketchbook.

When we turn from the external features to the contents of the loose

[19] It is true that Fishman says (Commentary, p. 13): "All the leaves are in place." But in his 1874 description Nohl, after referring to the loss of the upper half of pages 19 and 20 (see the facsimile), adds (p. 96): "At the end the grey wrapper is missing, and so far as one can tell, a total of five leaves." This doubtless refers to the stubs of torn-out pages.

[20] I am very grateful to Lewis Lockwood for drawing my attention to them.

[21] Max Unger, *Eine Schweizer Beethovensammlung* (Zurich, 1939), pp. 168-69.

[22] Cf., *inter alia*, Owen Jander, "Staff-liner Identification, a Technique for the Age of Microfilm," *Journal of the American Musicological Society*, XX (1967), 112. However these irregularity-patterns were produced, the particular pattern found throughout Wielhorsky and in the loose leaves discussed here is by no means rare in paper used by Beethoven at this period. Richard Kramer has drawn my attention to examples of it in scores and sketches of Beethoven dating from 1800 to 1806, and to an instance of it in some sketches of Haydn for *Die Jahreszeiten,* illustrated in Georg Schünemann's *Musikerhandschriften von Bach bis Schumann* (Berlin and Zurich, 1936), Plate 34.

sketches we see that they go some, but not all, of the way to make up for the lack in Wielhorsky of sketches for the last number.

I	Introduction	Mh 71(3)
II	Recitative: "Erzittre Erde . . ."	Mh 69^v
	Aria: "Preist, preist . . ."	Mh 69^r, 69^v
	"O heil euch . . ."	Mh 69^r
III	Recitative: "Verkündet, Seraph"	Mh 69^r (concept), 70^r, 71(1), Mod 2^v
	Duet: "So ruhe denn . . ."	Mh 69^v (concept)
IV	Recitative: "Willkommen Tod!"	No trace
	March: "Wir haben ihn gesehen"	Mh 70^v (*Hauptstimme* sketch)
V	Recitative: "Die mich zu fangen"	Mh 71(6), (7)
	Chorus: "Hier ist er . . ."	Mh 71(8), Mod 1^v
VI	Recitative: "Nicht ungestraft"	Mh 71(8) (scenario only)[23]
	Terzetto: "In meinen Adern"	No trace
	Chorus: "Auf, ergreifet . . ."	Mh 71(3), Mod 2^r
	Schlusschor: "Welten singen"	Mh 71(2), (3), (8), Mod 1^r
	Piano pieces in C minor, E major	Mh 71(1)
	Piano pieces in E major, C minor	Mh 71(4)
	Sketch for cadenza to C minor Concerto, Opus 37	Mh 71(7)
	"Fürchte Gott" (three notes only—cf. WoO 129)	Mh 71(5)

IX

In the light of what was said above about the "logical" position for sketches with a particular content to be located, let us try to place the Bonn page Mh 69 in Wielhorsky. In addition to two "concept" sketches (on the uppermost staves of each side) for the recitative and duet of the third number, it contains sketches for the recitative and aria of II.

The sketches for this second number in Wielhorsky occupy every page from 110 to 131, with further short drafts for the aria on pages 142, 146, and 149. But the only recitative sketches are on pages 111 and 113. This at least suggests a possible site for Mh 69, and further comparison reveals great similarities between the *verso* of Mh 69 and page 113, a *recto*: each offers a slightly different version of the orchestra's introductory bars. But we can get more help from the aria. Beethoven, I have already said, first tried to draft the opening in 2/4 time; these attempts can be found on pages 111 (staves 6-7), 112 (stave 11), 114 (stave 1) and — with unexplained perversity (perhaps it is another "concept" sketch) — 146 (staves 1-3 and 6-7). With the exception of

---

[23] See note 29, below.

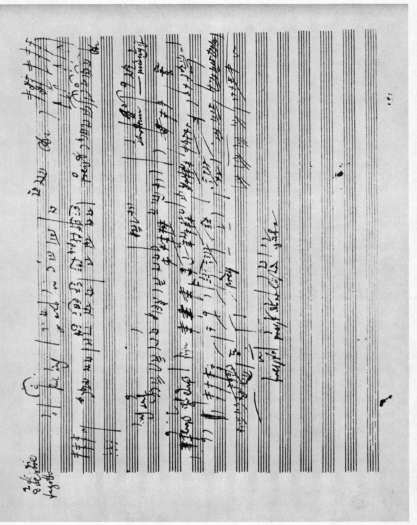

Plate V
Page 112 of the Wielhorsky Sketchbook, Moscow

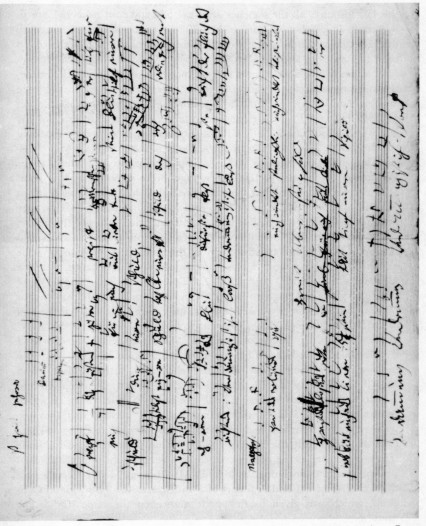

Plate VI
Sketch leaf, Bodmer Collection. *Recto* of Mh 69.

this last instance, all the sketches after the first stave on page 114 are in 3/8 time. Thus when we turn to Mh 69^r, we cannot fail to be struck by the fact that it contains drafts of the beginning of the aria both in 3/8 time (staves 3-5) and in 2/4 time (staves 13-14) — suggesting, therefore, a logical site near pages 112-14. And, by a stroke of good fortune, the inkblots on the lower part of page 112 (clearly shown in the facsimile and in Plate V) prove exactly to match some heavily inked passages on Mh 69^r (Plate VI). It is clear, for instance, that the last letter of the last word ("loos") on Plate VI has produced a blot of corresponding size and shape below the lowest stave (bottom, left) on Plate V.

Thus Mh 69 originally belonged between pages 112 and 113 of Wielhorsky. It is possible that other pages were removed at this point (the absence of detectable correspondence in inkblot impressions between Mh 69^v and the much-smudged page 113 is inconclusive);[24] if so, they have not yet been located. But lines of inference analogous to the above, based partly on the contents of the sketches and partly on blots and similar physical characteristics, help to determine the location of some of the other loose pages. It seems pretty certain, for instance, that the Modena pages, Mod 1 and Mod 2, follow directly after page 174 of Wielhorsky, the last page in the sketchbook; not only are the contents of Mod 1^r and 174 directly linked, but the indication "No. 100" at the end of the bottom stave of Mod 1^r appears to be picked up by the "No. 100" at the start of the top stave of page 174. And a number of blots on Mod 2^v correspond with blots or heavily-inked passages on Mh 70^r. Thus the last page of Wielhorsky was originally followed in turn by Mod 1 and Mod 2, and then by Mh 70, that other present from the generous Gräfin. I have not succeeded in determining the point in Wielhorsky at which the four pages of Mh 71 were withdrawn. It is possible that they too were removed from the end of the book or possibly from somewhere near the very lightly filled pages 158-61.[25] That they belong to the same series of sketches as the others can scarcely be in doubt, especially when we find that they include, like Mh 69, Mh 70, and Mod 2, sketches for the recitative of III and also part of a cadenza to the Third Piano Concerto, which was given its first performance on the same day as the oratorio.

[24] Nor can much help be got from the contents; but it is possible that the note g'-sharp to the word "Qual" on stave 4 of page 113 is intended to be picked up by the same note and the same word on stave 7 of Mh 69^v.

[25] There is reason to suppose that the facsimile of Wielhorsky has suppressed some of the marginal blots in the sketchbook. The margins are at any rate suspiciously spotless.

X

With a clearer idea of the Wielhorsky sketches — those that the sketchbook still contains and those that it once contained — we should be in a better position to tackle the question that we postponed at the end of section VI: were the recitatives of the fifth and sixth numbers (V:1-34 and VI:1-25) already in the version that was performed in April, 1803, or do they date from the revision of 1804?

But I do not think that we can answer the question with any certainty. The main difficulty here is that even with the addition of the loose pages the sketches for the end of the oratorio are very far from complete. And this is true (as a glance at the lists on pp. 67f. and 71 will show) not only of the two problematical recitatives but also of other sections which there is every reason to suppose were sung at the first performance. Hardly any sketches have survived, for example, of the complex terzetto "In meinen Adern wühlen" (VI:26-160),[26] yet there is no reason to doubt that it formed part of the version performed in April, 1803, and in the Berlin score, like the rest of the finale following it, it is all in the hand of Copyist A (in the London score: Copyist B). Where are these sketches? They must be presumed lost. What one evidently cannot do is to argue that since almost no sketches have survived in Wielhorsky the music did not form part of the April 1803 version.[27] An almost exactly contrary situation is to be found with the introduction to the first number. That is to say, the presence in the Berlin score of three deleted bars in the hand of Copyist A after I:62 is overwhelming evidence that the preceding material (all of which is in Beethoven's autograph) is a revised version. Yet the sketches that survive in Wielhorsky are detailed enough to show almost all the features of the present version — though not necessarily in their present order.[28] It may be that the

[26] All there is is the phrase "nur so gefällt ihr Gott" laid out for vocal trio (apparently in B-flat, but in 3/8 time) on page 147 (staves 3-5) of Wielhorsky; a setting, in the right meter and key, of the words "In meinen Adern wüthet [!] unbändig Zorn und Wuth," again on page 147 (stave 9); and a dubious phrase ("in meinen Adern"?) on page 133 (stave 6).

[27] The possibility cannot be excluded that there was a sketchbook of 1803, apparently no longer extant, in which Beethoven worked in the weeks between the Wielhorsky and the *Eroica* sketchbooks. One can speculate on what it might have contained: further sketches for the end of the oratorio and for the variation movement of the "Kreutzer" Sonata (the theme itself is worked out in Wielhorsky), the song *Der Wachtelschlag*, WoO 129 — cf. in this connection Mh 71(5) — and the Variations on "God save the King," WoO 78.

[28] The only phrase of which I can find no real trace is the one in G-flat, bars 33-35, but the whole of the passage from bar 33 to 42 is obscure. It appears that at

last-minute decision to add trombones to the scoring of the oratorio, something that adds great solemnity to the somber introduction, led him to rescore the whole of the opening. I suspect, however, that the structure of this section — the order in which various passages occur — was different in 1803.

So far as 1803 is concerned, the recitatives to V and VI — each in Beethoven's autograph in the Berlin score and in Copyist D's hand in the London score — would seem to stand or fall together, Of the recitative to VI not a word or a note is to be found in Wielhorsky,[29] but I have already argued that that in itself is not conclusive. For the recitative to V, on the other hand, we have all the words in Wielhorsky (page 154), though the music is at a primitive stage of development. We are taken rather further by two sides of the loose pages in Bonn, Mh 71(6) and (7), where there is a hint at the *Sturmwind* that calls forth a fortissimo in the final version, and where the recitative picks up the *tempo della marcia* (V:29-30) with a B (as in the final version), not with an A. But a gap still remains.[30] We can only speculate whether further lost sketches might have filled it. Until further evidence turns up, it seems better to assume that, like the rest of the autograph passages in the Berlin score, the music of these two recitatives owes its present form to a revision of 1804.

one stage the opening two bars of the work were planned to return at the recapitulation (page 165, stave 3). There is no *Hauptstimme* sketch, but the following thread through the maze may be of help: after the first eight bars, sketched in various places, start on page 164 at the beginning of stave 7 (= bar 9). Bars 9-29 are given by staves 7, 8, 10 (9 is deleted), and 11 up to the ✗ sign. The rest of bar 29 and bars 30 and 31 are by the ✗ sign on stave 15. The passage from bar 32 to the recapitulation is less clear, but is suggested by staves 12 and 13, where the ✗ sign leads to the ✗ sign on the next page (page 165, stave 3). The passage from bar 37 onwards is also shown (although deleted) on page 165, staves 5-6 (= bars 37-41). The rest of the introduction (bars 42-54) is on staves 6, 7, 8, 9, 10, and 12.

[29] The only hint of such a recitative is in a memorandum which Beethoven scrawled on one of the Bonn pages, Mh 70(8), and which appears to be an early scenario for the last number: "auch petrus recitativ die kriegsknechte petrus und Christus fallen / darin ein doch ohne die jünger darauf fällt das Recitativ des Seraph z. B. das Wort ist erfüllt / und der Chor der Engel. —" This may perhaps be understood as: "Peter as well — recitative — the soldiers, Peter and Christ come in but without the disciples; then comes the recitative of the Seraph, e. g., 'the Word is fulfilled,' and the chorus of angels." I am very grateful to Hans Schmidt, Bonn, for his help in deciphering this passage.

[30] Part of this gap is of course filled by the alterations that Beethoven made in the actual process of writing out the autograph (especially V:27-28). Another change in the autograph, involving the addition of a bar (V:15-16, formerly a single bar), was made at a later date since it had to be inserted later into the London score as well.

XI

It is clear from Beethoven's correspondence that the words as well as the music of the oratorio underwent reconsideration and revision between its first performance in April, 1803, and its publication in October, 1811.[31]

It is not difficult to reconstruct the libretto of 1803. If the preceding argument is sound, the words sung at the first performance can be found in those parts of the Berlin and London scores that were copied by A and B; and Wielhorsky provides a useful confirmation and supplementation, since, while it contains no part of a libretto that we do not recognize, it includes the words to the problematical recitative of V. Doubts are confined to the recitative of VI; to date there is no evidence that any of its words were sung in 1803, though they may well have been.

With the possible exception of this recitative, the revisions of 1804 apparently brought no changes to the words; the principal scrutiny of the libretto took place much later, between 1809 and 1811. What is probably the first hint is to be found in an entry in a sketchbook of 1809 (Landsberg 5, p. 47), now in the Deutsche Staatsbibliothek, Berlin: "gleich nach der Arie im Oratorium von Jesus muss ein neues Chor einfallen — Treitschke — kann Bernhard Musik." It is likely that the entry dates from May 1809, since the next *recto* page of the sketchbook contains the draft of a letter that Beethoven sent to Breitkopf & Härtel on May 26, 1809; doubtless he was hoping to get help from Georg Friedrich Treitschke or Josef Karl Bernard in revising the libretto.

Our main source for the revisions to the words is the London score. Broadly speaking, an alternative libretto has been written in. Throughout the score, though discontinuously, there runs either above or below the original words in the copyists' black ink (the "black text") a second line of words in ink that today has become pinkish red (the "red text"). Clearly the red text was intended as a possible replacement for the black text; in some passages no change was deemed necessary, and we find merely an initial word or phrase in red followed by a sign for "etc." [32] The score contains nothing to show who composed the red text; the nature of certain corrections in it suggests that it was written into the London score by its author.[33]

[31] Cf. in particular the letter to Breitkopf & Härtel of August 23, 1811, quoted in part above (p. 50).

[32] Some of the red text requires slight adjustments to the vocal note values; these too are marked in red ink.

[33] In a very few passages yet another hand has suggested small changes to the

Perhaps the most surprising feature of the red text is that — in spite of the evident intentions of producing a better libretto — the words were not for the most part adopted in the published score of 1811; in general the black text was retained. Much of the red text is in fact crossed out in pencil, and there are also penciled instructions (not in Beethoven's hand, and now very faint) in the margins of a few pages for the "old text" to be retained.

In three places, however, there are neat marginal notes in ink — again not by Beethoven — explicitly requesting the adoption of the red text. Who put them there? One's first thought is that these instructions were at any rate authorized by Beethoven. But there are great difficulties in maintaining this. No difficulty arises, it is true, with the request on page 48ʳ (II:77) for the black text of 1803 ("wenn ihr getreu der Lehre des Gott Vermittlers seyd") to be replaced by the red text ("wenn ihr getreu in Liebe, in Glaub' und Hoffnung seyd") adopted in the published score. But there are problems with the other two passages:

1. Page 129ʳ (VI:54). The red text requested here should be compared with the black text of 1803:

Black text	Red text
Du sollst nicht Rache üben!	Du sollst nicht Rache üben!
ich lehrt euch bloss allein	wer will mein Jünger seyn
die Menschen alle lieben,	muss seinen Feind auch lieben,
dem Feinde gern verzeihn.[34]	dem Irrenden verzeihn.

The red text was duly published in Breitkopf & Härtel's vocal score of the oratorio, published simultaneously with the full score (see source 7, above). But the full score contains the black text, and careful scrutiny of certain bars in copies of the full score reveals that the red text had originally stood there and had then been erased, probably at the proof stage.[35] This seems to be evidence that the adoption of the red text here was against Beethoven's wishes, and that he eliminated the change at the proof stage.

---

text (e. g., the substitution of "gerechter" for "unbändig" at the beginning of the terzetto of VI). Attention is drawn to most of these by a marginal "NB," and all were incorporated into the published score.

[34] These words are in A's hand in the Berlin score. In the London score they are not (like the music) in B's hand but in Beethoven's — B evidently having left them out.

[35] Those who are curious are invited to examine VI:67 in a copy of this edition. Where ♩ ♩, "Feinde," now stands there are traces of ♪. ♪♩, i. e., "Irrenden."

2. Page 95ᵛ (IV:35). Once again the red text requested in this number should be compared with the black text of 1803:

Black text	Red text
Wir haben ihn gesehen	Wir haben ihn gesehen
Nach diesen Berge gehen.	Nach diesen Berge gehen.
Schlag links den Weg nur ein,	Entfliehen kann er nicht,
Er muss ganz nahe seyn.	Seyn wartet das Gericht.

The red words were duly included in the full score and the vocal score. But that they were not what Beethoven wanted is clear from his letter to Breitkopf & Härtel of January 28, 1812:

In spite of my note in favor of the old text in the oratorio chorus "Wir haben ihn gesehen" you have again retained the *unfortunate* alteration. In the name of Heaven, do people in Saxony really believe that the words make the music? If an unsuitable word can ruin the music, which is quite certain, yet one should be delighted whenever one finds that music and words form a unit; and although the verbal expression in itself may be commonplace, one should not want to improve any word or passage — Dixi.

And a letter written a few weeks earlier to Joseph von Varena of Graz made more or less the same complaint against the publishers:

You are receiving herewith an oratorio. . . . In one chorus (i. e., after No. 4 in C major) the publishers have altered the words, completely disregarding the expression. Hence *the words written in pencil above* should be sung.

Even when allowance is made for Beethoven's changes of mind in matters where he felt unsure of himself, it seems clear that his wishes had been disregarded and that what he derided as a "Saxon" view, represented at any rate in his mind by the Leipzig critic Rochlitz (who had once found the C major chorus comical),[36] had prevailed. It looks, therefore, as though the marginal instructions in the London score were added by the publishers. Would it not be a courtesy to the composer to follow his instructions to Varena and insist that the original words of 1803 be sung whenever the oratorio is performed?

XII

Several passages in Beethoven's correspondence with Breitkopf & Härtel, quoted near the beginning of this article, betray his mixed feelings about the merits of the oratorio. And although for a time it became

---

[36] For Rochlitz's view of the chorus see Beethoven's letter to Breitkopf & Härtel of October 9, 1811.

popular with a broad public, the musical world in general has endorsed
his misgivings. Was it imprudent of him to undertake to write a major
work — a work at any rate containing over an hour [37] of orchestral and
dramatic vocal music — in a matter of weeks to meet a concert dead-
line? Since (except in his last years) Beethoven regularly set himself
challenges of this sort, he cannot have found it a distressing way in
which to compose; and a method that produces works like the Violin
Concerto and the "Kreutzer" Sonata can scarcely be regarded as ill-
considered. Yet there are reasons for supposing that in the case of his
only oratorio Beethoven had made something of a miscalculation.

The excuses that he was later to offer for its deficiencies are helpful
in pointing the way to what had gone wrong. It was, he said, his first
work in that style, and an early work; it was written in a fortnight (in
an earlier letter the time had been given as "a few weeks"); and the
composition had been disturbed by distressing events, including a very
serious illness of his brother. In this way he appealed both to stylistic uncertainty and to personal unhappinesses. It is the former that I want to
consider here. The distress in Beethoven's life at this time went far beyond the illness of his brother,[38] and the compositions of these years cannot be fully understood without reference to its principal cause, the
realization that his deafness was progressive and incurable. But I have
already discussed this elsewhere, attempting to draw parallels between
the ideas contained in the oratorio, which did not at first appear to stir
him greatly, and those of *Leonore,* which made the strongest sort of ap-
peal to his imagination.[39] Undeserved suffering, isolation, deprivation,
hopes and fears concerning deliverance — these themes link both oratorio and opera with Beethoven's own life.

The operatic style of the oratorio has often proved something of an
embarrassment to later generations. But for a work of this sort Beethoven had no immediately relevant models, and his only previous attempt at extended vocal writing on a sombre theme, the very impressive
Cantata on the Death of Joseph II of 1790 (WoO 87), written in Bonn

---

[37] According to Beethoven's letter to Treitschke of September 24, 1815, it "normally lasts . . . one hour and nine minutes."

[38] A letter to Breitkopf & Härtel that Caspar Carl dictated on March 26, 1803,
reveals that he had been prostrated for the previous eighteen days by a "violent
rheumatic fever."

[39] "Beethoven's Heroic Phase," *Musical Times,* February, 1969, p. 139. The
parallels are, I think, clear, but the contrast between the rapidity of the oratorio's
composition and the protracted labors on the opera also calls for an explanation.

when he was only nineteen, had never reached performance.[40] The example of Haydn's two late oratorios, which is perhaps less conspicuous than one might have supposed, is most obvious in the tone-painting of the introduction. It should be remembered that at this date, stimulated partly by the successes in the Viennese theater of French composers and of Cherubini, Beethoven was burning to write an opera, and even owed the opportunity of giving the concert for which the oratorio was completed to his appointment at the Theater an der Wien. It is also likely that certain stylistic features of opera seria, particularly in the duet in the third number and in the aria in the first, are traceable to Antonio Salieri's influence. The work that precedes the oratorio in the Wielhorsky sketchbook is a fine duet to words from Metastasio's *Olimpiade,* "Ne' giorni tuoi felici" (WoO 93), by which Beethoven marked the termination of his informal and irregular studies with Salieri in the setting of Italian words. An even more conspicuous influence is Mozart: particularly, perhaps, the Mozart of *Die Zauberflöte.* The Seraph's entry, to a roll on the timpani and opening words "Erzittre Erde," puts one in mind of the Queen of the Night's "O zittre nicht!" It may be added that Mozartean echoes continued to haunt Beethoven in the composition of *Leonore,* even if they produced the kind of number that he was obliged later to cut (e. g., the terzetto "Ein Mann ist bald genommen," or the duet with violin and cello solos "Um in der Ehe froh zu leben").

We have it on Schindler's authority that in his last years Beethoven blamed himself for having treated the part of Christ too dramatically [41] and would have dearly loved to be able to correct this "fault." This would have involved major changes in both words and music; they were not so ill-matched, as the sharp reviewer of the *Freimüthige* perceived. But some of the revisions of 1804 seem to have been directed at modifying certain of the more theatrical elements in the music. The 1803 version of the aria in the first number has not survived complete, but a sufficient number of deleted bars remain in the Berlin score to show that I:162 was originally followed by a tutti in E-flat forming the ritornello, and that after I:218 the expected cadence into

---

[40] Its subject matter precluded a performance at a later date; but it was not entirely forgotten, and in 1805 one number was adapted to form part of the third act finale of *Leonore,* "O Gott, O welch ein Augenblick!"

[41] A. Schindler (1840), p. 47: "zu dramatisch." In the third (1860) edition of Schindler's biography, Part I, p. 91, the phrase runs: "in moderner Singweise opernmässig." The London score contains a few stage directions in Beethoven's hand, e. g., at III:79, "Christus fällt nieder auf die Knie." None was included in the first edition.

C minor was interrupted by a plunge into A-flat. The formality of the E-flat cadential tutti and the self-consciousness of the later harmonic diversion were both eliminated by the 1804 changes; what was lost in staginess was actually gained in expressiveness and poignancy. The effect is to charge the words "Nimm den Leidenkelch von mir" with much greater intensity: words of anguish, surely, for a young man who found himself going deaf. It is as if Beethoven's deepening identification with his dramatic characters — by 1804 he was struggling with *Leonore* — had begun to reveal to him new profundities in the text. Other changes can be seen as mitigating theatrical formality or as intensifying the significance of the words. An example of the former is the introduction in 1804 of a chorus at the point of recapitulation of the Seraph's aria in the second number, and the deflection of its ending by a long *alla breve* fugato for this chorus. An example of the latter is the expansion of the phrase "damit die Menschen die er liebt von Tode auferstehen" in the recitative of the same number; this had been set rather perfunctorily in 1803 (Cf. Plate III).

Both aims seem to be achieved in the four bars added at the end of the third number in 1804. In the 1803 version the (solo?) cello in III: 78-79 had been two octaves higher than it is at present, so that the first note of 79 was a dizzy a"-flat, the number ending here with a fortissimo chord (Plate IV). In the changes this distracting instrumental virtuosity was eliminated, together with the fortissimo, and four quiet bars of unison, proceeding to the dominant of F, now ensure continuity with the F major recitative that follows. There were, however, limits to what could be done in this way; a certain triviality and perfunctoriness was less easy to eliminate. It seems to me that it was his experience with *Leonore* that taught Beethoven that he had in some ways shirked the responsibilities of the oratorio's theme. And thus there is no reason to doubt his confession in the year 1811: "What is quite certain is that now I should compose an absolutely different oratorio from what I composed then."

BEETHOVEN'S "NEW WAY"
AND THE *EROICA*

By PHILIP G. DOWNS

THE Heiligenstadt Testament marks a watershed in the creative life of Beethoven which is hard to parallel in the life of any other composer. Its effect is to be found not simply in Beethoven's relationships with his fellow-men, but is so profoundly spiritual that it is impossible to doubt the existence of a causal connection between Beethoven's despair and his contemporary dissatisfaction with the nature of his work. For we have it on the authority of Carl Czerny: "About the year 1800, when Beethoven had composed Opus 28 he said to his intimate friend, Krumpholz: 'I am far from satisfied with my past works: from today on I shall take a new way.' Shortly after this appeared his three sonatas Opus 31, in which one may see that he had partially carried out his resolve." [1] Czerny would never have thought that anyone, at a later time, might wish for a more accurate dating of his hearsay. For him, the statement "about the year 1800" is sufficient. But in order to narrow down the timing it is well to remember that Opus 28 was composed in 1801 and published in 1802, whereas the sonatas Opus 31 were composed during 1802 but not published until 1803 and 1804. It is, therefore, reasonable to assume a placing for Beethoven's alleged statement somewhere between the beginnings of 1801 and April of 1802, when the Opus 31 sonatas were completed. Although Beethoven several times comments upon the novelty of his compositions, his statement to Breitkopf, dated October 18, 1802, that his piano variations, Opus 34 and Opus 35, are each composed in an entirely new manner may add more strength to the idea that this period was for Beethoven one of reassessment. Although the symphony did not appear until 1804, it is no coincidence that the early work on the *Eroica* dates from this crucial year, 1802.

Since Beethoven nowhere committed to paper his own ideas on the

---

[1] Carl Czerny, *Memoirs;* cited in O. G. Sonneck, *Beethoven: Impressions of Contemporaries* (New York, 1926) p. 31.

connection between his Third Symphony and his objectives as a composer, his ideals and his idea of himself in relation to others as he writes
of these things in the Heiligenstadt Testament are particularly useful,
since they point to probabilities. The date on the Heiligenstadt Testament is October 6, 1802. This document is not the first in which Beethoven has expressed the kind of thoughts which are embodied in it;
rather it appears as the culmination of a wave of assessment and self-pity
which results in the acceptance of which Beethoven talks. The struggle to
achieve acceptance and the assumption of the burden of life in order to
fulfill the desire to create, which he felt so strongly, are in fact synchron-
ous with the move into new areas of creativity and musical function,
which Beethoven embodies in his Third Symphony. But in the development of the rationale of an artistic "new way," Beethoven never loses
sight of the ideal of "love for humanity and a desire to do good." Neither
his affliction nor his acceptance of it could make him withdraw into the
ivory tower which would have meant imprisonment behind doubly thick
walls for him. In the famous letter to Wegeler of November, 1801, he
says: "You will find me as happy as I am fated to be on this earth, not
unhappy — no, that I could not bear — I will seize Fate by the throat;
it shall certainly not bend and crush me completely — Oh it would be
so lovely to live a thousand lives — No indeed, I realize now that I am
no longer suited to a quiet life." [2]

In both art and life, at this point in his development, Beethoven was
committed to involvement. It is perhaps possible to gain some idea of
what this commitment may have implied musically, by examining two
things: firstly, Beethoven's relationship with a very close friend, Wenzell
Krumpholz; and secondly, Schindler's report of Beethoven's reaction
to the idea of a projected complete edition of his piano works. Krumpholz (1750-1817), according to Czerny, had attached himself to Beethoven as soon as Beethoven appeared in Vienna.

He was a musical enthusiast whose passion for music was carried to the most ex-
travagant lengths. Nature had endowed him to a high degree with a just and
delicate feeling for the beautiful in tonal art, and though he possessed no great
fund of technical knowledge, he was able to criticize every composition with much
acumen, and, so to say, anticipate the judgements of the musical world. [3]

Despite the fact that Beethoven called Krumpholz his jester, he nevertheless was very fond of him and used him as an intermediary between the

[2] Emily Anderson, ed. and trans., *The Letters of Beethoven* (London, 1961),
I, 68.

[3] Sonneck, *op. cit.,* p. 24.

world and himself, playing his new ideas to him and improvising for him every day. Concerning the second point, Schindler says, writing about Beethoven's intention of preparing a new edition of his piano works:

Apart from the material benefits accruing from such a project, there was an intellectual and artistic necessity underlying it. Beethoven hoped to convey the inner "poetic idea" that led him to compose each of his various works, and thus make possible a true understanding of them. As for performances that would reveal this inner poetry, there was much more to be done than meets the eye.[4]

And, further, Schindler reports Beethoven's reaction to his question about the key to the largo of the D major Sonata, Opus 10, No. 3:

He told me that at the time he had written it, audiences were more poetic than now (1823) and that for this reason it had not been necessary to supply them with the idea. Everyone, he continued, had sensed in the Largo the spiritual condition of a person consumed by melancholy and had felt the many nuances of light and shadow in this portrait of depression, in the same way that everyone had recognized in both Opus 14 sonatas the dispute in dialogue form between two principles, without the aid of words written above the score.[5]

Now, from the above statements it is possible to draw some general conclusions as a base for the discussion of the first movement of the *Eroica Symphony:* Beethoven, the man who wished to benefit humanity, knew very well that the symphony was the form in which he would reach the greatest mass of humanity; he was accustomed to receive penetrating criticism from someone of modest technical knowledge; at the point of crisis of will which Beethoven was undergoing he sees the necessity for embodying the power of will in the work of art, just as it has to be embodied in his own life. It follows that the symphony must not require anything from the listener other than the ability to concentrate for the length of a movement and to use the power of memory to recall salient features. The symphony is not designed by Beethoven as a communication to an élite unless that élite is chosen by virtue, and the particular means to virtue is the ability to listen reflectively.

A constant in Beethoven's assessment of the principle of the sonata is the necessity of adjusting the process of development with the process of recapitulation and making both of these dependent upon the exposition. It sounds like a truism to say the kind of exposition that the composer produces determines the kind of recapitulation, but the difference be-

---

[4] A. F. Schindler, *Beethoven as I Knew Him,* ed. Donald W. McArdle (Chapel Hill, N. C., 1966), p. 400.

[5] *Ibid.,* p. 406.

tween the early, grandiose yet diffuse works and the later, grandiose yet compressed works is dependent upon the composer's realization of this fact.

The *Eroica Symphony* shows signs arising from Beethoven's "new way" in that it succeeds in accomplishing a thing that Beethoven only once again succeeded in doing on such a vast scale. The first movement succeeds in reconciling the formal, spatial requirements of the traditionally conceived sonata form with a discursive, narrative, temporal drama. The sonata is almost invariably described as a dramatic form in music. Beethoven's achievement in the *Eroica* is to create in music something analogous to theatrical drama. In the theater it is generally admitted that characters who have undergone profound experiences of one sort or another can never be the same again. At the end of the play, King Lear is not the same man that he was in the beginning — he is sadder and wiser. Specific attacks on the personality as it is at the opening of the play result in specific modifications to it. There is sufficient evidence in the music of the first movement of the *Eroica* to show that similar considerations now begin to weigh heavily with Beethoven. The proposition can be formulated as follows: Beethoven acknowledges that the sonata principle is one of tension but recognizes it as specifically musical tension, since those elements which create tension, ideally, cannot remain as they formerly were when the tension is resolved. The will to introduce a musical analogy to theatrical drama creates an opposition within the structure of the sonata, for this basically is one in which recapitulation of material already heard and manipulated is necessary to ideas of formal balance and to formal time and space equations. Part of the structure serves one function and part serves another, and the adjustment of the two elements creates a problem of extreme complexity, which may ultimately result in the destruction of the sonata principle.

The tendency towards the grandiose was always a pronounced feature of the Beethoven style. In the earliest published works there is an obvious enlargement of the scale of operations of Haydn and Mozart which undoubtedly is prompted by the fashion of the times, but which one cannot help suspecting is also partly a conscious assertion of Beethoven's independence, if not superiority. The length of the first movement of the *Eroica* need not be dwelt upon except to say that its proportions come into being not simply as the search for impressiveness through size, but largely because of the conscious juxtaposing of the new and the organic with the traditional and the formal.

The movement opens with the well-known chords of E-flat major.

Whether one calls them introduction or not is immaterial, since, from the First Symphony, Beethoven has shown that the introduction can be given a function far removed from the relatively detached architectural ideas that Mozart's and Haydn's introductions most frequently represent. The onus rests with the listener to assess the chords in the light of what the music tells him, and what he knows of Beethoven's artistic goals.

It is worth remembering that Beethoven once thought of opening the symphony with chords similar to those dominants which open the First Symphony, but the idea was abandoned. What is Beethoven left with? The answer is deceptively simple. Tonality is not defined or even presented, although it would inevitably have been alluded to had he adhered to his earlier plan. Melody, which is the usual and most direct way of presenting the poetic idea, is absent. Rhythmic definition is absent also, since the relationship between the two chords and the first chord of the third measure is not clear — that is to say, whether they form three beats of one measure in slow tempo or one and a half measures at a somewhat faster tempo, or whether they occur as the first beats of measures and, in any event, whether the subdivision of the time between is to be into two parts or three. In the light of what I hope to show, it is not too much to say that the first two chords, by their very starkness, their lack of melodic content, and their failure to define a tonality, point to what is to be the major tension of the movement.

Beethoven added the chords as an afterthought. In a structure such as this, Beethoven is not concerned with an external matter such as silencing an audience, nor with imposing his will on his listeners, nor yet with giving an impression of heroic strength — all these suppositions are either naive or inconsistent with the facts. In the Sixth and the Eighth Symphonies, Beethoven has no scruple about starting *in medias res*. And how can one seriously propose a heroic function for the first two chords when the melody which follows them and which is metrically a continuation of them is gentle, if not pastoral, in rhythm and, although melodically arched, is unable to summon the energy to escape from the tonic. For the first four strong beats of the melody form a reiterated E-flat with the arches of the melody formed on the weakest beats of the measure (Ex. 1). The actual melody is four measures in length. The famous continuation of it is unique — it reinforces the sagging quality of the melody at this first appearance, but never again. In the context of the first six measures of the work, the afterthought chords become, as it were, a backward extension of the melody, which is so ordered to define a pulse which the listener only relatively slowly comes to realize, is subdivided

into three. The two chords have a function which extends beyond themselves insofar as the rhythm is concerned, and insofar as the drama is
concerned they act as portents of things to come. We do not yet know it,
but the crux of the drama is to be whether these chords are to be allowed
to stand in their opening relationship, separated by this time distance.

Ex. 1

It is not until the fifteenth measure that the tonality of E-flat is un-
equivocally established and the triadic part of the first melody, the first
four measures, is repeated on the secure tonal basis. But no sooner is this
done than modulations take place, using the pattern marked *b* in Ex. 1.
The listener expects that a principle of sonata will be followed and that
a modulation to the dominant area will take place, and this happens:
in measures 21-23 Beethoven slides into the key, using the chord of the
augmented sixth. Normally, this process would hardly call for comment,
but its later repetition makes one look more closely and call for explanations where it might pass by unnoticed in less complex surroundings. The
impression of B-flat major gives the listener the sense of the opening of
an orthodox second group, and the feeling is reinforced by the new melodic material. The impression of contrast and tension is most strongly
created by the modification that the meter undergoes, for, as Ex. 2 shows,

Ex. 2   mm. 23-35

the regularity of Ex. 1 is replaced by metrical irregularity, with measures
of two beats followed by three beats, and just at the point where one
feels a regular duple meter emerging, the melodic line moves back into
triple meter but fails to coincide with the bar line. The melodic material
of this section is apparently new and distinct from the opening material,
yet it shares with it the fact that it is built entirely upon harmony notes.
There is a kinship of the triad which underlies the tense relationship of
these two areas. In measure 37, Beethoven returns to his opening material

for the melody which is extended over another four measures, and then, by a process exactly analogous to that in measures 21-23, he moves into the second group.

Up to this point in the movement, Beethoven, who wants all his listeners to be where the action is, has given each listener several prods in the direction that will help him to realize the area in which the tension is going to occur. The first group is presented as a contained *ABA* form in which *A* (Ex. 1) occurs in the tonic and *B* (Ex. 2) occurs on the dominant. Since B is only on the dominant and not in it (to use Tovey's distinction), Beethoven does not disrupt the accepted generalized principle of the form but uses the distinction to call attention to the fact that tension is to be created between a conflict of meters. The matter cannot consist in the melody (although finally its resolution can only be seen in the melody) since, while the *A* and *B* sections are melodically distinct, they are united by their triadic nature. The whole course of the second group goes to prove the identity of the melodic material of the first group by remaining ostentatiously aloof from anything resembling first group material, until measure 109. The matter cannot consist in tonality, since the naiveté which Beethoven made use of to draw attention to the *B* section of the first group is counterbalanced by the subtle difference between in and on the dominant, which Beethoven fully acknowledges. In other words, if Beethoven was planning to build a structure dependent upon tonal tensions, his first trick would be useless, for none of his listeners would believe in his first tonal move. The afterthought of the first two strokes can now be seen as something designed to make assurance doubly sure. The first sounds give a pulse, the next sounds divide the pulse into a rhythm, and the next sounds move to modify the rhythm. One remembers Beethoven's statement about his listeners in 1823 and their reaction to his sonatas, and one wonders whether he would have said that in his younger days everyone recognized the principle involved in the opening of his Third Symphony.

Now follows the second group, which concerns the present argument less than the first group, for reasons which will follow. Here Beethoven appears to be intent on creating an area in which maximum differences in texture, melody, and rhythm are juxtaposed closely while still giving an appearance of flow from one to the other. The creation of a second group of similarly enormous proportions and differences by means of an organic process is not accomplished until the Ninth Symphony. In the *Eroica* the material can be readily split up into its components, and it is staggering in its variety. The identity and close kinship of the first group, its repetitions and developments, is immediately impressed upon the memory of the naive listener. The second group is already so large, so different in its components, and so lacking in repetition that Beethoven cannot allow it to take part in his new dramatic development — he can only use it to fulfill the recapitulatory principle. It can go through a process of what may be called "formal" development, in which elements from one part are heard as counterpoints to elements from other parts, but the elements which are so put together are taken apart again without the least damage to either — nothing is broken or restored, nothing is lost or gained. In the recapitulation, the whole of the second group is repeated with only the most minor changes in orchestration made necessary by the change in register and key. It is at this point that Beethoven's intuitive appreciation of the psychology of listening dictates his formal procedures, for where his exposition material is simple and memorable he can modify in development and recapitulation; where his exposition material is complex he is restricted to less development and to literal recapitulation.

There is one problem area in the second group which seems to stand in relation to the metrical tension that the first group brings into existence. This is the area from measure 45 to 56, and it is clear that Beethoven means to draw the naive listener's attention to this passage, since

Ex. 3   mm. 45-49

he introduces it exactly as he introduced the first problematic passage of meter in the first group, with the chord of the augmented sixth. The passage in question is one of extreme delicacy and charm, and with seductive orchestration. It is in itself the complete antithesis to any sense of tension. The one feature which causes a degree of anxiety is the fact that its constant rhythmic figure, which occurs eleven times without interruption, while in triple meter, places the stress of the meter, the strong beat, on the second beat of the measure. Up to this point, the only dislocation of the triple meter has involved the placing of the strong beat of the meter on the third beat of the measure (see Ex. 2). Even so, this material would appear to be the most "feminine" of the whole first movement, and certainly the least likely to be an agent. The first sign of the ability of this figure to modify any other material is experienced when, in measure 109, the listener hears material which, because of its triadic nature and its rhythm, immediately recalls the opening of the work (Ex.

4). Beethoven writes a sforzato on the second beat, and this appears to prompt the rhythm of Ex. 3 to superpose itself upon the triadic melodic

Ex. 4   mm. 109-16

line. And from this point until measure 131 there is no doubt about the metrical irregularities. But I must repeat here that Beethoven forces one to question the dramatic function (not the artistic or sonata function) of material which is recapitulated without modification. Since the second group is subject to the formal function of recapitulation this metrical irregularity still exists when the dramatic tension is resolved, hence it must be assumed that Beethoven requires the listener to recognize this force of Ex. 3 and Ex. 4 as something external, something that has always been and will always be. The force of will that resolves the dramatic tension is powerless to resolve this, which, as will be shown, has a positive force in the drama nevertheless.

The division of the development into four sections has long been noticed and studied, and commentators have remarked that the first two sections form a thesis and antithesis while the last two form the synthesis. The discomfort of believing in the necessity of applying the Hegelian triad to a quadripartite structure is something the writer would personally wish to avoid experiencing — his capacity for vicarious suffering tells him it must be acute, and another interpretation has to be proposed.

The first section of the development, from measure 170 to 223, follows an orthodox pattern, and starting with material from the beginning of the second group (the material of Ex. 3), it modulates to a section which combines modified elements of groups one and two in counterpoint. There is a deal of sound and fury, but the fact that it signifies little is shown when the second section begins in measure 224 with material virtually identical with the first sixteen measures of the first section. One must ask why this section is placed where it is if it serves no dramatic purpose, and while the answer is a complex one, its main component is that Beethoven's "new way" nowhere assumes that the creation of a narrative or dramatic technique shall be thought to demote formal function in any way. The two can exist side by side, and this section in question stands in such a relationship to the rest of the development that it provides a balance, permitting the height of dramatic tension to occur at the midpoint in the time scale — that is to say, that its function is ideally formal. Secondly, I suggest that Beethoven intends its failure to develop certain of its material, i. e., the material in Ex. 3, to act as a foil for the actual development of the same material which comes about in the second section. Also, in the first section of the development there are repetitions of material and procedures (giving it a form which may be described as *ABCDCD*) which again tends to prove that the developmental process here is conventional and formal and that it has no effect upon the drama, since it modifies nothing.

The two-measure link (measures 222 and 223) between the first section of the development and the second is one which Beethoven expects his naive listener to grasp both in its occurrences and in its implication. Three times in the first movement of the *Eroica,* Beethoven uses the harmonic process of an augmented-sixth chord resolving to a dominant, and each time following this progression something important for the drama takes place. On the first occasion, the central part of group one (Ex. 2) was exposed as apparently new material and the meter suffered its first attack. On the second occasion, the first part of the second group, that charming, lyric, delicately off-beat melody was introduced, which became the start of another separate attack on the meter. The peculiar force of the progression lies in the way it appears to change the harmonic flow very suddenly, giving the effect of the sleight of hand that brings the rabbit out of the hat. Now, in using this same progression to introduce the second section of the development, Beethoven is about to show relationships, alliances, perils, and threats which to this point have not been remotely suspected. The rhythmic figure, which when it occurred in the exposition appeared eleven times without interruption, in the first section of the development occurred twelve times successively. It is interesting to note that in opening the second section of the development, the first thirty measures of that section are given over to it. After the first sixteen measures of the second section, a fugato develops from the rhythmic figure which insidiously moves to change the meter from the conditioned

	1	2	3	1	2	3	
through	1	2	3	1	2	3	
to the dislocated		1	2	3	1	2	3.

As soon as this happens, in measure 252, everyone, not simply the naive listener of Beethoven's conception but also even the most highly-trained observer, has sensed that the battle is joined, but the reason for the battle, whether it really is a battle, what is at stake, and who the antagonists are, seems to have remained at a lower level in the mind than that of conscious perception, despite all Beethoven's efforts.

Ex. 5   mm. 252-75

Ex. 5 gives an indication of the process from measure 252 until the height of tension, which follows after measure 276. This example shows an orderly arrangement of dislocated triple meter for two measures, followed by six measures of duple, which is followed by two measures of triple and six of duple, and so on. The orderly arrangement of these elements suggests alliance rather than battle and the force which should stand opposed to these two elements, that is to say, the solid triple meter of the opening of the symphony in triadic shape, is quite absent. It is remarkable that the sound of the triad unelaborated (just root, third and fifth) occurs only twice in this passage (through measure 283), and on one of those occasions it is heard as a minor triad; otherwise the chords are chords of tension which contradict normalcy. Following the seventh chord on the flattened supertonic of the key to come, the link with the next section which starts at measure 288, is formed by the dominant chord sounded eleven times.

The well-known passage which follows and which opens the third section of the development has, for the naive listener, a character of supplication or intercession — it certainly forms the sharpest contrast with the section that immediately precedes it. But it is not sufficient to assume that its purpose is simply contrast. Both metrically and melodically, this material is something which has not been heard before. Its sinuous upper line is balanced by the bass line which supports it in classic contrary motion. Between them, they create a chromaticism, a major-minor mode interchange which is quite unlike any previous melodic or harmonic element.

For the naive listener, the greatest confusion seems to arise at this point, for if this material is to have any effect on the drama, if it is to offer any possibility of resolution (and since we feel sympathy with it, we want this to be the case), how is the outburst which follows it and its own repetition in the key of E-flat minor to be reconciled with the course of the narrative? The character of the music is so pronounced that a more intense search of its substance is necessary. Ex. 6a shows the two parts of the melody as they occur. Ex. 6b shows that the bass line is created from a filling-out of the first five notes of the first melody of the work (*a* in Ex. 1) but set in the minor mode. Ex. 6c shows that the upper line is made by the same process of melodically filling-out the line of the fifth, sixth, seventh, and eighth notes of the same melody. At the same time as Beethoven presents this very convincing allegory of a theme cut up and changed beyond recognition melodically, he also makes it lose its original rhythmic identity while yet preserving a triple meter. It almost appears as though this enormous "compromise" has to be made in order to preserve this modicum of identity in the face of the onslaught of the opposing meters.

Ex. 6   mm. 288-92

It would appear that the compromise offers no means of resolving the tension, for immediately after its repeat in the key of A minor, a sudden and abrupt modulation to C major sees the re-emergence of the opening theme (*a* in Ex. 1) in a full orchestral unison, with no harmony and with the addition of a pasage of uncontrolled turbulence and excessive energy. This can only be interpreted by Beethoven's listener as a denial of the previous passage of compromise, since this is such an overforceful assertion of itself.

Why, then, does Beethoven make the "compromise" passage into music which compels audience sympathy? Perhaps it is possible that Beethoven has committed something of a dramatic blunder, for if we, the naive listeners, are to follow Beethoven through his musical (and, by analogy, conceptual) arguments, we must be made to sense the unworthiness of this potential solution and reject it as Beethoven does. I suggest that Beethoven has here set himself an impossible task in terms of the naive listener, for in order to make the unsuitability of the solution clear Beethoven has presented what is to him a compromise which denies the self (the self being represented by analogy with the opening material, Ex. 1). The listener, however, probably hears the material as completely new, and with the connection not grasped the point is missed. Where the listener grasps the connection of Ex. 1 and Ex. 6, aurally, then there is no flaw in the plan. The third section of the development closes with a repetition of the material which opened it, this time in the key of E-flat minor. Just as the "compromise" is denied by the assertion of the opening theme (Ex. 1), so the subsequent restatement of the compromise must be seen as a rejection of the unison assertion.

At this point, it is worth remarking that the second section of the development used only material which involved the creation of metrical tension, and any mention of Ex. 1 was strictly avoided. The culmination of that section was the orderly alliance of duple meter and dislocated triple meter. Now in the third section of the development, only material from Ex. 1 is dealt with. In one form this material is aggressively itself, and in the other form it is unrecognizably modified. In the context, it is apparent that neither of these solutions can resolve the tension which is the dramatic means of the music and its didactic purpose.

The fourth and last section of the development begins at measure 342 and the naive listener knows that the resolution of the tension is now at hand, for the tonality, which functions as a subliminal means of reinforcing the more conscious means of communication (rhythm, melody, and harmony), settles imperceptibly from the regions of E-flat minor through G-flat major onto the original dominant of B-flat major. It is apparent that all the winds, with the exception of the trumpets, gradually follow the lead of the bassoon and accept a modification of the opening theme that appears as *a* in Ex. 7. From now on, with the exception of two

Ex. 7   mm. 342-45

recollections in the recapitulation, every time the opening melody appears, it appears in modified form. In effect, what has happened to it is a notable gain in energy, sufficient to escape from its bond to the tonic note, and with this it has become balanced and buoyant, strong and assured — well able, in fact, to sustain its conclusion on the fifth degree. In the violas, cellos, and basses, there occurs the expanding, leaping figure (*b* in Ex. 7) which, although it recalls other parts of the movement, has not been heard in its present form before and appears as new material. Its relation to duple meter is obvious, and it is also clear that the duple meter moves along side by side with the original figure with no tension. Since no musical event has intervened between the apparent rejection of the previous solution, it is reasonable to assume that Beethoven intends the listener to connect the appearance of the bass with the new-found strength of the original material. The means of communicating this gradual realization on the part of the orchestra is the classic and obvious one of a crescendo in which the new form of the old figure is adopted by more and more instruments.

The power of the leaping bass figure to promote such well-being must prompt the question why such power should reside in such a figure, and in order to answer this question, the ancestry of the figure must be traced. To be sure, the naive listener, that Rousseau-esque figure referred to so frequently, will realize the effect without necessarily understanding why, but in order for the complete communication of the symphony's purpose to be received, the listener has to reflect on this point.

The obvious triadic nature of *b* in Ex. 7 connects it immediately with the first group material from the exposition, and its duple meter connects it at once with the material from the middle of the first group of the exposition. This material was earlier referred to as obviously differing from the other material of the group. The device Beethoven used to call attention to the duple material has been noticed: the augmented sixth was used to slide onto the dominant at the point where the listener expects the dominant to occur. At this same point, the principle of sonata structure dictates (more often than not in Beethoven's time) that new material shall occur. The new material does apparently occur, and the orthodox expectancy is fulfilled, for Beethoven uses this new material to create the tension with the original material. It was pointed out that the deception occurs because Beethoven has not, in fact, left his first group, but he needs to emphasize that right here, in the first thirty-four measures of the symphony, is the nub of the major drama. Further examination of this middle section shows that, while it embodies differences, the melodic and metrical profile of the original material is built into the fabric of the new material. The disguise is complete because the material appears out of phase with its original self (Ex. 8). The implication of this point for the spiritual communication of the symphony will be discussed later. At this point, it must suffice to say that the strength of the bass figure from the opening of the fourth section of the development and its power to reconcile the tensions that have been created during the course of the movement reside in its extension from the two measures (*a* in Ex. 8) to the four measures (*b* in Ex. 7) and the coincidence of the strongest beats of both entities. The additional strength comes from the fact that now each element contributes to the other rather than standing opposed to it.

Ex. 8   mm. 27-31

The actual return to the tonic key and the recapitulation principle takes place in measure 402. The last twenty measures of the final section of the development have been taken up with a clear dominant pedal. It is, however, arguable that the dominant is achieved at the beginning of the final section, and that the harmony of the dominant persists as background throughout the whole section. If this argument is followed, an interesting arrangement of the whole development section is obtained. The two outer sections can now be seen as serving primarily a formal function, whereas the two inner sections would be seen as serving a dramatic narrative function. Thus, Beethoven's "new way" integrates the two essential elements of the temporal (dramatic, discursive, narrative) and the spatial (formal, recapitulatory).

If this kind of examination of the symphony is to have any validity whatsoever, then it must be expected that the evidence of the struggle, the tension and the changes which it has brought about, will also be seen from this point on. The recapitulation, in its first four measures, presents sounds identical with the opening of the symphony. This is one of the two remaining occasions on which we can hear the *a* of Ex. 1 in its original form. The bass line falls, as before, to C-sharp, but whereas in the exposition the C-sharp was compelled to rise again, by force of will, from a situation of weakness, back to the tonic, here it falls further, sagging down to C-natural as an introduction to F. How can it happen that music which is interpreted one way at one point can be differently interpreted when the same music occurs again? The first answer to this question would point to the fact that in the most formal recapitulations the literally repeated material is differently interpreted, the listener having heard the exposition. In this symphony, the different interpretation also arises from the fact that there is no longer any threat, hidden or exposed, to this material, and its repetition in this shape is owing to a formal principle. As if to make this distinction quite clear, Beethoven commits one of the most glaring stylistic solecisms in all of music. (The act is completely intentional, but it is clear that Beethoven intends reaction to be as strong as if it had been unconsciously committed.) In the two measures (410-11) preceding the cadence in F, the first violins and the violas play the only trill of the whole movement, following a turn of three quarter-notes. Together, these two measures stand out from the remainder of the texture as something that might well have fitted into a dancing minuet of thirty years earlier. Now that the conflict within the first theme is over, self-assurance makes humor a possibility. It is this humor that makes the repetition of the plodding version of the first theme something which can be heard as a sham, a mockery, an unreality. Formally, the recapitulation is perfect and serious in intent: dramatically it is equivalent to the tolerant looking-back on former weaknesses. As if to show the reality of the situation, the French horn now takes its melody, which it so desperately wanted to take at the start of the recapitulation. (The famous horn anticipation can now be seen as a stroke of humor in which the formality of the recapitulation of the old version of the theme forces the new version to give way to it, and the new version has the strength to stand back and await its due place.) A more complete presentation of assurance cannot be found than that in measures 415 onwards, in which the horn holds its final note on the fifth degree for five whole measures. The flute follows suit with a similar demonstration of a superabundance of energy. The two keys chosen for this section are also of interest since they are equally spaced, two steps on either side of E-flat in the cycle of fifths — a further demonstration of assurance. On the return to E-flat for the repeat of the last section of the *ABA* form, which the first group still is, Beethoven presents the old version (*a* in Ex. 1) for the last time.

Now the first group in recapitulation is still basically an *ABA* form, but it is remarkable — not simply interesting but vital — that Beethoven has omitted any reference to the original *B* section (Ex. 2). The reason is clear. That material which presented the initial tension, which was the cause of the major conflict, was removed when the tension was resolved, and thus it cannot appear again. In its place, Beethoven sets the final version of the opening theme with the emphasis on the long-held fifth degree. This part of the drama is over. With the disappearance of this dissident material, there is no possibility of using the chord of the augmented sixth to draw attention to it. And since there is no need to indicate similarities or orthodox relationships, the second augmented sixth, which Beethoven used to introduce his real second group, also disappears. Now the second group is introduced by an ordinary strong dominant. As it was primarily the first group material which created the dramatic action, it is the first group which has been modified by it in the recapitulation. The second group is here presented, as already stated, with not a melody or a rhythm changed.

The coda provides Beethoven with an opportunity for fulfilling the sonata principle of recapitulation; therefore its function in this symphony is virtually entirely formal. To look upon it as a second development is quite mistaken if, by development, dramatic development is implied. Only insofar as it does not literally repeat earlier forms of all its material can the term be justified.

Since the central drama has been resolved, Beethoven cannot do anything in that area. However, a forum for the re-exposure of all the material that first came to light in the development has to be found. The best thing Beethoven can do to make the point clear and to give his coda the appearance of tension is to repeat and extend the most formal procedure of the whole symphony. The sudden forte of the first five notes of the theme in D-flat and the hammered fortissimo of the same melody on C are paper tigers that alarm no one. Everything in the recapitulation has been too settled to allow for any fears that there might be an unsettling process in store. For this is a harmonic extension of that moment in the bass line of the recapitulation when the cellos allowed their melody to sag from C-sharp down to C-natural. The glance into these tonal areas provides just sufficient mock tension to allow Beethoven to look, for the last time, at the purely formal developmental process from the first section of development which counterpointed Ex. 1 with second group material. By definition, there can be no reference to the material from the second section of the development for that was involved with forces of destruction or tension, or whatever they may be called, and they have all been disposed of. The next material to recapitulate is the so-called compromise material, which still cringes in the minor mode in

F and E-flat. An eight-bar link connects that material with the extended leaping figure which, it has been postulated, contained the key to resolution. Its appearance here, in formal recapitulation, occurs in deference to the fact that, although its ancestry was made clear, in the development it was perceived as a new thing. That Beethoven repeats it here stands as proof that he wanted it to be heard as a new entity. In the coda the leaping figure appears alone, and this is yet another confirmation of its role, for, with its dramatic function having ended when it was accepted by the whole orchestra, it cannot be repeated in that role. The passage that follows, in which Beethoven extends the carefree coexistence of duple and triple meter stands as the formal climax of the movement, in the same way as the end of the second section of the development represents the climactic tension.

It appears as though everything in the first movement is concluded, as the four-measure theme, now mirrored by its four-measure equivalent on the dominant, moves through the various sections of the orchestra in a great crescendo. The repeat of the classic process of acceptance already described in connection with the last section of the development calls for comment, for now the rocking from tonic to dominant and back again has become so assured that there is never the least doubt as to what the next move may be.

Yet for some listeners the final measures, from measure 677 to the end, can be the most important. Every point which has had a bearing on Beethoven's method of musical dramatization has been emphasized by the composer, has been made to stand out from its surroundings by one means or another. Now, in the last nineteen measures of this movement, Beethoven rapidly has four of the major elements of the drama pass before our eyes (advisedly eyes, as well as ears). Firstly, eight measures are occupied with a two-part element from the second group, which Tovey once saw as occupying a position of cardinal importance. Since Beethoven uses it once in the exposition and once in the recapitulation and once in the final measures, nowhere modifying a note and only slightly strengthening the color in the final appearance, I can only assume that this material stands as representative of the second group in its unchangeability — analogous to that which was, is, and will be. In other words, it stands for the necessary formality of the sonata principle. The next four measures raise a destructive spirit from the tomb, and the ghost of a dislocated triple meter and a duple meter is heard in the full orchestra. If any listener has been so naive as to miss Beethoven's point, he makes it for the last time by setting beside this forgotten destructive

4-8771

force the positive power that silenced it. The last three chords now can be seen in relation to the first three sounds of the symphony — the two forte chords and the first chord accompanying the opening melody. All the doubt and questioning that marked their first appearance is forgotten, for their relationship, as a pulse subdivided into three has been the stuff of the drama. Their function as dramatic portent has been fulfilled, and the dangers which threatened to modify their relationship have been overcome. The last eleven measures of the movement contain a harmless miniature picture of the whole drama.

No music has ever stated an argument in purely musical terms and simultaneously in extramusical terms so clearly as the *Eroica*. In one of the Brentano-Goethe letters there occurs the following famous passage:

He himself said: "When I open my eyes I must sigh, for what I see is contrary to my religion and I must despise the world which does not know that music is a higher revelation than all wisdom and philosophy, the wine which inspires one to new generative processes, and I am the Bacchus who presses out this glorious wine for mankind and makes them spiritually drunken. When they again become sober they have drawn from the sea all that they brought with them, all that they can bring with them to dry land. I have not a single friend; I must live alone. But well I know that God is nearer to me than to other artists; I associate with him without fear; I have always recognized and understood him and have no fear for my music — it can meet no evil fate. Those who understand it must be freed by it from all the miseries which the others drag about with themselves.[6]

These words could apply to the *Eroica Symphony*'s first movement. Beethoven's "new way" undoubtedly involved very much the kind of considerations which are embodied in this new sonata form. The music has to be more than music — it has to be a means to a way of life, and the dramatic purpose of the *Eroica Symphony* is to provide a lesson on the conquering of self. It is fruitless to talk about the hero of the symphony being Napoleon or General Abercrombie or even Beethoven himself. The work of art is not the author of it, although it certainly is a projection of part of the author. The forces which so nearly overwhelmed Beethoven, and which ultimately resulted in the Heiligenstadt Testament and the rejection of suicide as a way out of difficulty, certainly appear in the musical parable. The music presents the listener with a musical entity which is anything but heroic, since it lacks the strength to escape from the tonic. A destructive force which threatens the existence of the first musical entity is found to be identical with it, but, as it were, out of phase with it. What a musical allegory of those forces which psycho-

[6] Sonneck, *op. cit.*, p. 80 (Bettina von Arnim to Goethe; letter of May 28, 1810).

logical jargon labels as *ego* and *id!* In addition to the internal forces that threaten strength and adjustment, there are those forces which threaten from outside. The heroism involved in the first movement is that which, when threatened to the point of extinction, rejects the solution which requires total suppression of the individuality (compromise solution) and rejects that which requires the uncontrolled expansion of self (the turbulent passage which rejects the compromise and is in turn rejected by it). The heroism lies in the rational adjustment of that which is out of phase, and the result is security.

Many commentators have speculated as to who the hero of the symphony may be, for heroism there certainly is. But it is not the heroism of the military hero, for the man who has the strength to overcome himself is the rarest kind of hero. Beethoven's wish to benefit humanity is realized. The new way which was revealed was one in which Beethoven was able for perhaps the only time in music, to show the listener an analogue of his own potentiality for perfection. *A higher revelation than all wisdom and philosophy.*

BEETHOVEN'S PASTORAL SYMPHONY
AS A *SINFONIA CARACTERISTICA*

By F. E. KIRBY

THE problem of formal organization in large-scale multimovement instrumental compositions of Beethoven — and indeed of all such works of the Classic period, for that matter — continues to be perplexing. There seem to be two important aspects to the question: the first concerns the matter of unity, of formal coherence in the constitution of such compositions, while the second has to do with the question of expression, with the character and, in a way, the artist's purpose or intention in the work. Ordinarily scholars have dealt with these two aspects separately, with the first getting most of the attention, as is clear, for instance, from Ludwig Misch's admirable attempt to formulate a systematic basis for investigations of this kind.[1] Yet there are cases in which it is possible to take the two aspects in combination, and the *Pastoral Symphony* provides a good opportunity to do this.

That Beethoven had specific expressive intentions of some sort with each of his major instrumental works seems clear enough. We have the firsthand reports of both Ferdinand Ries and Carl Czerny, both of whom were at one time or another in close association with Beethoven. Ries maintains that Beethoven, in composing, always had a "definite object"[2] in mind, while Czerny states that Beethoven's compositions always express a "mood or point of view."[3] The Darmstadt composer Louis Schlösser has handed down Beethoven's notion of a "fundamental idea"

---

[1] Ludwig Misch, *Die Faktoren der Einheit in der Mehrsätzigkeit der Werke Beethovens. Versuch einer Theorie des Werkstils.* (Veröffentlichungen des Beethovenhauses in Bonn, Neue Folge, Vierte Reihe, III; Munich, 1958).

[2] Franz Wegeler and Ferdinand Ries, *Biographische Notizen über Ludwig van Beethoven*, rev. ed. Adolf Kalischer (Berlin, 1906), pp. 92-93 (the book originally appeared in 1838).

[3] Carl Czerny, *Die Kunst des Vortrags (Vollständige theoretisch-praktische Pianoforte-Schule*, Op. 500; Vienna, 1847), p. 33.

which allegedly controls the organization of each of his works.[4] It seems
likely that Anton Schindler's conception of poetic ideas which are said to
underlie each of Beethoven's major works belongs here as well, even
though the exact nature of these poetic ideas is far from clear.[5] We also
know that Beethoven himself was deeply concerned with expressive character in his compositions. He provided many of his works, either in whole
or in part, with explicit designations of their expressive quality: *Sonate
pathétique, Sinfonia eroica, Pastoral-Sinfonie, Quartetto serioso, La malinconia, Das Lebewohl, Heiliger Dankgesang eines Genesenen an die Gottheit, Der schwer gefasste Entschluss,* and so forth.

But just exactly how all this is to be interpreted has given rise to
considerable difference of opinion. One such opinion takes its point of
departure from Schindler's poetic ideas. Referring to conversations he
allegedly had with Beethoven himself, Schindler claims that Beethoven
intended to affix programmatic titles to all of his compositions — after
the fashion of the *Pastoral Symphony* — in order to make his intentions
explicit, thus to provide for each of them what Schindler calls a "key."[6]
In a similar vein, Karl Amenda, a close friend of Beethoven around
1800, reports that the adagio of the String Quartet in F major, Opus 18,
No. 1, was explicitly associated by Beethoven with the tomb scene of
Romeo and Juliet; and in a preliminary draft the close of this movement
appears with the annotation "les derniers soupirs." [7] Other examples
could also be mentioned.

It is clear that such an idea would find great resonance among nineteenth-century musicians and writers on music, and indeed E. T. A.
Hoffmann, Friedrich Rochlitz, Ludwig Rellstab, Robert Schumann,
Franz Liszt, and Richard Wagner — to name only a few of the more
prominent among them — have regarded Beethoven and his works in
this light.[8] More recently scholars such as Paul Bekker [9] and Arnold

---

[4] The account of Louis Schlösser, originally published in 1885, has often been
reprinted, as in *Ludwig van Beethoven: Berichte der Zeitgenossen, Briefe und persönliche Aufzeichnungen,* ed. Albert Leitzmann, I (Leipzig, 1921), 253-54. The passage
has often been translated into English.

[5] See Anton Schindler, *Beethoven As I Knew Him,* ed. Donald W. MacArdle,
trans. Constance Jolly (Chapel Hill, N. C., 1966), pp. 400-408.

[6] Anton Schindler, *Life of Beethoven,* translated by Ignaz Moscheles (Boston,
n. d.), pp. 133-36, 140.

[7] See Alexander Wheelock Thayer, *Life of Beethoven,* ed. Elliot Forbes (Princeton,
N. J., 1964), I, 261, and Paul Mies, *Die Bedeutung der Skizzen Beethovens zur
Erkenntnis seines Stiles* (Leipzig, 1925), pp. 150-51.

[8] See Adolf Sandberger, "Zur Geschichte der Beethovenforschung und Beet-

Schering [10] have given similar interpretations. By all odds the most drastic is the one offered by Schering, who set out from the premise that Schindler's poetic idea was the same as a literary program, so that in this view Beethoven's works become virtual symphonic poems, the specific programs for which were not identified by the composer. Schering took it upon himself to uncover these alleged hidden literary programs by moving from a detailed analysis of the music to a hypothetical program which by means of intuition (*Spürsinn*) is then connected with a specific literary work.[11] In this way Schering made the following associations among others: the *Sonate pathétique* with portions of Schiller's *Hero und Leander;* the Sonata in C minor for Violin and Piano, Opus 30, No. 3, with Goethe's *Die Leiden des jungen Werthers;* the *Eroica Symphony* with Homer's *Iliad* (the obvious links to France and Napoleon notwithstanding!); and the three Razumovsky quartets, respectively, to Goethe's *Wilhelm Meisters Lehrjahre,* Jean Paul's *Flegeljahre,* and Cervantes's *Don Quixote* in the translation by Ludwig Tieck. The *Pastoral Symphony* itself is specifically associated with James Thomson's *The Seasons.*

Such an extremely programmatic approach to the problem of the poetic ideas has, to be sure, not found widespread acceptance. A number of arguments indeed may be raised against it, even against the whole idea of any association between Beethoven's works and literary works. It must be noted, for instance, that most suggestions alleging that such relationships exist do not go directly back to Beethoven himself, but rather to people who knew him — Amenda and Schindler. Furthermore, it would seem that if Beethoven really had such elaborate literary allusions as Schering suggests in mind when composing his works, then some — even a great deal — of evidence for this would necessarily be found in the sketchbooks: while in fact there is virtually nothing to substantiate this interpretation. It may, on the other hand, be objected that the sketch for the adagio of the String Quartet in F major, Opus 18, No. 1, has the annotation at the close of the movement "les dernier soupirs," thus apparently confirming the association with *Romeo and Juliet;* but at the same time the passage in question consists merely of conventional

hovenliteratur," in his *Forschungen, Studien und Kritiken zu Beethoven und zur Beethovenliteratur (Ausgewählte Aufsätze zur Musikgeschichte,* II; Munich, 1924), pp. 8-80.

[9] Paul Bekker, *Beethoven* (Berlin, 1912); English ed., trans. M. Bozman (London, 1925).

[10] The principal books are *Beethoven in neuer Deutung* (Leipzig, 1934) and *Beethoven und die Dichtung* (Berlin, 1936).

[11] *Beethoven in neuer Deutung,* pp. 13-14.

"sob" figurations which in themselves would entirely justify the remark in the sketch without any need to bring in *Romeo and Juliet*. Finally, we know Beethoven's intensely negative reaction to the extensive poetic interpretations by the Bremen poet Karl Iken of his Second and Seventh Symphonies, and how he instructed Schindler to make a public protest against such interpretations: "Should explanations be necessary, they should be restricted to characterizing the piece in a general way, something that a well-educated musician should not find it difficult to do correctly." [12]

Since the *Pastoral Symphony*, with its obvious expressive intention and "programmatic" titles affixed to the various movements, has played such an important part in the development of this particular line of interpretation, it is well to realize that the work can also be viewed in an entirely different fashion, as the present essay will endeavor to demonstrate. This is done by establishing a relation between the fundamental, poetic idea underlying the composition as a whole and the older conception, handed down from the Baroque, that a musical composition should be unified by the expression of a single emotional character or quality throughout. The latter idea was espoused by a number of German writers around the turn of the eighteenth century, and with particular force by a group of conservative musicians in Berlin, including Johann Friedrich Reichardt, Carl Spazier, and Carl Friedrich Zelter. Zelter, for instance, refers to a "total idea," which he variously calls also "total feeling" and "total sensation," which is to govern an entire musical composition.[13] This would seem to imply that the overall unity of a large instrumental composition in several movements is somehow bound up with expression of a particular character, emotion, or affective quality. But this idea requires considerable modification before it can readily be applied to the major works of Beethoven, to say nothing of those of the Classic period generally. At the same time, there are several works by Beethoven to which the idea is more readily applicable, and the *Pastoral Symphony* is one of them.

Among the sketches Beethoven made in 1818 we find the following annotation: "*Adagio cantique*. Pious song in a symphony in the ancient modes — Lord God we praise thee — alleluia — either alone or as

[12] Quoted by Adolf Sandberger in the *Neues Beethoven-Jahrbuch*, VII (1937), 173.

[13] See Paul Mies, "Zur Musikauffassung und Stil der Klassik: eine Studie aus dem Goethe-Zelter Briefwechsel 1799-1832," *Zeitschrift für Musikwissenschaft*, XIII (1930-31), 432-43 (especially 434).

introduction to a fugue. The whole 2nd symphony might be characterized in this manner...." [14] As we know, the two symphonies planned here were never composed, but elements of them clearly appear in the Ninth Symphony and in the String Quartet in A minor, Opus 132. Although there are but few compositions of Beethoven that display a single expressive character throughout, the possibility of such a work in his mind is clear enough; indeed, we hope to show that he had already composed at least one work of this kind, exceptional to be sure, but an example nonetheless, the *Pastoral Symphony*. In the London sketchbook (1808), which contains the principal sketches for this work, we find, right at the bottom of the first page the annotation *sinfonia caracteristica*.[15] This qualification was applied by him to no other completed symphony, although he did apply it to the Overture in C major, Opus 138, originally intended for the opera *Fidelio;* and he also, as we have seen, contemplated a symphony characterized by the use of the church modes. Zelter, moreover, used the term "characteristic" with reference to Beethoven in his correspondence with Goethe.[16]

A search for the explanation of the term "characteristic" in art and music leads naturally to aesthetic and musical writings of the late eighteenth century, especially in Germany. Just as we now recognize a number of different meanings for the word "character" — among them a graphic symbol, a style of handwriting, or perhaps more commonly an attribute or set of attributes that makes up or distinguishes an individual or a group of objects or persons — so also in the eighteenth century the term had several connotations. In aesthetics, however, it is the last — an attribute or set of attributes that distinguishes or characterizes something — that was ordinarily meant. But even this meaning is open to further interpretation, since such characterization may underline the uniqueness of an individual or object, in which case the element of individuality — and often emotional expression — is stressed, or it may serve to typify the individual or object, to mark him or it with typical features that belong to a particular group, type, or class. Both interpretations are encountered

[14] English translation as given in Thayer-Forbes, II, 888.

[15] MS London, British Museum, Add. 31766, fol. 2ʳ. Published in *Ein Skizzenbuch zur Pastoralsinfonie op. 68 und zu den Trios op. 70, 1 und 2,* ed. Dagmar Weise, II (Veröffentlichungen des Beethovenhauses in Bonn, Neue Folge, 1. Reihe; Bonn, 1961), 5.

[16] See his letter of May 16, 1820, in *Der Briefwechsel zwischen Goethe und Zelter,* ed. Max Hecker, II (Leipzig, 1915), 62: "Haydn in der 'Schöpfung' und in den 'Jahreszeiten,' Beethoven in seinen Charaktersinfonien und in der 'Schlacht von Vittoria' haben das Seltsamste auf die Tafel gestellt und ausgezeichnet."

in eighteenth-century German aesthetic writings.[17]

The same two possible meanings appear when the term is used with respect to music. Often the word "character," "characterized," or "characteristic" refers to the expression of individual subjective emotions; or it refers to the manifestation in the musical composition of some typical and generally recognized quality. The two are not mutually exclusive.[18] As an example we may take the description given by Carl Friedrich Cramer in his review of Georg Christian Füger's *Charakteristische Clavierstücke:* "These characteristic pieces differ from sonatas thus: in the latter several different characters are presented mixed up together; in the former, however, in general only one definite character is expressed throughout the piece." [19] Thus, according to Cramer, in such a characteristic piece not only is a single expressive character displayed throughout — and thus may be associated with the Baroque doctrine of the expression of the affections — but its character is also definite, and, we may add, in most cases explicit. Cramer's description is borne out by keyboard compositions published in the eighteenth century under the name of characteristic or characterized pieces, such as those by C. P. E. Bach in Birnstiehl's serial anthology *Musikalisches Allerley* (Berlin, 1761-63), or Daniel Gottlob Türk's *Handstücke* (two volumes; Leipzig, 1792), to name only two.[20]

Türk, for his part, has given definitions not only of "characteristic piece," but also of "characteristic symphony." The former designation,

[17] A comprehensive discussion of the problem is Ferdinand Denk, *Das Kunstschöne und Charakteristische von Winckelmann bis Friedrich Schlegel* (diss., Munich, 1925); see also Denk, "Ein Streit um Gehalt und Gestalt des Kunstwerkes in der deutschen Klassik," *Germanisch-Romanische Monatsschrift,* XVIII (1930), 427-42.

[18] The subject needs further investigation. Two works that seem especially close to Beethoven and his circle are: Christian Gottlob Neefe, "Das Charakteristische der Instrumentalmusik," in his *Dilettanterien* (n. p., 1785); excerpt in Ludwig Schiedermair, *Der junge Beethoven,* 2nd ed. (Weimar, n. d.), pp. 89-90; and Christian Gottfried Körner, "Über Characterdarstellung in der Musik," *Die Horen,* I. Jahrgang 1795, 5. Stück, pp. 97-121; in the facsim. reprint ed. (Darmstadt, 1959), Vols. I-II, 585-609; also reprinted in Wolfgang Seifert, *Christian Gottfried Körner als Musikästheiker* (Forschungsbeiträge zur Musikwissenschaft, IX; Regensburg, 1960), pp. 147-58. It should be noted that the distinction between "tone-painting" and "the characteristic" drawn by Hugo Goldschmidt, *Die Musikästhetik im 18. Jahrhundert* (Zurich, 1915) is not always reflected in eighteenth-century writings.

[19] Füger's pieces were published in Tübingen, apparently in 1783 or 1784, and not in 1751 as some earlier references have it. Cramer's review appears in his *Magazin der Musik,* II (Hamburg, 1786), 1308-10.

[20] See Willi Kahl, article "Charakterstück," *Die Musik in Geschichte und Gegenwart,* II (Kassel, 1952), cols. 1094-1100.

he says, "is used primarily for those individual compositions in which either the character of a person, etc., or of any sort of emotion (feeling, passion), such as joy, yearning, compassion, pride, love, etc., is expressed." [21] Again the emphasis is put on the musical representation of particular emotional qualities. As composers of characteristic pieces Türk names C. P. E. Bach, Carl Ferdinand Friedrich Fasch, and Johann Abraham Peter Schulz, in addition to Füger, of whose pieces, incidentally, he says that "they could have remained unpublished without doing art any harm whatsoever."

In Türk's explanation of characteristic symphony the term is associated with the overture to a theatrical or dramatic work of some kind: "Characteristic symphonies is a name that could primarily be given to those symphonies which instead of the usual overtures [i. e., which lack a specific expressive character] are intended to open an opera, an oratorio, or something of the sort. But the term may be applied to a symphony only when it stands in [close] relation to the principal content, or even merely to important individual parts of the opera that is to follow, or when a certain action that is to take place immediately is expressed in the symphony." [22] As examples he mentions the overtures to Gluck's *Alceste,* Naumann's *Cora,* Mozart's *Don Giovanni,* and Reichardt's *Geisterinsel.* Presumably Mozart's overture to *Die Zauberflöte,* as well as several of Beethoven's overtures, could also be included. In any case, the term "characteristic" seems, once more, to refer to a composition whose emotional quality can be exactly determined and explicitly stated in words.

Cramer, in his review of Füger's keyboard pieces, also goes on to name individual composers of characteristic pieces, mentioning first Johann Friedrich Klöffler (who composed a well-known battle symphony) and Justin Heinrich Knecht (who composed an equally well-known pastoral piece), and then adds the names of Telemann, Dittersdorf, and with particular emphasis, C. P. E. Bach. He then makes the assertion that Haydn has also composed such pieces, but that he has omitted the

[21] *Klavierschule,* 2nd ed. (Leipzig, 1806), p. 444. The first edition of Türk's treatise (1789) is available in a modern facsim. reprint, ed. Erwin R. Jacobi (*Documenta musicologica,* I. Reihe, XXIII; Kassel, 1962). The passage corresponding to the one just quoted appears here on p. 395.

[22] *Ibid.,* p. 440: "Charakteristische Sinfonien könnte man vorzugsweise diejenigen Sinfonien nennen, welche, statt der sonst gewöhnlichen Overtüren, zur Eröffnung einer Oper, eines Oratoriums &c. bestimmt sind. Die erwähnte Benennung kommt aber der Sinfonie nur alsdann zu, wenn sie auf den Hauptinhalt, auch wohl bloss auf einzelne wichtigere Theile der darauf folgenden Oper &c. Beziehung hat, oder wenn eine gewisse unmittelbar vorhergehende Handlung in der Sinfonie ausgedrückt wird." (In the first edition the corresponding passage appears on p. 392.)

descriptive titles. Presumably an example of this would be Haydn's Symphony in F minor, No. 35a or 49, composed in 1768, which displays the passionate character throughout, so that it was (and is) known as *La passione,* a title that does not come from Haydn.

Thus we have clearly reached the second of the two principal connotations of the qualification "characteristic": a composition possessing certain typical features that mark it as belonging to a particular genre or type. Such a piece, then, must make use of a musical style that has explicit associations with a definite expressive character. The repertory of such musical styles and associations seems to have been rather small. As examples we may suggest: the passionate, the *pathétique,* the melancholy, the churchly, the military, the heroic, the battlefield, the hunt, and the pastoral-idyllic. Different national characters were frequently expressed through dances.

That Beethoven's understanding of the characteristic was in conformity with this seems clear from an annotation associated with sketches for the Piano Sonata in A-flat major, Opus 26. This unusual composition begins with a set of variations, continues with a scherzo and then a funeral march, and concludes with a rapid finale. After giving the theme used for the variations Beethoven wrote in the sketches, "varied throughout — then a minuet or some other characteristic piece, as, for example, a march in A-flat minor, and then this," and there follows a sketch for the theme of the last movement.[23] A minuet or, better, a march, especially a funeral march, was for him a characteristic piece. Hence, when Beethoven used the designation *sinfonia caracteristica* or, later, *sinfonia pastorella,* it is obvious that he intended a particular kind of characteristic work, one associated with the pastoral character.

Many years ago Adolf Sandberger presented a comprehensive discussion of the pastoral style,[24] so that it is necessary here only to recapitulate the main points of his survey of this tradition. As the principal elements in the pastoral style we may mention bird-call themes, hunting-

[23] Gustav Nottebohm, *Zweite Beethoveniana,* p. 237: "variée tutt a fatto — poi Menuetto o qualche altro pezzo characteristica come p. E. una Marcia in as moll e poi questo."

[24] Adolf Sandberger, "Zu den geschichtlichen Voraussetzungen der Pastoralsinfonie," in his *Forschungen, Studien und Kritiken zu Beethoven und zur Beethovenliteratur (Ausgewählte Aufsätze zur Musikgeschichte,* II; Munich, 1924), pp. 154-200. See also Willi Kahl, "Zu Beethovens Naturauffassung," in *Beethoven und die Gegenwart. Festschrift des Beethovenhauses Bonn Ludwig Schiedermair zum 60. Geburtstag,* ed. Arnold Schmitz (Bonn, 1937), pp. 220-65 and 324-37; Karl Schönewolf, *Beethoven in der Zeitwende,* I (Halle, 1953), 417-21, and Hans Engel, article "Pastorale," *Die Musik in Geschichte und Gegenwart,* X (1962), cols. 937-42.

horn themes, shepherds' pipes (*pifa* or *pifferari*), and shepherds' calls (*ranz des vaches* or yodeling), country dances, the representation of flowing water and of bleating sheep, and the imitation of that characteristic instrument of country life, the bagpipe with its drone bass, In the eighteenth century the lilting dotted rhythm of the siciliano was frequently associated with the representation of the pastoral, as were flutes, oboes, and horns. Melodic motion in parallel thirds was also common. That such features were recognized at the time as having a pastoral character seems clear, for example, from a passage in Goethe's *Italienische Reise,* where a "Pastoral Music" which he heard (January 6, 1787) is described as being characterized by "the shawms of the shepherds," "the twittering of birds," and "the bleating of sheep." [25]

Pastoral compositions of this type had a long history, as has been abundantly demonstrated by Sandberger and Engel. Sandberger gives examples of pastoral subjects (for instance, *Il pastor fido*) in theatrical presentations from the sixteenth through the eighteenth centuries; obviously many operas and intermezzos could be included. Portrayals of the Annunciation and the Nativity are also often pastoral in character, as exemplified, for instance, by Bach's cantata for Annunciation, *Wie schön leuchtet der Morgenstern* (BWV 1), or Handel's *Messiah,* which contains a short instrumental piece called *Pastoral Symphony.* We may also find examples in works by Vivaldi, Boccherini, Leopold Mozart, Dittersdorf, and countless others. Often related to the pastoral piece is the *chace* or *Jagdstück* (the hunt piece).[26] Parts of Haydn's oratorios, *Die Jahreszeiten* in particular, may be connected with this tradition. It is not uncommon to have the naive-idyllic calm interrupted by a brief thunderstorm, as pieces by Freystädtler,[27] Vogler, Knecht, or even Vivaldi testify. The famous overture Rossini wrote for *Guillaume Tell* belongs here, since it presents in succession dawn, a storm, a pastoral, and the quick march as finale.

Even Beethoven himself, apart from the *Pastoral Symphony,* composed works of this kind. There is the early set of *Variations sur un air suisse* (WoO 64), composed around 1790. Then, among a collection of songs Beethoven arranged for the Edinburgh published George Thomson in the winter of 1815-16 under the title *Lieder verschiedener Völker*

---

[25] Goethe, *Werke* (Hamburger Ausgabe), XI (1960), 156.

[26] See Alexander L. Ringer, "The Chasse as a Musical Topic in the 18th Century," *Journal of the American Musicological Society,* VI (1953), 148-59.

[27] See H. W. Hamann, "Zu Beethovens Pastoral-Sinfonie," *Die Musikforschung,* XIV (1961), 55-60.

(WoO 158), are found five Tirolean songs based on yodeling themes and one Swiss song, a duet setting of Goethe's poem in the Swiss dialect *An ä Bergli bin i gesässe;* two of these were subsequently used for sets of variations for piano and flute or violin, Opus 107. Furthermore, it is not impossible that the so-called *Namensfeier* Overture in C major, Opus 115, which was known as *La Chasse* at the time, belongs here, even though Beethoven himself denied the association. Another possible example would be the finale of the Violin Concerto.

When one turns specifically to the *Pastoral Symphony,* it is easy to see that themes connected with the traditional elements of the pastoral style underlie and at the same time unify the entire composition in a most explicit fashion. Two such elements are mentioned by Anton Schindler in his account of the work: the obvious bird calls at the close of the second movement (one of the two plain examples of tone-painting in the symphony, the other being the thunderstorm) and the peasants' dance with its humorous adumbration of the playing of rural musicians. (Here one might refer to Mozart's *Ein musikalischer Spass,* K. 522, which not only contains humor of this sort but is known as *"Dorf-musikanten-sextett."*) Schindler also points to a figure used repeatedly in the first movement, which, he states without giving any evidence, makes use of a pattern characteristic of Austrian folk music.[28]

But there is much more. Perhaps most important is the *ranz des vaches,* the yodeling theme. Common features of *ranz des vaches* melodies are: triadic motion, dotted 6/8 meter (reminiscent of the siciliano), frequent use of grace notes, all harmonized mainly by the tonic triad. There can be no question that the description of a typical *ranz des vaches* melody is at the same time a good description of the principal theme of the finale of Beethoven's *Pastoral Symphony,* the *Hirtengesang.* In fact, as Alexander Hyatt-King has shown, Beethoven employed here a real Swiss *ranz des vaches* melody, the one known as the Rigi tune.[29] Among the sketches for the theme we find the annotation "siciliano," in

---

[28] Schindler, *Beethoven as I Knew Him,* pp. 144-47. Other themes in the symphony have been associated with Slavic, or more specifically, Croatian folk music; but there has been much debate on the problem, and a satisfactory resolution has yet to be reached. See, among others: B. Sirola, "Haydn und Beethoven und ihre Stellung zur kroatischen Volksmusik," *Beethoven-Zentenarfeier. Internationaler musikhistorischer Kongress* (Vienna, 1927), pp. 111-15, and K. Schönewolf, *Beethoven in der Zeitwende,* I, 421 and 695.

[29] A. Hyatt-King, "Mountains, Music and Musicians," *The Musical Quarterly,* XXXI (1945), 401-3.

Ex. 1a   Ranz des vaches (Rigi version, after Hyatt-King)

Ex. 1b   Hirtengesang from *Pastoral Symphony*—Beginning

reference to the rhythm of that dance which Beethoven also uses.[30]

[30] London Sketchbook, fol. 14ʳ. See *Ein Skizzenbuch zur Pastoralsinfonie op. 68*, **II**, 29.

The drone-bass accompaniment to this theme right at the beginning of the finale is worth special attention. First, the clarinets suggest the *ranz des vaches* theme in C major, accompanied by the sustained fifth C-G in the violas; then, the horn echoes the clarinets an octave lower, but joined by the cellos, which play the fifth F-C, thus creating dissonance with the violas. While this may be intended as rustic in character, suggesting the bagpipe, it must also be remembered that, since such dissonances occur in other compositions of Beethoven, notably in the *Eroica Symphony* and the piano sonata *Das Lebewohl,* this character is not to be inferred simply from the mere presence of the dissonance. The passage recurs in varied form immediately preceding the development (bars 56-63).

Elsewhere in the symphony are found themes and passages that depend on the combination of the *ranz des vaches* melodic type and the drone bass. It appears prominently right at the beginning of the symphony, in the principal theme of the first movement. This theme features the drone bass in fifths (as in the finale) and melodic material that may be divided into three segments (which we designate X, Y, and Z), but the underlying basis is clearly triadic. The third segment (Z) moves in parallel thirds, a feature of the pastoral style, while the second part (Y) displays the rhythm Schindler associates with Austrian folk music.

Another example, completely different in character, is the peasants' dance in the third movement, the passage in 2/4 time marked "In tempo d'Allegro ($\quad = 132$)" beginning at bar 165. Here the upper voices are marked by repetitions of a strongly accented rhythmic figure (see Ex. 3c, below) while the bass has heavily accented slow-moving notes (the interval of the fourth predominates here) in a way reminiscent of the bagpipe accompaniment. Furthermore, the first principal theme in this movement, in the D major section (bars 8-16 and 24-32), has something of the same quality.

Many examples from other parts of the symphony could be introduced here to testify to the importance of this type of construction in the composition as a whole. Reference could, for example, be made to the transitional and secondary passages in the exposition of the first movement (bars 94-110), where the bass has the same character; and the same is true of the closing theme (bars 115-35). There are also long stretches in the development section which belong here, especially bars 151-75 and, again, bars 197-221. While the combination of the *ranz des vaches* with the drone bass is less important in the slow movement (the scene by the brook), elements derived from it are not entirely absent, as

Ex. 2   First Movement of *Pastoral Symphony*—Beginning

may be seen from the prevailing character of the bass part.

The *ranz des vaches,* however, is by no means the only interesting feature presented by the finale. The lyrical theme of the movement as stated at the outset consists of an eight-bar phrase played by the first violins and accompanied primarily by pizzicato cellos and sustained chords in the clarinets and bassoons (see Ex. 1). The theme is then repeated two more times, first with the melody in the second violins (bars

17-24) and finally in the violas, cellos, horns, and clarinets (bars 25-32);
with each statement of the theme goes an intensification: the dynamic
level rises and the rhythmic action in the accompanying figuration in-
creases. In short, we have a crescendo in stages, each stage comprising
a complete statement of the theme. This repetitive structure is maintained each time the theme appears during the course of the movement.
In the development the theme commences in the main key, F major, but
its repetitive presentation is broken off during its second statement (bars
64-75). In the recapitulation, the threefold presentation of the exposition is
heard, but the theme is here submitted to figural variation (bars 117-24,
125-32, and 133-40), then followed by the concluding passage (bars
140-64), which is substantially the same as in the exposition.

While such a repetitive structure is perhaps somewhat unusual in a
work of this kind, there are a number of other compositions in which
Beethoven employs it, as, for instance, in the coda of the first movement
of the *Eroica Symphony,* the allegretto of the Seventh Symphony, the
principal themes in the finales of the "Waldstein" Sonata and the Violin
Concerto, as well as, to a lesser extent, the *Coriolan* and *Egmont* overtures. More pertinent here, however, as will be seen, is the use of this
repetitive structure in the finale of the Ninth Symphony, as well as in the
Choral Fantasia, and it is this use that seems to provide a clue to Beethoven's intentions in the *Pastoral Symphony.*

Beethoven's own title for the movement according to the annotation
he put on the original concert-master's part was "The Shepherd's Song.
Joyous feelings with thanks to God after the storm." [31] In the sketchbook
known as Landsberg 10 (formerly in the Prussian State Library, now in
the possession of the Stiftung Preussischer Kulturbesitz in West Berlin)
this theme is characterized by Beethoven as "Expression of thanks. O
Lord, we thank thee. Slide softly throughout." [32] The idea of an expression of thanks to God is of particular interest here, since something of the
sort is also suggested on a single sheet containing sketches for the symphony in the Bodmer Collection at the Beethovenhaus in Bonn, where
the theme is described: "Prayer. 4 voice-parts." [33] Furthermore, in the

[31] Nottebohm, *Zweite Beethoveniana,* p. 378: "Hirtengesang. Wohltätige mit
Dank an die Gottheit verbundene Gefühle nach dem Sturm."

[32] Quoted by Weise, in *Ein Skizzenbuch zur Pastoralsinfonie op. 68,* I, 17:
"Ausdrucks des Danks [.] O Herr wir danken dir [.] schleifen durchaus sanft." See
also p. 10. Compare the slightly different and less correct reading given by Nottebohm, *Zweite Beethoveniana,* p. 375.

[33] See Willi Kahl, "Zu Beethovens Naturauffassung," pp. 253-54: "Gebeth.
4 Stimmen."

sketchbook Grasnick 3 (formerly in the Prussian State Library, Berlin, but apparently no longer extant) there were to be found on a leaf containing references to the *Pastoral Symphony* the words "Praise be to God on high — in the church style — holy in the church style." [34] In view of all this, one might connect the repetitive structure of the theme with the strophic form characteristic of the hymn, as is surely the case with the "Joy" theme of the Ninth Symphony.[35] Sandberger, in his survey of pastoral compositions, makes reference to the symphony by Justin Heinrich Knecht already mentioned, dated around 1784, the outline of which is similar to the *Pastoral Symphony;* its finale bears the title "inno con variazioni." [36] It is entirely possible that Beethoven had a similar conception in the finale of his symphony.

It seems plausible that Beethoven further unified his symphony by employing this repetitive construction, sometimes in conjunction with a crescendo and sometimes not, in all movements of the work. It shows itself primarily in extensive passages characterized by incessant repetition, often almost in the nature of ostinatos, and, by extension, in numerous themes formulated in repetitive phrase structure. One may raise the objection that such formulations appear elsewhere in Beethoven, and so they do, but in this particular composition they seem at the same time to dominate the construction.

A few examples may be given to illustrate this point. In the first movement this kind of construction plays the largest role — apart, of course, from the finale. We can point first to the principal theme itself, where for ten bars the same bar of music is repeated ten times, with a crescendo and then a decrescendo (bars 15-25). Then, in the transition, there is a section characterized by repetition, an eight-bar period presented three times, followed by a cadence of two bars (bars 67-93). But most striking is the development, where we find a long passage (bars 151-80) based on incessant reiteration of the same material, in which the primary phrase unit is four bars in length: this phrase comes first in B-flat and is repeated twice, then in D, where it is also presented three times and associated with a crescendo, and finally a single cumulative

[34] Sketchbook Grasnick 3, fol. 16ᵛ. See *Ein Skizzenbuch zur Chorfantasie op. 80 und zu anderen Werken,* ed. Dagmar Weise (Veröffentlichungen des Beethovenhauses in Bonn, Neue Folge, 1. Reihe; Bonn, 1957), p. 92: "Ruhm sej Gott in der Höh im Kirchenstil heilig im Kirchenstil."

[35] See F. E. Kirby, "Beethoven and the *geselliges Lied,*" *Music and Letters,* XLVII (1966), 116-25, as well as Joseph Müller-Blattau, "Das Finale der Neunten Sinfonie," in *Von der Vielfalt der Musik* (Freiburg im Breisgau, 1966), pp. 269-84.

[36] Sandberger, "Zu den geschichtlichen Voraussetzungen," pp. 190-94.

statement in D, followed by a relaxing passage of eight bars. The whole is then restated in G and E (bars 198-225). Had Beethoven composed this in the 1820s, he would doubtless have marked the section "ritmo a quattro battute." Elsewhere in the symphony repetitive phrase structure prevails in the most important thematic material. In the second movement we may observe it in the principal and secondary themes. In the third movement, where this procedure would accord well with the country-dance character of the composition, we find it in each of the themes: the opening theme, with its opposition of F major and D major, in the village musicians' episode (bars 87-161), and finally in the peasants' dance (bars 165-204). Repetition and sequential structure likewise appear in the fourth movement, the storm.

There are two other factors that promote overall unity in the work but are not specifically associated with the pastoral character. Both have to do with rhythm. The first involves the use of a rhythmic motive in all movements of the symphony. The motive consists of the alternation of eighth-notes with groups of two sixteenth-notes, the sixteenth-notes forming the weak part of the beat. But the motive appears in two forms according to whether the meter is duple (as in the first and third movements) or triple (as in the others). In the first, second, and last movements the motive forms a part of the principal theme, while in the third it dominates the peasant dance episode. As already mentioned, we have Schindler's unsupported statement that this rhythmic pattern is found in Austrian folk music. If true, then the use of this pattern would provide yet another instance of the use of elements of the pastoral style in the symphony.

Ex. 3   Recurring motif in *Pastoral Symphony*

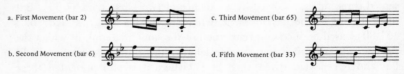

a. First Movement (bar 2)   c. Third Movement (bar 65)

b. Second Movement (bar 6)   d. Fifth Movement (bar 33)

The second has to do with the accompaniment. In this symphony we frequently find ternary subdivision of the beat, as goes without saying in the second and fifth movements, in 12/8 and 6/8, respectively. But it is also prominent in the first movement, in 2/4 time, especially in the long repetitive passages in the development that have already been discussed, where the triple rhythm is continuously maintained in the violas and cellos (bars 151-74 and 196-220); this triplet rhythm in the accompaniment is prepared for in the exposition, as may be seen from the transition and closing themes (bars 54-63 and 115-30). Finally, reference may be made to the conflict in rhythms that characterizes the village musicians' episode in the third movement.

To draw all this together, it seems clear that in the *Pastoral Symphony* the expressive character that promotes unity is explicit: the pastoral style. This character depends upon the use of certain stereotyped thematic types, the *ranz des vaches,* the bagpipe, the country dance, the brook, the bird calls, the storm, and so on, along with an almost systematic use of repetition in the phrase-structure which may be associated with the strophic form characteristic of the hymn. The consistent use of such materials explains why Beethoven called the work a *sinfonia caracteristica*. Hence, in the *Pastoral Symphony* what Schlösser called the "basic idea," what Zelter called the "total idea," Ries's "definite object," Czerny's "basic mood or point of view," or what Schindler referred to as the "poetic idea" of the work does not seem to be a single theme or motive, but rather a complex of elements, all of which are associated with the expression of the pastoral character. It is of such elements that the entire work is composed, and hence this symphony is unified in a way that does not appear to be typical of most of Beethoven's compositions. The symphony rather fulfills one of Cramer's requirements for a characteristic piece: a single expressive character is manifested all the way through.

Thus, it may be suggested that if the symphony is characteristic in the sense here described, with its expressive character manifested by consistent use of elements of a readily recognized pastoral style, this would shed light on some of Beethoven's annotations concerning the work that appear among the sketches. In the London sketchbook (1808), which contains sketches for the entire symphony, we find right on the first page: "it is left to the listener to discover the situations for himself." [37] The sketchbook known as Landsberg 10, which originally was part of the London sketchbook, contains still other written annotations: "even without description one will recognize the whole, which [is] more feeling than tone-painting"; and "Sinfonia pastorella — anyone who has ever had an idea of country life can imagine for himself what the author [intends]." [38] Apart from the usual explanations of these passages, which involve the difference between tone-painting (*Malerei*) and expression of feeling (*Ausdruck der Empfindung*),[39] it seems equally clear that the listeners

[37] Weise, *Ein Skizzenbuch zur Pastoralsinfonie op. 68,* II, 5.

[38] *Ibid.,* I, 17.

[39] Sandberger, "Mehr Ausdruck der Empfindung als Malerei," *op. cit.,* pp. 201-12. See also Willi Kahl, "Zu Beethovens Naturauffassung."

would grasp Beethoven's intention simply because they would recognize the characteristic use of the pastoral style throughout the composition.

The point is especially important in view of interpretations advanced in the nineteenth century, and not infrequently today, according to which the *Pastoral Symphony* is a piece of Romantic program music pure and simple. The fact that Beethoven gave descriptive titles to the various movements of the symphony is often cited in support of this view. On the other hand, we may refer once more to the complete conventionality of these descriptive titles in the context of the tradition of compositions in the pastoral style. But beyond this there remains the fact that the work is a symphony which respects the principal formal requirements of that genre. The tonal organization of the work, for instance, is precisely what would be expected in a symphony: all movements are in F (the storm is in F minor), except the slow movement, which is in B-flat, the sub-dominant relation to the main key. Furthermore, the sonata form, the structure *par excellence* of instrumental music of the Classic period, rules the symphony, appearing everywhere except for the third and fourth movements (the "Gathering of the Peasants" and the storm). It is also worth noting that the realistic bird calls in the second movement are introduced only as an appendage, once the course of the recapitulation has been completed.

Even the undeniable changes in organization made by Beethoven in this work do not basically affect its constitution as a traditional symphony. Among the more prominent changes to be noted here are the added movement (the storm), the peculiar organization of the third movement, the scherzo, and the running together of the last three movements, which follow one another without a pause. The storm, while clearly an example of tone-painting (*Malerei*), is dominated by a single motivic theme, so that the principle of thematic consistency is left undisturbed. As for the peasant dance, we have here a scherzo, but instead of the conventional arrangement with a trio Beethoven gives us a succession of three dances, the first at the very beginning, the second (beginning at bar 87) featuring the village musicians passage already mentioned, and the third (beginning at bar 165), a stamping dance in duple time (see Ex. 3c). Since such successions of dances are important in the historical background of the symphony, their incorporation here does not represent a departure from the traditions of the genre: the dances merely give a pastoral character to the symphonic scherzo. Furthermore, one could regard the third of the dances (or possibly the second and third taken together) as constituting a trio which is heard twice, between three statements of the scherzo proper, a procedure familiar from the Fourth and Seventh symphonies and other compositions. The last statement of the scherzo proper, then, is' broken off and runs directly into the storm, with which, moreover, it is thematically related.

This brings us to a most important point, the sense of continuity, the progression achieved by the last three movements of the *Pastoral Symphony,* which are to be played without pauses between them: peasants' dance — storm — hymn of thanksgiving. While instances of running movements together are by no means unknown in the instrumental music of the time, as works by Haydn, C. P. E. Bach, and Beethoven himself readily testify, here it is essential to note that the procedure followed in the *Pastoral Symphony* corresponds closely to the second half of Beethoven's Fifth Symphony, which was composed at the same time. In the Fifth Symphony the progression moves from the martial scherzo through the vigorous trio and the muted restatement of the scherzo, which ends in a gradual diminuendo, leading to the mysterious pianissimo passage with the sustained A-flat chord in the strings and the soft pulsation of the timpani, culminating after a gradual quickening of activity and an exhilarating crescendo in the triumphant affirmation of the finale. In the *Pastoral Symphony* the sequence of expressive characters is entirely different, moving from the naive dances of the peasants through the tumult of the storm (which thus, although it is considerably longer and is designated by Beethoven as a separate movement, structurally corresponds to the transition passage in the Fifth Symphony) to the quiet affirmation of the hymn of thanksgiving. The two symphonies thus have much in common, however much they differ in character.

The *Pastoral Symphony,* then, *is* a symphony. But it is a particular kind of symphony, a characteristic symphony, consistently incorporating traditional — and, for the audiences of the time, readily recognizable — elements of the pastoral style, even to the inclusion of virtually stereotyped titles for the various movements and of the most obviously pictorial components of the style — bird calls and the thunderstorm — but in such a way that the normal constitution of the symphonic form is left intact. The consistent use of the pastoral style provides the fundamental idea that underlies and unifies the symphony as a whole.[40]

[40] Work leading to this article was supported in large measure by research grants made through Lake Forest College in the summers of 1965, 1967, and 1968 by the Irene Heinz Given and John La Parte Given Foundation, Inc., and by the Ford Foundation.

BEETHOVEN'S UNFINISHED PIANO CONCERTO OF 1815: SOURCES AND PROBLEMS

By LEWIS LOCKWOOD

THE composition under discussion here [1] would have been the Sixth Piano Concerto if it had been brought to completion, and although it is one of the longest and most developed of Beethoven's unfinished works, it has had surprisingly little notice in the vast Beethoven literature. Nottebohm made passing references to sketches for it in his descriptions of two sketchbooks,[2] and in a brief essay entitled "Ein unvollendetes Clavierconcert" he gave a concise account of the autograph manuscript — the chief source preserving the work — and published a reduced transcription of the first twenty measures.[3] Beyond this the piece has been neither written about at length nor published in facsimile or extended transcription, and only a few accounts of Beethoven's sketches or general activity around 1815 have mentioned it.[4] Among bibliographers it is listed only by Willy Hess, who includes the autograph as No. 15 in his *Catalogue of Works by Beethoven Not Published in the Collected Edition* (Wiesbaden, 1957), a listing designed for finished works, not sketches. Hess suggested there that the autograph materials be added to the complete edition, and while it may indeed eventually be published in his supplementary volumes to the Breitkopf *Gesamtausgabe* or in the new edition of the *Werke,* the critical fact here is that it is still inaccessible.

---

[1] An earlier version of this study was read at the annual meeting of the American Musicological Society held in December, 1967, at Santa Barbara, California.

[2] G. Nottebohm, *Zweite Beethoveniana* (Leipzig, 1887), Chapters. XXXIII and XXXIV, especially pp. 312 (incipit only); 314-15 ("kleine abgebrochene Entwürfe"); 321f.: Von Miller=Scheide sketchbook, with transcription of thirty-seven measures of one of the single-staff drafts for the solo exposition.

[3] *Ibid.,* pp. 223-24.

[4] An exception is the note by Elliot Forbes in his revised edition of *Thayer's Life of Beethoven* (Princeton, N. J., 1964), II, 613.

In consequence it is an obvious and conscious limitation of this paper that it will have to resort to assertions about the work and its sources that cannot be readily checked. Perhaps by way of extenuation it should be stressed that the primary concern of this paper is not the analysis and evaluation of the work as a whole, but rather an interpretation of the network of problems raised by the autograph and sketches in their manifold interrelations.

Documentary evidence beyond the musical sources is scarce. Had the work been finished, it would have been not only the last of Beethoven's piano concertos but the last of his concertos for any instrument — and the evidence of the sketchbooks is that it was begun at some time late in 1814 or early in 1815, worked out intensively in several sources and in several ways, and finally abandoned. For whom it may have been intended, exactly when it was started and dropped, what external motivations may have suggested it — about all these questions we can only speculate. None of Beethoven's letters mentions it, presumably because it never reached the point at which he felt it ready to be suggested to a publisher, a matter in which he was not ordinarily reticent. Yet it cannot be wholly irrelevant to this work to cast a larger glance at the changing performance functions of his piano concertos. The first three concertos were written exclusively for his own public performance during his early years as a pianist, and they were even withheld from publication for some years after their composition.[5] In March, 1807, he gave the first known performance of the Fourth Concerto (composed in 1805-1806), and he played it again in 1808. But of the Fifth Concerto the first performance seems to have been that by a little-known pianist named Friedrich Schneider in Leipzig in 1811, and there is actually no evidence that Beethoven himself ever played it in public. Observers tell us that by 1814 his increasing deafness had evidently affected his perception of his own dynamics at the keyboard, and Thayer reports a performance of the "Archduke" Trio in May, 1814, in Vienna as being the last public occasion in which he took part as a pianist except as accompanist.[6] Less than a year later, an impromptu accompaniment to *Adelaide* at a special festival concert (in January, 1815) seems to have been his very last public appearance as pianist.[7] Since he had never performed his piano sonatas publicly, subsequent composition of them did

[5] See Erich Hertzmann, "The Newly Discovered Autograph of Beethoven's *Rondo a Capriccio*, Op. 129," *The Musical Quarterly*, XXXII (1946), 193-194.

[6] See Thayer-Forbes, I, 577-79.

[7] *Ibid.*, I, 610.

not imply concert performance;[8] but it is worth speculating on the possibility that in starting work on this concerto he may have harbored aspirations to play it himself, and that its incompleteness signals in effect a final abandonment of his career as a concert performer.

As a composition attempt it belongs to that twilight stage of his career that divides the "second" period from the "third," roughly 1815-17, extended by some biographers. This is the period which is variously regarded as one of decline or gestation, depending on the point of view, but which is undeniably marked by a decrease in the steady production of finished major works. It lies between two poles: earlier, the intense activity that had culminated in the large works of 1811-12 (the Seventh and Eighth Symphonies, the "Archduke" Trio, and the violin sonata Opus 96) and the revision of *Fidelio* in 1814; later, the composition of Opus 106 in 1818-19. Admittedly, important achievements can be attributed to this period, including in 1815 the overture *Zur Namensfeier* Opus 115, the cello sonatas Opus 102, Nos. 1 and 2, and in 1816 the piano sonata Opus 101 and the cycle *An die ferne Geliebte*. But the major sketchbook for 1815, that which is the primary source of sketches for this concerto, also contains extensive studies for a host of other projects that never materialized, ranging from short, abortive entries to lengthy sketches for an unfinished F minor piano trio. These combine with other evidence to reinforce the impression that for a considerable period Beethoven's earlier pace of achievement had been broken and that he was working not only more slowly but with a different approach.

Since only the most cursory glance at the content of this concerto movement is possible here, a brief outline of its superficial organization and a set of examples must temporarily suffice. It is clear that it was to have had some obvious elements in common with the Fourth and Fifth concertos: an opening introduction with contrasting statements by tutti and solo before the main exposition; also, the first entrance of the solo at its own exposition was to dovetail with the end of the first long orchestral tutti. At the very beginning the two contrasting statements present the theme first in the tutti, measures 1-10, then (elaborated) in the solo, entering at measure 11 on a prolonged V that prepares the return to I at measure 17 by long arpeggios expanding through the total range

[8] Schindler states categorically that "of all Beethoven's sonatas, this Opus 101 is the only one that was publicly performed during the life of the composer"; it was performed by the pianist Stainer von Felsburg at a concert arranged by Schuppanzigh in February, 1816. See Schindler's biography of Beethoven, as translated into English by C. S. Jolly and edited by D. W. MacArdle under the title *Beethoven as I Knew Him* (Chapel Hill, N. C., 1966), p. 209.

of the instrument. In outline the movement is laid out as follows (with indication of appended brief musical examples):

Pages	Segment	Measures	Example
1-4	Introduction		
	Tutti	1-10	1a
	Solo	11-17	
	Exposition		
	Tutti		
5-8	Group 1	17-31	
8-12	Transition	32-51	1b
12-14	Group 2	52-65	1c
15-21	Extension of 2 and concluding figures	66-101	1d
	Solo		
21-24	Dovetailed entrance and preparation of I	102-114	
24-29	Group 1	115-128	
30-37	Transition (alternating tutti and solo)	129-155	
38-40	Group 2	156-169	
41-46	Extension	170-195	
	Development		
47-52	Solo & tutti elaboration of 1 and 2	196-230	
53-56	Solo cadenza on V (sketched)	231-237	
	Recapitulation		
57-58	Tutti introduction in modified form		
	(begins in measure 5)	238-247	
59	Solo	248-252	
60	Tutti Group 1	253-	
		(breaks off at 256)	

Ex. 1a   Concerto, mm. 1-8 (reduced from autograph score)

Ex. 1b   mm. 32-36

Ex. 1c   mm. 52-59

Ex. 1d   mm. 68-75

The rising arpeggiation of the tonic triad in the first subject (Ex. 1a) is reminiscent of other familiar Beethoven uses of the directly ascending major triad for an opening subject, but it has its closest parallel in the contour of the secondary subject in D-flat major in the slow movement of Opus 59, No. 1 (measures 71ff.), written in 1805-1806. Similarly, the primary subject of Group 2 of this concerto movement (Ex. 1c) recalls figures in the Violin Concerto (1806) more readily than it does such finished works of about 1815 as the two violoncello sonatas Opus 102, Nos. 1 and 2. The instrumentation of the opening subject shows a careful calculation of sonority in its pianissimo statement by winds in octaves plus solo double bass. But the primary impression created by the thematic material, if abstracted from the larger context, is that it is decidedly retrospective for 1815, and in many details of linear and rhythmic structure recalls compositions of about ten years earlier. This too may well have been a factor in Beethoven's decision to abandon the project.

Sources

A. The Autograph Manuscript.

The primary and indispensable source for the composition is the autograph score: Berlin, Deutsche Staatsbibliothek, Artaria MS 184. This is an integral manuscript of sixty pages containing the greater portion of the first movement of the concerto — the only movement preserved here and the only one worked out at length in the sketches, though they contain jottings that may be hints for a slow movement and finale. The manuscript is entirely in Beethoven's hand and consists of a fully consecutive orchestral score that breaks off suddenly at a point some twenty-five measures into the recapitulation of the movement (measure 256). Since format is a matter of some moment in this discussion, it should be emphasized that in its basic design this is a full score, not a sketch, and that it is laid out in the normal form familiar from autographs of other Beethoven orchestral works using sixteen-staff oblong paper.[9] The manuscript is entirely uniform in layout, characteristically confining the score to the upper thirteen staves and framing these with a long sweeping vertical brace at the left, with amply spaced bar lines drawn freehand on every page. The manuscript shows no signs of preparation for copying: it has neither title, signature, date, nor other identification anywhere, and even lacks all indication of instruments at the left margin on page 1. But the instrumentation is the same throughout, and the distribution is that familiar from many Beethoven middle-period scores: violins I and II and violas at the top; then in descending order flutes, oboes, clarinets, bassoons, horns, trumpets, timpani; two staves for the solo pianoforte; and at the bottom the basses (single staff).

Although "autograph score" is the convenient and familiar term with which to describe the manuscript, it is far from being in any sense a finished product, complete or even wholly conclusive in all its details, let alone a fair copy of the movement such as might be imagined to have been copied out from amply developed score antecedents.[10] On the contrary, the state of the material leaves no doubt that this is an example

---

[9] See, for example, G. Schünemann, *Musikerhandschriften,* Plate 59 (Fifth Symphony autograph, p. 1); R. Bory, *Ludwig van Beethoven: His Life and Work in Pictures,* p. 114 (March from *Fidelio*); p. 120 (Violin Concerto); p. 121 (*Coriolanus* Overture); E. Winternitz, *Musical Autographs from Monteverdi to Hindemith,* Plate 91 (Ninth Symphony, first page of the slow-movement autograph).

[10] On the problem of the concept "autograph" in Beethoven's works see H. Unverricht, *Die Eigenschriften und die Originalausgaben von Werken Beethovens in ihrer Bedeutung für die moderne Textkritik* (Kassel, 1960), p. 13.

of the rarest type of document of Beethoven's compositional process: it is a "composing score" or "rudimentary score" that occupies what we would generally take to be an intermediate position between the first studies for a piece or movement, in sketch form, and the final, fully developed "autograph" — the *Fassung letzter Hand* — that we normally accept as the final compositional product. The evidence for this view of the manuscript runs through the whole score in gross and subtle forms: its first page begins with a characteristically clear and boldly written version of the opening figure, measures 1-4 (see Ex. 1), and despite a corrected lapse in the staff location of the oboes and a double change of mind over the inclusion of the solo double bass with the winds, the first page alone looks deceptively like the beginning of a final version. But immediately thereafter the assurance of the opening is transformed into a notation heavily laden with corrections, cancellations, insertions, gaps, patching-in of doublings, etc.; in short, a version not merely revised but very much in the process of formation. As the movement proceeds further, even the main line of the material becomes at times obscure. For each small segment of the movement Beethoven puts down the primary ideas for the leading voices on the appropriate instrumental staves, sometimes canceling and changing both content and instrumentation and sometimes sketching in elements of accompaniment on other staves, but never indicating rests for silent measures in secondary instruments or showing clear continuations of the secondary entrances, which form a haphazard pattern of elements that come and go from page to page.

So far as the collective evidence would indicate, this manuscript should be distinguished from the sketches as representing what must be the earliest stage in the composition process at which Beethoven felt himself ready to set the movement into full score. Working with great economy, he left intermittent space for some material that would have to be elaborated in detail later: for instance, at page 5 he had reached a place at which the opening arpeggiated quasi cadenza by the solo pianoforte would resolve back from V to I to begin the first main orchestral tutti — and he accordingly left the first half of page 5 blank to hold the additional arpeggios and scale figures that would form the transition. Still more significant is an empty score-page at page 49, at which he left several measures blank at a point early in the development (measures 210-215) with the obvious intention of returning later to fill them in, while in the meantime going on to the next page. Particularly revealing is that two peripheral notational elements *are* included on this blank page 49, and these have an importance considerably beyond their content. First, the bar lines for these measures are drawn down through all the staves. Second, at the bottom of the page (on the lowest staff, the sixteenth, three staves below the bottom of the score) is visible in small notation what looks at first glance like a series of jotted corrections but turns out to be a species of "cue-staff" (as I shall call it) that has a special importance for the score. This "cue-staff" is the least conspicuous but at the same time most continuous element in the notation of the entire manuscript, and I shall come back to it shortly in discussion of the presumed relationships of the sources. Suffice it to say for the time being that the "cue-staff" first appears on page 6 of the score and continues sporadically through the following few pages; it begins again on page 12 and then runs on with only the most minor interruptions consecutively to page 53, near the end of the whole manuscript. It extends, in effect, from the beginning of the first tutti exposition to the pianoforte cadenza that was intended to close the development and supply a transition to the opening of the recapitulation. The accompanying plate shows page 13 of the score (measures 52-59), marking the point just after the resumption of the "cue-staff." Ex. 2 supplies a complete transcription of the material shown on the plate, to which we shall return later in the discussion.

B. The Sketches.

This review of the known sketches for the concerto can only be cursory, although it covers all the known available material. But in an area that suffers well-known inadequacies of bibliographical information there is always the chance that isolated new material may turn up; furthermore, some sketches that once existed and were mentioned by Nottebohm can no longer be located, while most of what is known is unavailable in any published form. Still, what is argued here is based on transcription of all extant pages, and it is hoped that enough can be gleaned from these to support the present arguments. Sketches for the concerto are known to me in these sources:

1. The Scheide sketchbook, pages 4-32 (and possibly more in seventeen lost leaves following page 32). This is the sketchbook previously known as the Von Miller, Koch, and Flörsheim sketchbook, after its former owners. It is now the property of Mr. William Scheide and is housed in the Scheide Library at Princeton University. Descriptions: Nottebohm, *Zweite Beethoveniana,* pages 321ff.; Georg Kin-

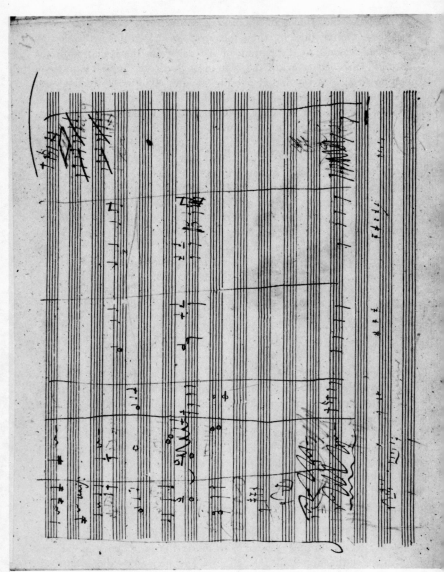

Plate I
Berlin, Deutsche Staatsbibliothek, Artaria 184, page 13, measures 52-59.
(See Ex. 2 for a transcription of this page.)

Ex. 2 Transcription of p. 13 of autograph score of unfinished Concerto (Berlin, Deutsche Staatsbibl. MS Artaria 184), mm. 54-59 (see Plate I).

sky, *Manuskripte, Briefe, Dokumente . . . Katalog der Musikauto-graphen-Sammlung Louis Koch,* pages 69-71. This is the major extant Beethoven sketchbook for 1815, containing material for this unfinished concerto; for the song cycle *An die ferne Geliebte,* Opus 98; the A major Pianoforte Sonata, Opus 101; and the D major Violoncello Sonata, Opus 102, No. 2, as well as for other works both finished and incomplete. Aside from the concerto the most extended sketches in the latter group are for the previously mentioned F minor piano trio that would have postdated the "Archduke" by four years and would have been the last of Beethoven's piano trios. Along with many jottings for works that never developed at all, it also contains the earliest version of what later became the theme for the scherzo of the Ninth Symphony (in 1815!). The sketches for the concerto form a large number of entries for all parts of the first movement. Brief jottings that may allude to a slow movement and finale appear on a few pages, while the first-movement material is spread over twenty-nine pages and consists principally of short and moderate-length variant readings for single ideas rather than extended drafts for lengthy sections — though at least two of these do appear. Especially prominent are a large number of entries for the first subject of the movement (at least twenty-nine entries involve it), many with continuations not represented in the autograph version and in keys not even hinted at in the autograph. The sketches crisscross back and forth among these pages in complex patterns, some of which are connected by an elaborate series of symbols (including the familiar "Vi-de," special symbols such as circles with crosses, and numerical signs such as "1000," "2000," "3200," etc.), at times connecting sketches several pages apart. These sketches reveal anything but a single clearly planned and executed schema; the notation is largely single-staff, occasionally double-staff.

2. Berlin, Deutsche Staatsbibliothek, "Mendelssohn" sketchbook of 1814, perhaps extending into 1815. Description: Nottebohm, *Zweite Beethoveniana,* pages 307-313, with brief mention of some sketches for this concerto near the end of the sketchbook. The sketchbook is reported to have been missing since the end of World War II.[11]

3. Berlin, Deutsche Staatsbibliothek, "Mendelssohn" pocket sketchbook, attributed by Nottebohm to the year 1815. Description: Nottebohm,

[11] Communication from Dr. Karl-Heinz Köhler, Director of the Music Division of the Deutsche Staatsbibliothek.

Zweite Beethoveniana, pages 304-320, with sketches for this concerto towards the beginning of the volume. According to Nottebohm, a portion of this *Skizzenheft* formed a penciled parallel to the Scheide sketchbook (in ink almost throughout), and would have represented the "pocket" variety of sketchbook Beethoven carried with him out-of-doors, while the Scheide is the larger kind of sketchbook used indoors. This volume also is reported to have been missing since World War II.

4. Berlin, Staatsbibliothek der Stiftung Preussischer Kulturbesitz, Musik-abteilung, MS Landsberg 10, pages 79-82. Description: Dagmar Weise, *Beethoven. Ein Skizzenbuch Zur Pastoralsymphonie und zu den Trios Op. 70, 1 und 2* (Bonn, 1961), *Erster Teil,* page 10, note 25; also Nottebohm, *Zweite Beethoveniana,* pages 533-34. This "sketchbook" is actually a mixture of originally separate gatherings from different periods and originally different sketchbooks ranging from ca. 1805 to ca. 1817. Some pages once formed part of the British Museum sketchbook Add. 31766. Pages 79-82 of Landsberg 10 contain a three-staff "continuity draft" of measures 1-72 of the concerto first movement (i. e., the introduction and about three quar-

Ex. 3   Transcription of beginning of three-staff continuity draft of the unfinished Concerto (MS Landsberg 10, p. 79).

ters of the exposition), each system being set up as follows:

> Staff 1: treble-range material (with a few indications of instruments).
> Staff 2: for corrections or additions to staves 1 or 3; also for solo pianoforte sketches.
> Staff 3: bass-range material.

This "short score" in draft form is laid out consecutively on four pages of twelve-staff oblong paper, four systems to the page. Ex. 3 provides a transcription of the beginning of this sketch.

5. London, British Museum Add. 29997, folios 41^r-41^v-42^r. Description: A. Hughes-Hughes, *Catalogue of Manuscript Music in the British Museum,* I, 381; II, 9, 399, and 626; III, 10 and 129 [12] This is a sheaf of forty-two folios of sketches bundled together in no clear order, containing material ranging from before 1800 to the period of the C-sharp minor Quartet (1826), and evidently belonging to at least four different sources. Some of the material from ca. 1815 may be related to the Scheide sketchbook. On folios 41-42 appears isolated material from the very end of the exposition of this movement (approximately measures 94-104) in the form of a three-staff draft, followed by sketches on one or two staves. These pages are twelve-staff oblong like Landsberg 10, pages 79-82, and they may originally have formed part of the same gathering, with these pages tentatively assignable to a position about one full page beyond the point at which Landsberg 10, page 82, now breaks off.

6. Berlin, Staatsbibliothek der Stiftung Preussischer Kulturbesitz, Musikabteilung, MS Grasnick 20b, folios 21-23. Description: Wilhelm Virneisel, "Zu Beethovens Skizzen und Entwürfen," in *Studien zur Musikgeschichte des Rheinlandes: Festschrift zum 80. Geburtstag von Ludwig Schiedermair* (Cologne, 1956), pages 150-55. Folios 21-23 are all sixteen-staff oblong sheets, written in ink throughout. They contain one extended "continuity draft" of measures 1-102 of the concerto movement (that is, from the introduction to the beginning of the solo exposition). This entire draft is written on two-staff systems throughout, in contrast to the three of Landsberg 10. The systems are consecutively laid out on the pages, without any intervening blank staves that could have been used for corrections; where there are alterations, these are crowded into the two-staff systems. The beginning of the sketch is shown in Ex. 4.

[12] A new listing of the Beethoven sketch material in the British Museum is provided by Joseph Kerman, "Beethoven Sketchbooks at the British Museum," *Proceedings of the Royal Musical Association,* XCIII (1967), 77-96.

Ex. 4   Transcription of beginning of two-staff continuity draft of the unfinished Concerto (MS Grasnick 20b, fol. 21ʳ).

Interrelations of Sources

In brief review, the sources just described can be divided into these categories:

1. Sketches, preserved on separate sheets, in gatherings, and in large extant sketchbooks, consisting mainly of nonconsecutive (often, widely separated) variant readings and elaboration of discrete structural units: themes, motives, progressions of several measures, etc. These are the varieties most commonly thought of as "typical Beethoven sketches," thanks chiefly to the great pioneering publications of Nottebohm and the few modern transcription publications (Mikulicz, Schmidt-Görg, Weise, Fishman). The characteristic format of these sketches is the compression onto a single staff (often without clefs) of both upper- and lower-range material written in a very rapid and highly abbreviated notation that exhibits no apparent intent to be legible to anyone but Beethoven. Occasionally, two staves are used where temporarily convenient, but the pattern of alternation of one- and two-staff units is unpredictable. For the unfinished piano concerto movement this type is represented by the sketches in the Scheide sketchbook and probably also by those in the two lost Mendelssohn sketchbooks (to judge from Nottebohm).

2. Sketch-like drafts ("continuity drafts") in which larger sections of a movement, at times even a whole movement, are set forth in consecutive order but in reduced form (in this case a two- or three-staff score). The notation resembles the sketchbook style as do also (in the sketches of the concerto) the extensive corrections, for which in the three-staff version one staff is provided throughout. The three-staff type is represented by Landsberg 10, pages 79-82, and the two-staff type by Grasnick 20b, folios 21-23.

3. The "autograph manuscript": an ideally complete representation of the movement, though the concerto movement is left incomplete, broken off before the end. The distinctive feature of this version, which separates it sharply from the "continuity draft" of Landsberg 10 and Grasnick 20b, is that the entire score of the piece is fully and consistently accounted for throughout the movement. This distinction is of course sharper in the case of a composition for full orchestra than a piano or chamber work, but in principle it should be visible in those categories as well.

If these three types of sources make up the bulk of evidence for Beethoven's compositional process, it needs no emphatic reminder that they are as yet unequally familiar: sketches and sketch-like drafts are fairly well-known, but "rudimentary" scores resembling the score for this concerto are entirely exceptional. Very few remain, probably either because they were elaborated into a final form (from which a copyist could prepare a final copy for the printer) or because they were superseded by other, physically independent scores for given works. Since for orchestral works these rudimentary scores were probably always independent physical units, they are likely to have disappeared once Beethoven had no more use for them — in contrast to the sketchbooks, which formed a vast treasury of ideas and elaborations that always grouped material for many different works within the contents of a single book or booklet, and consequently were carefully preserved. From what has been generally known of the character of Beethoven's sketch material a more or less consistent view has come to be widely held about the nature of the compositional process, a view that envisages a normally steady path of progress from sketches to score, from rudimentary beginnings to a fully developed state. In dealing with specific evidence from this standpoint, one would generally assume a genetic progression leading from Group 1 to Group 2 to Group 3: from initial sketches to more developed ones, then to sketches that are readily definable as continuity drafts, and eventually to the autograph score. A model for this view can be suggested:

Sketch A ⟶ Sketch B ⟶ Sketch N ⟶ Autograph
(continuity draft)

While there are some, perhaps many, compositions for which this model may be plausible, applicable, and illuminating, it does not appear that this concerto is one of them. For the straight-line genetic model is not really adequate to cover the relations of sketches and autograph as we see them here, with consequences that may well extend beyond this composition to other complexes. What it fails to suggest is the possibility that not all the material in the sketchbooks can be assumed to have been worked out before the autograph was begun but that some may have been developed concurrently with the autograph (as "rudimentary score"). On this view the relationship of sketch to autograph may have taken either of two possible forms. On the one hand, they may have stood as antecedent to eventual consequent. On the other, they may have formed alternative compositional work areas, representing complementary and virtually simultaneous purposes, and Beethoven could have proceeded in part by shifting back and forth from rudimentary score to sketchbook, and from sketchbook to rudimentary score, as demanded by the particular character of his material and its compositional problems. In this way, the process of shaping the final paths of elaboration of his material would be recorded in several sources that can be seen as counterparts to one another, rather than as members of a single causal chain. To put these possibilities in the form of theses for wider study:

1. Some sketches doubtless represent a pre-autograph phase of activity, in the familiar sense, and contain versions of musical ideas more "primitive" than those employed in the autograph.

2. The autograph (as "rudimentary score") may have been begun at a relatively early stage of the process, before all the material for the composition had been elaborated in final form and even before all the details were settled. Indeed, in many instances the beginning of an autograph may have been an indispensable precondition to the final formulation of some of the material. And in some cases the very distinction between "sketch" and "autograph" is obscured by the nature of the sources.[13]

3. Other sketches, at times in the same sketchbooks and even perhaps

[13] For an extended discussion of this problem see my study "On Beethoven's Sketches and Autographs: Some Problems of Definition and Interpretation," *Acta musicologica*, XLII (1970), 32-47.

on the same pages as some preliminary entries, may have served for the elaboration of musical ideas concurrently with work on the autograph, and may even in rare instances record some details in a form more nearly final than that of the autograph.

A model reflecting this would suggest a circular or reciprocal relationship between later sketches and the autograph in such a form as this:

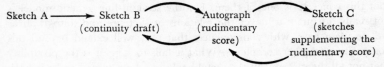

Sketch A ⟶ Sketch B   Autograph   Sketch C
          (continuity draft)   (rudimentary   (sketches
                              score)   supplementing the
                                                rudimentary score)

The loops and connections suggested here are of necessity highly abstract and entirely speculative so far. Many other hypotheses can of course be substituted for this one. But while this model preserves the initial linear sequence of the first, it also reflects, at least in bare outline, something of the variety and potential intricacy of the sources that are beginning to emerge from the still too little-known domain of the so-called Beethoven "sketches."

To submit evidence from the unfinished concerto in support of such a view we should turn first to the autograph, since the critical assertion made earlier is that it represents an unusual example of a rare type — a truly rudimentary score that harbors solid evidence through which we can confidently assign it to a relatively early phase of the creative process. That this autograph represents a still unsettled phase of composition is generally obvious from its sparse content and the extensive corrections and cancellations visible throughout. Even the most enthusiastic admirer of the movement is likely to agree that, despite several very striking thematic ideas, the quality of motivic and harmonic elaboration represented in it at this stage would hardly have survived intact into a later version. Yet even beyond this, the physical layout of the manuscript also shows us something revealing about the sketch process in relation to the autograph. I mentioned earlier that a small but legible "cue-staff" runs almost throughout the entire score at the bottom of each page (sporadically from page 6 to page 12, then continuously from page 12 to page 53, ending at the sketch for a main cadenza by the solo pianoforte; see plate). This "cue-staff" represents for every measure a condensed linear version of the same material that is then distributed above through the orchestral score. Moreover, it is not a revision staff; for it appears from several pages of the manuscript that the cue-staff could not have been entered after the instrumental material above it, but must have been put in first. This is discernible from the blank page (page 49) mentioned earlier: here the page contains nothing but the score bar lines drawn down freehand for six measures, with the cue-staff at the bottom with the material corresponding to each measure. Further, the single line is segmented here in such a way that each string of notes within a measure fits neatly into the middle of the measure. From this page (and from similar spacings on many others) we can reconstruct the steps by which the score was written: first Beethoven drew the bar lines; then he filled in the cue-staff at the bottom; then, using the cue-staff as a guide, he began to distribute the material into the upper orchestral staves. In short, the formation of the score proceeds from the bottom of each page upward into the orchestral fabric — from the cue-staff to the instrumentation of its content.

It should also be obvious that this cue-staff is identical in its format, its content, and even its details of notation to the linear sketches with which we are familiar from many sketchbooks and discussions since Nottebohm (in this case those of the Scheide sketchbook and related sources). In fact it is not too much to say that the cue-staff *is* a species of sketch line that has been transferred, in effect, from sketchbook to autograph score; it is a kind of "missing link" between the two types of redactions and, consequently, between the two types of work areas. The "cue-staff" occasionally uses figured bass numerals as abbreviations (exactly as in many sketches), and has its own corrections, *especially near the end of the unfinished concerto movement,* near the point at which the whole composition broke down (pages 50-51). At page 50 Beethoven writes a new continuation for the cue-staff and labels it "Meilleur," again a typical sketchbook entry; in the next pages the score breaks down into a sketch because the basic decisions about the material at this point have not yet been made.

An attractive inference from this complex bundle of evidence is that the autograph cue-staff goes back to the principal consecutive versions for the movement which we possess: the composition drafts for the exposition in Landsberg 10 (evidently continued in the last pages now bound into British Museum Add. 29997) and Grasnick 20b. This in turn would suggest a straight-line progression from linear sketches to two- and three-staff drafts to autograph (via the cue-staff). The model would be:

| Schiede Sketchbook (single-staff sketches) | → | { Grasnick 20b and Landsberg 10 (continuity drafts) } | → | Autograph (cue-staff) |

This schema is superficially reasonable, and absolutely conclusive evidence cannot be marshalled against it. But the evidence at hand leads me toward a different interpretation, one that would associate the autograph with one stage of a total process that may well have carried beyond it and gone back into the sketches when the particular version entered in the score was broken off. The cue-staff material is at times closer to the monolinear drafts in the Scheide sketchbook than it is, in all details, to Landsberg and Grasnick, though the differences are admittedly minute.

One concrete example may fortify this line of argument. The principal "second subject" of the first exposition of the movement is found in all sources: in the Landsberg 10 draft, in the Grasnick 20b draft, in the

Ex. 5a   Concerto, second subject: MS Landsberg 10, p. 82.

Ex. 5b   Concerto, second subject: MS Grasnick 20b, fol. 21ᵛ

Ex. 5c   Scheide Sketchbook, second subject, "A" (p. 5, staff 7)

Ex. 5d   Scheide Sketchbook, second subject, "B" (p. 6, staff 11)

Ex. 5e   Scheide Sketchbook, second subject, "C" (p. 7, staves 3-6)

Ex. 5f   Scheide Sketchbook, second subject, "D" (p. 13, staves 3-4)

Ex. 5g   Scheide Sketchbook, second subject, "E" (p. 31, staff 5)

Ex. 5h   Concerto, second subject: Autograph cue-staff (see Plate I)

Staff 15

autograph (both cue-staff and score), and in part or whole in five entries in the Scheide sketches. Ex. 5 gives all these readings; from them I infer what I take to be a reasonable chronological sorting, in which the progress of certain problems in the material is more or less sharply visible. The ordering suggested is as follows:

Ex. 5a: Landsberg 10.
  5b: Grasnick 20b (Local correction of measure 7.)
  5c: Scheide A (Local correction of measure 7 of Landsberg 10, corresponding to an alternative reading in Grasnick 20b.)
  5f: Scheide D (A plausible but unattractive solution for the second phrase, of which measures 5-7 remain unused while measure 8, when approached as in the later readings, is accepted.)
  5e: Scheide C (A sketch of the second subject in the dominant, for the Solo exposition, showing the final contour of the upper line.)
  5h: Autograph cue-staff (measures 52-59; the possibility of combining a repetition of measures 52-53 with 54-55 is not prefigured in the preserved sketches and may have been worked out in the cue-staff for the first time.)
  5d: Scheide B (An elaboration of the second subject that is not used in the autograph.)
  5g: Scheide E (A continuation of the first phrase that leads in the direction of F major, not used in the autograph.)

The evident problems of linear direction visible in measure 7 of the Landsberg 10 version form the point of departure for the remaining interpretations. Scheide A is a totally isolated entry, one of those that look like a completely random jotting until one sees the link with the corresponding measure in Grasnick 20b and Landsberg 10 (measure 7). The remaining assignments before the cue-staff version are admittedly based on internal evidence alone — but the physical characteristics of the Scheide sketchbook are so complex that I can say here only that they do nothing to contradict these assignments. As for the hypothetical pair of sketch-entries I place after the autograph version, these are obviously possibilities for passages later in the movement than the first exposition, and they represent figurations and harmonic elaborations beyond the scope of this autograph version.

I would suppose that the elaborate mixture of monolinear sketches in the Scheide sketchbook represents at least two stages of the process: one stage likely to have been about concurrent in development with that of the Landsberg 10 draft (which is different in format and paper from the Scheide sketchbook and could not have come from it), the other concurrent with the autograph. I assume that the three-staff draft in

Landsberg 10 was begun in order to afford more clarity in details than the first single-line sketches could do and that the two-staff draft of Grasnick 20b is close to the same phase, though slightly later. In both of these we see a draft of the first large segment of the movement, from the introduction to the solo exposition. The development and the recapitulation were evidently left to be worked out elsewhere. That "elsewhere" may well have been the score itself, presumably now begun with the "cue-staff" as the basic guide to the larger physical dimensions of the score in full panoply. Along with this I would further assume that Beethoven concurrently entered a number of rapidly flashing new elaborations that are found sandwiched in on pages of the Scheide sketchbook. These entries often deal with the material in ways that seem radical in comparison to the score, e. g., versions of the opening theme in keys far removed from the simple patterns of the score: C major (Scheide, pages 12/15-16), B minor (page 13/9), B-flat major (page 19/1). It is even possible that some of these represent late thoughts about the material that were set down after this score had been given up — then, when Beethoven turned away to other projects, he would have kept the sketchbook as part of his enormous store of sketches and also kept this score, perhaps with a passing intention of returning to it some day. On this view, a model stemma would be:

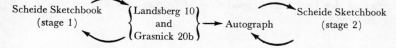

Deciphering and discriminating the putative layers I call stages 1 and 2 of the Scheide sketchbook material for this work is no mean task, and inevitably this scheme is offered as a provisional one. Yet it may help to focus attention on the possibility, perhaps even the necessity, of examining sketches not only in themselves but in connection with their autographs whenever possible, and of regarding all the relevant genetic evidence for individual compositions not only as constituting broad classes of evidence which we seek to label "sketches" or "autographs" but as forming for each work networks of potentially intersecting sources that may shed light on one another and that may embody diverse patterns of compositional procedure.

Since the main feature of evidence for these speculative probings is the cue-staff in the autograph, one may immediately wonder whether the concerto autograph is unique in preserving this link with the sketches. Ample evidence is not yet generally available owing to the well-known scarcity of published reproductions of autographs to date. But at least some support can be mustered.

In a study of the autograph and related sources for the Violin Concerto (1806) published in 1967, Alan Tyson referred to "jottings on the lowest staff in the last movement and in a few places in the first movement as well . . . they are a rough *aide-mémoire* for writing out the work in score." [14] While Tyson's observation of these jottings in the Violin Concerto and my own of those in this unfinished piano concerto were made entirely independently of one another, it seems to me that they corroborate one another in showing Beethoven's special use of the empty lower staves of orchestra scores for compositional purposes. Lacking extensive studies of the autographs of the orchestral works — indeed of works in any category — it is much too soon to say how widespread his use of these cue-staff jottings may have been. But a number of instances in the autographs of works separated by many years, suggest that it may have been a habit of long standing: these include the autograph revision of the ending of the *Coriolanus* Overture (1807), the entire trio of the scherzo of the Fifth Symphony (completed 1808), and the entire Kyrie of the *Missa Solemnis* (1819-23). It seems to me obvious that despite the immense subtleties and difficulties we face in the study of source material of this kind, it is towards the identification and analysis of evidence of this kind that a good deal of further investigation could well be directed.

[14] Alan Tyson, "The Textual Problems of Beethoven's Violin Concerto," *The Musical Quarterly*, LIII (1967), 484.

BEETHOVEN AND ROMANTIC IRONY

By REY M. LONGYEAR

MANY of Beethoven's musical devices strike even today's listeners as being arbitrary, eccentric, or capricious, and have aroused bewilderments and misunderstandings too numerous to mention. Attempts at explaining these effects have ranged from citation of Beethoven's deafness as the reason for his works becoming "immer barocker, unzusammenhängender und unverständlicher" [1] after 1815 to description of his humor, the "Beethovenian jokes which walk on two left feet." [2] Yet his flouting of musical conventions, his contrast of prosaic roughness and poetic beauty, his blunt destruction of sublime moods, and his practical jokes on musicians and audiences can be interpreted within the framework of a literary device which attained its peak during Beethoven's young manhood: romantic irony.

The connection between Beethoven and romantic irony has been missed not only by commentators on Beethoven's music but also by the Germanists who have studied the early Romantic movement and even by previous investigations of German Romantic writers and music. [3] In a recent statement of Beethoven's relationship with romantic irony I discussed only one of the most obvious examples, the string quartet Opus 131, [4] but will show in this study that his use of this device extended back to shortly before 1800, to the time when Friedrich Schlegel (1772-1829) was formulating his concepts of romantic irony and Ludwig Tieck (1773-1853) was independently utilizing romantic irony in his literary comedies.

---

[1] Folker Göthel, ed., *Louis Spohr: Lebenserinnerungen* (Tutzing, 1968), I, 180.

[2] George R. Marek, *Beethoven* (New York, 1969), p. 608.

[3] E. g., Wilhelm Dilthey, *Von deutscher Dichtung und Musik* (Leipzig, 1933); Linda Siegel, *The Influence of Romantic Literature on Romantic Music During the First Half of the Nineteenth Century* (Ph.D. diss., Boston University, 1964); Emil Staiger, *Musik und Dichtung,* 3rd ed. (Zurich, 1966).

[4] R. M. Longyear, *Nineteenth-Century Romanticism in Music* (Englewood Cliffs, N. J., 1969), pp. 31-32.

Though irony has been an essential constituent of German literature from the Minnesinger to Günter Grass, a special type arose at the close of the eighteenth century which critics have usually termed "romantic irony," although "poetic irony," "künstlerische Ironie," and "auto-ironie romantique" have been used as synonyms for this effect. Whereas an earlier view of this concept embraced even Jean Paul Richter's novels and Heine's poems,[5] the general focus of research during the past twenty years has emphasized the works of Schlegel and Tieck.[6]

Schlegel's theories of irony have received many critical interpretations. Though he is credited with having coined the term "romantic irony," he used it seldom, and was equally chary with examples to illustrate his theories. The aphoristic fragments in which he stated his ideas are stimuli to thought rather than elucidations, and he admitted that the irony in these fragments was the cause of much of their incomprehensibility.[7] Yet from these fragments we can compile a description of the concept of romantic irony.

Irony is paradox,[8] instinctive throughout, and impossible either to feign or to explain to one who cannot understand it. It should be all jest and all earnestness (*alles Scherz und alles Ernst*), and a good sign it is when one who cannot understand irony takes the joke seriously and the serious elements as a joke.[9] "Really transcendental buffoonery" is, internally, a mood that perceives everything and rises over all limitations, even those of its own art, virtue, and originality; externally, it is "the

[5] Raymond Immerwahr, "The Subjectivity or Objectivity of Friedrich Schlegel's Poetic Irony," *Germanic Review*, XXVI (1951), 175. This essay contains an extensive review of previous investigations of this topic.

[6] Separate studies are needed to show the reflection of the later ironists in the works of Beethoven's successors. Heine's irony is best paralleled in some of Mendelssohn's works, like his setting of *Neue Liebe* and the second movement of the cello sonata Opus 58. Robert Mollenauer, in his essay "The Three Periods of E. T. A. Hoffmann's Romanticism," *Studies in Romanticism*, II (1963), shows (pp. 222-23) that in Hoffmann's second stage, beginning in 1814, he developed irony "as a concept to replace Romanticism," and Hoffmann's *Kater Murr*, which Karl Wörner ("Schumanns 'Kreisleriana,'" *Sammelbände der Robert-Schumann-Gesellschaft*, II [1966], 61-64) considers the most probable model for Schumann's *Kreisleriana*, belongs to this period of Hoffmann's "negative attitude" toward Romanticism.

[7] Friedrich Schlegel, "Über die Unverständlichkeit" [1800] in *Kritische Friedrich-Schlegel-Ausgabe* (Munich, 1967), II, 368 (hereafter abbreviated *KFSA*). Immerwahr, *op. cit.*, p. 180, cautions the reader against taking Schlegel's statements too literally. References in previous studies of Schlegel's irony have been made to Jakob Minor, *Friedrich Schlegel, 1794-1802: seine prosaischen Jugendschriften* (Vienna 1882).

[8] 48th Lyceum Fragment, *KFSA*, II, 153.

[9] 108th Lyceum Fragment, *KFSA*, II, 160.

expression of the mimic manner of an ordinarily good Italian buffo." [10] Irony is the "clear consciousness of eternal agility, of infinitely full chaos," [11] a capricious appearance of self-annihilation, a playing with the contradictions of form and practice, the introduction of the fortuitous and the unusual, a flirtation with unlimited caprice (*Willkür*) [12] — all as a means to annihilate the self, for self-limitation, the Alpha and Omega for the artist, is a result of self-creation and self-annihilation. [13] Many writers have considered the destruction of illusion a central element in the theory of romantic irony. [14]

To introduce the correlation of Beethoven's music with the concept of romantic irony, let us examine the coda of the last movement of the string quartet Opus 95, which Beethoven himself termed "serious quartet." [15] While commentators on Schlegel's Forty-second Lyceum-Fragment have regarded the "mimische Manier eines gewöhnlichen guten italiänischen Buffo" as a reference to the clowns of the *commedia dell'arte*, they have not considered the Italian opera buffa. Mozart, in the finale of his G major Quartet, K. 387, used the buffa melodies of his closing themes (measures 92-124) as an effective foil for a "learned" fugue, but Beethoven, in ending Opus 95, destroys the illusion of seriousness which has hitherto prevailed with an opera buffa-like conclusion. This ending exemplifies many of the other characteristics of romantic irony which Schlegel described: paradox, self-annihilation, parody, eternal agility, and the appearance of the fortuitous and unusual. Kerman's idea that "the seriousness seems kicked in the rear" [16] is anticipated by Schlegel's description of "extrafeine Ironie" wherein Scaramouche will feign friendliness in a serious conversation while awaiting the moment when he can deliver a kick in the pants. [17]

The central paradox of romantic irony is that the artist, as an individual, animates his work and is constantly perceivable in it, yet must

[10] 42nd Lyceum Fragment, *KFSA*, II, 152.

[11] 69th of *Ideen*, *KFSA*, II, 263.

[12] 305th Athenäum Fragment, *KFSA*, II, 217. We shall subsequently see the importance of *Willkür* as central to romantic irony.

[13] 37th Lyceum Fragment, *KFSA*, II, 151; 28th Lyceum Fragment, *KFSA*, II, 149.

[14] E. g., Immerwahr, *op. cit.*, p. 174; Ingrid Strohschneider-Kohrs, *Die romantische Ironie in Theorie und Gestaltung, Hermaea*, Neue Folge, VI (1960), p. 18, where she equates Schlegel's "buffo" with the destruction of illusion.

[15] Beethoven's autograph "Quartett [*sic*] serioso / 1810" cited in Georg Kinsky and Hans Halm, *Das Werk Beethovens* (Munich, 1955), p. 267; Emily Anderson, ed. and trans., *The Letters of Beethoven* (London, 1961), II, 503.

[16] Joseph Kerman, *Beethoven's Quartets* (New York, 1967), p. 183.

[17] Schlegel, "Über die Univerständlichkeit," *KFSA*, II, 369.

detach himself from it and regard it objectively, almost as if it were an illusion. Romantic irony can therefore be both "irresponsible caprice" and "self-restraint and detachment," [18] with the author as sovereign creator. Such sovereign individuality is expressed by a contemporary of Schlegel, Tieck, and Beethoven, the philosopher Johann Gottlieb Fichte (1762-1814):

I conceive of my independence as I. I ascribe to myself the power of originating a conception simply because I originate it ... by the absolute sovereignty of myself as intelligence. ... I am beforehand as a *thinking* what I am afterwards as an *active* being. I create myself; my being by my thought, my thought by thought itself.[19]

And, as one writer has commented, the artist is to play an essential role in enabling man to become an individual.[20] Evident in Beethoven's own life and conduct is this conception of individuality, as expressed by one who knew him well: "absolute freedom in the commission or omission of any deed, limited only by the laws of morality: such was the guiding principle of this unique character." [21] The moral law which limited Beethoven derived from Immanual Kant and his "categorical imperative" (never act unless you can also will your principle of action into the rank of universal law), with which Beethoven may have become acquainted during his early years in Bonn [22] and which was later to occasion his statement "The moral law within us and the starry heavens above us ... Kant!!!" [23]

Associated both with the independent individual and with romantic irony is the word *Willkür,* which bears the connotations of free will with overtones of arbitrariness and caprice. This is the act of the creating person toward his creation: not an absolute and anarchic license to do and permit everything, but a path to self-determination.[24] Through ro-

[18] Immerwahr, *op. cit.,* pp. 177-78.

[19] Johann Gottlieb Fichte, *Die Bestimmung des Menschen* [1800]; English trans. by Roderick M. Chisholm, *The Vocation of Man* (New York, 1956), pp. 85, 29.

[20] W. Schmidt, "Fichtes Einfluss auf die ältere Romantik," *Euphorion,* XX (1913), 679.

[21] Anton Schindler, *Beethoven as I Knew Him,* ed. and trans. Donald MacArdle, (Chapel Hill, N. C., 1966), p. 238.

[22] Ludwig Schiedermair, *Der junge Beethoven* (Leipzig, 1925), p. 333.

[23] The most complete citation is in Friedrich Kerst, *Beethoven,* trans. H. E. Krehbiel (1905; reprint ed., New York, 1694). See further (and also for a correction of Schiedermair, *loc. cit.*), Robert L. Jacobs, "Beethoven and Kant," *Music and Letters,* XLII (1962), 242-51.

[24] Helga Slessarev, "Die Ironie in Friedrich Schlegels 'Idylle über den Müssiggang,'" *German Quarterly,* XXXVIII (1965), 292.

mantic irony the artist can strive to endure his critical position in a disrupted and finite world; through renunciation and revaluation he seeks a point of view outside himself and raises himself above the division that separates his individuality and the appearance of the world.[25] Romantic irony is therefore *Willkür* in its paradox, its play, "transcendental buffoonery," and yet it corrects the excesses of arbitrariness by providing a means for self-criticism and detachment.

Tieck's early works show this clearly. In his novel *William Lovell* the protagonist writes in a letter, "Everything is subjugated to my will [*Willkür*]....I *myself* am the only law in all of nature; everything obeys this law," [26] and this exaggerated individualism is shown also in the hubris of the anti-hero Scaramuz in *Die verkehrte Welt*.[27] Tieck, moreover, "lays stress upon the element of '*Willkür*' in the workings of the mind of the creative genius." [28]

Arbitrary caprice seems dominant in Tieck's three literary comedies *Der gestiefelte Kater* (1797), *Die verkehrte Welt* (1798), and *Prinz Zerbino* (1800). These "satirical comedies . . . the product of a brief period of time and of one creative mood," [29] are the focal point of Tieck's romantic irony. These plays can be perceived on several levels: as harbingers of the "theater of the absurd" of Pirandello and Dürrenmatt; as literary satires attacking "Bestseller als Kitsch"; [30] as parodies not only of the sentimental plays and novels beloved by the Biedermeier class but also of Shakespeare, Sterne, and Mozart's *Die Zauberflöte;* and, in Tieck's subsequent evaluation of these plays in 1812, as "das Theater parodieren . . . ein Spiel mit dem Spiele . . . sich selbst zu ironisieren." [31]

Parody is not the only element of romantic irony in Tieck's comedies. Contrast is achieved by the incongruous juxtaposition of the ultraserious with the ironic or even with slapstick comedy, the poetic with the pro-

---

[25] Peter Szondi, "Friedrich Schlegel und die romantische Ironie," *Euphorion,* XLVIII (1954), 406.

[26] Ludwig Tieck, *Schriften* (Berlin, 1828), VI, 179.

[27] Karl Pestalozzi, *Ludwig Tieck: Die verkehrte Welt,* Komedia, VII (1964), 127-28.

[28] Alfred E. Lussky, *Tieck's Romantic Irony* (Chapel Hill, N. C., 1932), pp. 113-14.

[29] Harvey W. Hewett-Thayer, "Tieck's Revision of his Satirical Comedies," *Germanic Review,* XII (1937), 147.

[30] Marianne Thalmann, "Der Manierismus in Ludwig Tiecks Literaturkomödien," *Literaturwissenschaftliches Jahrbuch,* V (1964), 345. Neither here nor in her more extensive discussion of these plays in her biography, *Ludwig Tieck* (Bern, 1955), pp. 97-120, does she discuss Tieck's romantic irony.

[31] Ludwig Tieck, *Phantasus* in *Schriften,* V, 280.

saic, and commonplace reality with flights of imagination. There is iron-
ical treatment of the hero, the play, the actors, the readers, and the
audience — Schlegel's "self-limitation" from "self-creation and self-annihilation." Illusions are repeatedly destroyed, not only by sharp contrast
of moods, but also by comments on the plays from the actors and
even from the audience. (Actors situated among the audience under the
guise of spectators interrupt the action and even come from the pit onto
the stage to participate.) Puns, often complex plays on words, abound;
Immerwahr finds the "most ingenious" one in *Prinz Zerbino* to turn on
Nicolai's novel *Sebaldus Nothanker,* which serves as an "emergency
anchor" for the foundering rationalism of Nestor.[32] Even musical ideas
and structures are the subject of word play, for the "overture" and
"entr'actes" in *Die verkehrte Welt* are assigned musical directions (*Andante aus D dur; violino primo solo; Adagio, As moll*) and the sections
marked "rondo" and "menuetto con variazioni" are literary equivalents
of the musical forms, with the words closely following the musical structures.

Interruptions in the plays are frequent and are achieved either by
rapid changes in scene and mood or, within a scene, by the introduction
of incongruities (an essential ingredient of Beethoven's romantic irony,
too); here the comments from the audience, usually of the most philistine type, assist in the creation, destruction, or false "explanation" of
illusion. Tieck further destroys illusions by baldly exhibiting the conventions of the stage, unmasking the machinery through which effects are
created, and making the audience conscious that it is seeing a play; the
playwright, machinist, director, and prompter frequently appear on stage
as part of the dramatic action. Self-deprecatory romantic irony is to be
seen in the attacks on the play delivered by the characters, the stage
personnel, or the acting members of the audience. These often include
the most outrageous slapstick, as in the epilogue to *Der gestiefelte Kater*
when the playwright is driven from the stage by a barrage of paper wads
and spoiled fruit.[33] Certain of Beethoven's works aroused reactions that
would not be out of place in Tieck's comedies — for example, with reference to the second movement of the string quartet Opus 59, No. 1, Bernhard Romberg's "trampling [the cello part] under foot," or a contempo-

[32] Raymond Immerwahr, *The Esthetic Intent of Tieck's Fantastic Comedy* (St.
Louis, 1953), p. 69.

[33] Lack of space does not permit citation of further illustrations from Tieck's
comedies. An antiquated and abridged English translation of *Der gestiefelte Kater*
("Puss in Boots") by Lillie Winter is included in Kuno Francke, ed., *The German
Classics* (New York, 1913), IV, 194-251.

raneous English cellist's calling the piece "patchwork by a madman." [34]

Romantic irony can, in short, be interpreted in a number of ways. It is subjective in its capricious destruction of illusion and mood, yet objective in representing the author's detachment from his work, over which his sovereign control is best shown by "an arbitrary playing with it." [35] Contrasts of scene and mood, interplay of poetry and prose or seriousness and humor, play with dramatic conventions and forms (in *Die verkehrte Welt* the epilogue comes first and the prologue last, and in 1796 Tieck wrote *Ein Prolog*—to nothing),[36] and the "self-representation of art . . . over which no external principle has the power of assertion," [37] — all these contribute to a literary device which at first glance seems to outrage the very idea of art.

* * *

In seeking elements of romantic irony in Beethoven's music, we are hampered by a paucity of statements by him regarding his own music or his intent therein.[38] Criticisms by contemporaries and anecdotes from Beethoven's life provide some supporting evidence, but none as strong as the music itself. Some incidents in Beethoven's life show that he was temperamentally attuned to the concepts of romantic irony. As a young man in 1800 he insulted the virtuoso-composer Daniel Steibelt (1765-1823) when he "picked up the cello part of Steibelt's quintet in passing, placed it (intentionally?) upside down upon the stand, and with one finger drummed a theme out of the first few measures." [39] Twenty-two years later Rochlitz observed that ". . . once [Beethoven] is in the mood, rough,

[34] Alexander Wheelock Thayer, *Thayer's Life of Beethoven*, rev. ed. by Elliot Forbes (Princeton, N. J., 1964), I, 409-10. Yet the close association of Beethoven and Bernhard Romberg since their days in Bonn leads one to believe that this anecdote may well fall in the category of *petite histoire*.

[35] Lussky, *op. cit.*, p. 29. In no other composer's music is the creator's personality more evident than in Beethoven's, yet his irony is a means of giving it an "objective" cast. This is one of the principal differences between the music of Beethoven and that of his more "romantic" contemporaries Dussek, Spohr, and Weber, in which objective and ironic detachment is lacking.

[36] Szondi, *op. cit.*, pp. 406-9 finds "Vorläufigkeit" (with *Ein Prolog* as representative) and consciousness of self the two main ingredients of Tieck's romantic irony.

[37] Strohschneider-Kohrs, *op. cit.*, p. 236.

[38] ". . . being a state of mind, [intent] is rarely susceptible of direct proof, but must be inferred from the facts." Henry Campbell Black, *Black's Law Dictionary*, 4th ed., rev. (St. Paul, Minn., 1968), p. 947.

[39] Franz Gerhard Wegeler and Ferdinand Ries, *Biographische Notizen über Beethoven*, ed. A. C. Kalischer, 2nd ed. (Berlin, 1906), p. 97. The translation in O. G. Sonneck, *Beethoven: Impressions of Contemporaries* (New York, 1926), is less accurate.

striking witticisms, odd notions, surprising and exciting juxtapositions and paradoxes suggest themselves to him in a steady flow." [40] Self-deprecatory are Beethoven's response to the publishing firm of Bernhard Schotts Söhne in Mainz when he described the quartet Opus 131 as a "bit of patchwork" and the frequent references in his letters to his bagatelles Opus 119 and Opus 126 as "trifles." [41] Beethoven delighted in puns, even for serious incidents ("Ich schreibe Noten aus Nöten"), and on the names or titles of his friends he jokingly devised plays on words that ranged from the scatological to the sacred.[42] Many of his surprising modulations, tonal shifts, and unexpected resolutions of dominant harmonies can only be considered puns in music, with the same effect on the hearer. Seyfried testified that "listening to wretched, execrable music appeared to cause [Beethoven] the utmost joy, which he at times proclaimed with roars of laughter ... [in which] he ... was a virtuoso of the first rank" [43] and that he took "almost childish pleasure in the fact that he had been successful in unhorsing such routined orchestral knights," [44] especially in his scherzos. We shall subsequently see two examples of his practical jokes on his musicians.

It is manifestly impossible to list all of Beethoven's compositions in which he had recourse to romantic irony; we shall restrict ourselves to representative instances that give a good idea of his use of this principle. Most of the works to be cited date from 1810 onwards. One more prefatory note is needed, however, before we can take up the musical application of romantic irony; it concerns Beethoven's humorous works. Several of these contain not romantic irony but a playfulness that stems from the Haydn of the finales of the string quartets Opus 33, No. 2, and Opus 76, No. 5, and Symphony No. 102. Playfulness in Beethoven, as opposed to romantic irony, can best be seen in the first movement of the piano sonata Opus 10, No. 2, where the recapitulation is begun in the "wrong key" and a subsequent adjustment made for the return to the home tonic; in the introduction to the finale of the First Symphony; in the canonic trio of the

[40] Friedrich Rochlitz, *Für Freunde der Tonkunst*, 3rd ed. (Leipzig, 1868), IV, 235.

[41] Anderson, *op. cit.*, III, 1295.

[42] See L. Zolnay, "Miklós Zmeskál, Beethovens ungarischer Freund," *Studia musicologica*, VIII (1966), 214 ("Zmeskallität; Baron von Aron; nicht Musikgraff, sondern Fressgraf; Liebster Baron Dreckfahrer"); Donald W. MacArdle, "Beethoven und Karl Holz," *Die Musikforschung*, XX (1967), 21 ("Dem holz christi oder dem span des Holz christi ... sieh unser Mahagoni-Holz ...").

[43] Ignaz von Seyfried, *Beethovens Studien* (Vienna, 1832), cited in Sonneck, *op. cit.*, p. 41.

[44] *Ibid.*, p. 42.

scherzo of the violin sonata Opus 30, No. 2 (a contrast to the awesome canonic minuets in Haydn's Symphony No. 44 and string quartet Opus 76, No. 2); and in the deliberately delayed statement of the tonic in the third movement of the piano sonata Opus 78. One need but compare these movements with those in which similar devices are used ironically: the introduction of the First Symphony finale with that of the Third, the recapitulations of the first movement of the piano sonata Opus 10, No. 2, and the second movement of the string quartet Opus 59, No. 1, and the delayed tonic statement of the third movement of the piano sonata Opus 78 with the "reflective preliminaries" [45] of the openings of the piano sonata Opus 31, No. 3, and the quartet Opus 135. There are a few borderline cases between playfulness and romantic irony, among them the rhythmic complications (incredible for their time) of the syncopated scherzo in the string quartet Opus 18, No. 6, or the unexpected sforzandos in the second movement of the piano sonata Opus 31, No. 3. Incidentally, one work would seem to epitomize romantic irony: the Rondo a Capriccio, Opus 129. It has been shown, however, that the title "Rage over the Lost Penny" was added by Schindler; that the original title was "Alla ingharese [sic] quasi un capriccio"; that the work is an arrangement of an unfinished composition, most likely a "provisional notation on which [Beethoven] based improvisations," written between 1795 and 1798; and that the clumsy dissonances are not Beethoven's.[46]

A few detailed illustrations from Beethoven's music will show the application of several of the concepts of romantic irony. The juxtaposition of the prosaic and the poetic is an essential ingredient in the destruction of illusion that characterizes romantic irony, and sharply contrasting movements, such as the scherzo of the violin sonata Opus 96 (one of Beethoven's few scherzos in minor for a work in major) as it follows the adagio, to which it is directly linked, or the ironic bagatelle Opus 126, No. 4, which destroys the sublime mood created by the preceding bagatelle, are large-scale examples. Conversely, the second movement of the quartet Opus 18, No. 4, contains extreme contrast within a phrase. The rude sawing of the musicians on the principal motive a measure 33 is followed, without transition or preliminaries, by the "poetic" theme at measure 37. The rudeness in measures 33-36 also makes the listener conscious that the motive is being treated in stretto, and this deliberate highlighting of a contrapuntal artifice is analogous to Tieck's

[45] Strohschneider-Kohrs, op. cit., pp. 286-87, based on Szondi, op. cit., p. 409.
[46] Erich Hertzmann, "The Newly Discovered Autograph of Beethoven's Rondo a Capriccio, Op. 129," The Musical Quarterly, XXXII (1946), 171-95.

purposely making the audience aware of the machinery of stage effects, such as the references to trap doors after the hilarious naval battle in Act IV of *Die verkehrte Welt*. Contrapuntal artifice is further highlighted in the recapitulation of this movement (measures 147-66) when the motive is treated in an intricate triple counterpoint.

Beethoven's exuberant delight in displaying his contrapuntal skill culminates in his late works, especially in the fugal finale of the piano sonata Opus 106 and the *Grosse Fuge*. What has been described, in these two works, as "unprecedented, almost exaggerated employment of contrapuntal artifices" [47] is treated with romantic irony in the very titles of the two works: "Fuga a tre voce, con alcuna licenza" in the finale of Opus 106 and, on the title page of the first edition of the *Grosse Fuge*, "Grande Fuge, tantôt libre, tantôt recherchée." Beethoven's exhibitions of contrapuntal artifice can best be compared, not with Schumann's B-A-C-H fugues, Opus 60 (1847), but with Tieck's "naive pleasure in exercising prodigious powers of virtuosity."[48]

The interruption of a mood can be achieved not only by contrasting the prosaic and poetic but also by surprising tonal shifts, a frequent occurrence in Beethoven's music. Most of these sudden shifts, however, are not ironic, but fulfill both dramatic and architectonic functions, usually in going from the submediant to the dominant of the home key at the close of the exposition, as in the first movements of the piano sonata Opus 111, the Ninth Symphony, and the string quartet Opus 130. Yet the sudden dislocations of an apparent tonal stability are treated ironically in the rondo finale of the violin sonata Opus 30, No. 3. Toward the end of the second episode, that is the developmental portion of the sonata-rondo form, Beethoven states the rondo theme as a "false recapitulation" in the major mediant (B major, measures 133-36) after the careful preparation of this tonal center, and then suddenly leaves it (measures 136-38) by an abrupt shift from a unison B to a unison D, the dominant of the home key, to prepare for the statement of the theme in the home tonic at measure 141. In the coda Beethoven not only repeats this joke but tops it: after an extensive dominant preparation climaxed by a sforzando dominant seventh chord that is emphasized with a fermata (measures 165-77), out of nowhere comes the flat submediant tonality, stated in a "vamp" accompaniment (measures 178-

[47] Warren Kirkendale, "The 'Great Fugue,' Op. 133: Beethoven's 'Art of Fugue,'" *Acta musicologica,* **XXXV** (1963), 23.

[48] Robert Minder, "Redécouverte de Tieck," *Etudes germaniques,* **XXIII** (1968), 540.

81), preceding the statement of the rondo theme in this "wrong" key. The listener does not perceive the idea of a tonal axis (B major balanced by E-flat major); rather, he experiences the arbitrary "destruction of illusions" through deliberate playing with the key, the form, and his sense of tonal stability.

Ex. 1   Violin Sonata, Op. 30, No. 3, third movement, mm. 172-83

It is necessary to separate Beethoven's depictions of musical inept-ness from passages in which virtuoso writing for awkward instruments or a working within external limitations is demanded by musical or programmatic exigencies. In the trio of the third movement of the Fifth Symphony the difficult scrambling of the basses, though giving the im-pression of clumsiness, is needed for the creation of a mood of musical exuberance.[49] (Beethoven's encounter in 1799 with the string-bass vir-tuoso Domenico Dragonetti, rather than romantic irony, was the most likely stimulus for this bravura writing for such unwieldy instruments.)[50] And in portraying the musicians of a village orchestra in the scherzo of his Sixth Symphony (measures 91-161)[51] Beethoven had no need to

[49] Noteworthy that E. T. A. Hoffmann, in his review of this symphony in the *Allgemeine Musikalische Zeitung*, XII (1810), found no irony here; he rather no-ticed the abbreviation of the theme when treated by the violins (E. T. A. Hoffmann, *Schriften zur Musik* [Munich, 1963], p. 46).

[50] Thayer-Forbes, *op. cit.*, I, 208.

[51] That he was depicting a village band is shown in Schindler-MacArdle, *op. cit.*, p. 146.

resort to the slapstick comedy of Mozart's *Musical Joke,* nor was he striving to represent musical incompetence.

In the scherzo of the string quartet Opus 131 (measures 444-69) Beethoven creates the effect of musicians who have gotten lost and are trying to get back together; when they do (measures 470-86), they scrape away *sul ponticello.* Previous statements of the initial motive, at the opening and at measures 167 and 333, give the impression of an overeager cellist who starts before his colleagues are ready. The Beethoven literature is filled with accounts of ensembles that broke down or became lost while playing his music, and the composer seems to be here depicting what must have frequently happened in rehearsal and even in performance.

A more subtle example takes place in the final movement of the cello sonata Opus 102, No. 1. The opening of this movement (see Ex. 2a) illustrates, in its first four measures, a "reflective preliminary" [52] to the theme: can't the musicians get together? The development (measures 59-77) gives the impression of a fugato that cannot get under way until the two performers know what they are going to do, and the same preliminary effect is repeated in the coda (measures 168-85; see Ex. 2b). Here the contrast between the "prosaic" (measures 168-83) and "poetic" (measures 184-201) is even more pronounced, but the "poetic" effect is somewhat vitiated by another practical joke, the sustained open fifths in the cello.

The most pronouncedly sustained example of romantic irony in Beethoven's music is the second movement of the string quartet Opus 59, No. 1. Some initial reactions to this movement have already been cited, and of the commentaries on this movement I have seen, only Gerald Abraham's captures the element of arbitrary caprice in this musical embodiment of *Willkür* and the irony which Abraham calls "wit . . . unex-

Ex. 2a   Cello Sonata, Op. 102, No. 3, fourth movement, mm. 1-8

Allegro vivace (♩ = 120)

[52] See note 45, above.

Ex. 2b   mm. 166-86

pected juxtapositions, the relation of the apparently unrelated." [53] A lack of space prevents a detailed analysis of this complex and unprecedented movement, which incorporates aspects of sonata and rondo processes,[54] nor is it possible to indicate more than the most striking examples of romantic irony in this movement.

1. The opening part (A/1) of the first theme is a drum rhythm, virtually insulting to the cellist.[55] Subsequently, as shown in Ex. 3, A/1 is "made melodious" (Ex. 3b), and in the recapitulation appears disguised with a countersubject (Ex. 3c) which is inverted at measures 304-8.

[53] Gerald Abraham, *Beethoven's Second-Period Quartets* (London, 1942), p. 21. A further comparison can be drawn with this movement and Hans Eichner's statements on *Witz* and *Scharfsinn* in his introduction to *KFSA,* II, xxxvi-xxxvii.

[54] Most writers have regarded this movement as a sonata form but the recurrence of the tonic at mm. 68-77 and 101-07 vitiates this principle. Kerman's analysis (*op. cit.,* p. 106) as a scherzo with two trios is an over-simplification. The closest category is the "improper rondo" as defined by Malcolm Cole, "Rondos, Proper and Improper," *Abstracts of Papers Read at the 35th Annual Meeting of the American Musicological Society* (St. Louis, 1969), pp. 28-29.

[55] Thayer-Forbes, *op. cit.,* I, 409, contains an account of a general outbreak of laughter when the cellist "played his solo on *one* note" at a performance in St. Petersburg around 1817.

2. The recapitulation is distorted not only by the countersubject to A/1 and the spiky accompaniment of A/2, but also by the restatement of these ideas in the wrong key; the tonic does not return until the statement of A/3, this time accompanied by a trill. This recapitula-

Ex. 3a   String Quartet, Op. 59, No. 1, second movement, mm. 1-8

mm. 23-28

and

Ex. 3b   mm. 177-83

Ex. 3c

tion may be compared with the "playful" one of the first movement of Beethoven's piano sonata Opus 10, No. 2. There, what appears to be the retransition prepares D minor or D major; the opening theme, after a double bar and a change of key signature to two sharps at measure 117, is then stated in D major. An almost apologetic corrective (iv of D as ii of F) appears at measure 131, and the recapitulation continues in the proper key with the restatement of measures 121-29, now in the home key of F (measures 137-44). But the pivot chord in the quartet movement is an abrupt interruption rather than an apologetic correction.

3. The musical equivalent of a pun is a humorously sudden modulation achieved by the irregular resolution of dominant harmony, a large-scale example being the sudden tonal shift to the submediant which introduces the second theme in the finale of the Eighth Symphony (measures 48 and 224). Such an effect is heightened by the irregular resolution of a diminished seventh chord that is ostensibly functioning as dominant harmony, and a most surprising example of this occurs in the coda of the quartet movement under discussion. Whereas immediately following the statement of A/3 in the exposition and recapitulation (measures 23-28 and 259-64) there is a fortissimo statement of A/1 in the tonic (measures 29-32 and 265-68) which serves as a springboard for a modulation to the tonal area of the first episode (measures 39-64, iii; measures 275-97, vi), in the coda there are surprisingly unexpected irregular modulations emphasized by silences, a statement of A/3 in the remote key of E minor, and an unpredictable return to the tonic, as shown in Ex. 4.

4. The exaggerated pathos of the second episode (measures 115-47 and 354-86) is ironically concluded by the rhythm of A/1 (measures

Ex. 4   String Quartet, Op. 59, No. 1, second movement, mm. 442-60

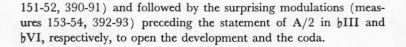

151-52, 390-91) and followed by the surprising modulations (measures 153-54, 392-93) preceding the statement of A/2 in ♭III and ♭VI, respectively, to open the development and the coda.

5. A muddy and apparently purposeless mock fugato at measure 404-19 intervenes between tonic minor (measure 400-404) and tonic major (beginning at measure 420).

An altogether different type of irony permeates the string quartet Opus 135, a work which many have considered the conclusion not only to Beethoven's last quartets but to his entire life's work. Several explanations have been given for the inscription "Muss es sein? Es muss sein!" in the finale: stories about a gruff housekeeper, the reluctance of an amateur musician to pay for the rental of parts, or the frustration of the desire of a music-loving bureaucrat to have the first performance of the quartet Opus 130 in his home without paying Schuppanzigh an indemnity, or, again, claims that the theme of "Es muss sein!" is the inversion of the "Muss es sein?" motive. Cooke has aptly compared with the technique of G. K. Chesterton Beethoven's "use of a phrase with an originally humorous connection as a text for a highly serious disquisition touching lightly on fundamentals," [56] and Llewellyn has seen an analogy between Beethoven's late works, especially the quartets, and Goethe's late novel *Wilhelm Meisters Wanderjahre*, in that in these works "the polished artifice is deliberately eschewed," "the conventional, the cliché almost, becomes peculiarly startling," and there are periods of a "laconic and enigmatic" style.[57] These elements are strikingly present in the finale of the quartet Opus 135.

The irony in Goethe's works has been described as not being the "auto-ironie romantique" which at its worst conceals defects, but as "skepticism turned against itself," filled with a melancholy born of personal inadequacy, yet showing a smiling serenity of self-knowledge that dominates the division between the practical and poetic world.[58] Such is the irony in this final movement of Opus 135. And the real solution of the "schwer gefasste Entschluss" is not the "Es muss sein!" theme, but

[56] Deryck Cooke, "The Unity of Beethoven's Last Quartets," *Music Review,* XXIV (1963), 46. Alfred Einstein, in "Opus Ultimum," *Essays in Music* (New York, 1956), p. 80, rhetorically asks whether the finale is "in jest or in earnest? Cannot gayety be sublime?" — a possibly unconscious reflection of Schlegel's "alles Scherz und alles Ernst" in the 108th Lyceum Fragment.

[57] R. T. Llewellyn, "Parallel Attitudes to Form in Late Beethoven and Late Goethe: Throwing Aside the Appearance of Art," *Modern Language Review,* LXIII (1968), 408-10.

[58] Hans-Egon Hass, "De l'Ironie chez Goethe," *Etudes germaniques,* XXII (1967), 30-33. Hass's description of "auto-ironie romantique" seems to describe better Hoffmann's second period as depicted in Mollenauer, *op. cit.,* pp. 222-34, than the romantic irony of Schlegel and Tieck.

the childlike simplicity of the second theme and its treatment in the coda.[59]

* * *

Romantic irony did not arise from any influence by Friedrich Schlegel on Tieck, nor from their impact on Beethoven. Immerwahr has conclusively shown that Schlegel and Tieck attained their conceptions of irony "from the independent development of similar inclinations in their two personalities," [60] and Schlegel was subsequently unable to recognize Tieck's *Der gestiefelte Kater* as an embodiment of his concepts of irony, for in the 307th Athenäum-Fragment he took the play to be only a literary satire, with its tomcat hero "walking around the roof of dramatic art." [61] Beethoven, for his part, knew of Friedrich Schlegel only as a translator of Shakespeare and, according to Schindler, considered his translations inferior to Eschenburg's earlier versions,[62] and the names of Fichte and Tieck are absent from his conversation books and letters.

The essential question is not that of influence, but of affinity. "Influence" is loosely used to mean that certain salient characteristics beyond the merely technical exist in the works of more than one writer, but the true meaning of these similarities which are more than coincidences derives not from their causation, but from affinities for similar ideas, concepts, or techniques.[63] Influences, in the common sense of the term, are, moreover, impossible to determine when certain ideas are "in the air" — and romantic irony was one such idea. The dying Classic and emerging Romantic styles, and the pedestrian attitudes of musicians and audiences, were as ripe for parody, satire, and pranks as were the sentimental theater and the philistine actors and playgoers of the time. Beethoven, attuned temperamentally to the idea of romantic irony, expressed it in tones much as Schlegel and Tieck represented it in words.

---

[59] Is there not a similar irony in such *opera ultima* as the endings of Monteverdi's *L'incoronazione di Poppaea* and Verdi's *Falstaff?*.

[60] Immerwahr, *Esthetic Intent,* pp. 102-3.

[61] 307th Athenäum Fragment, *KFSA,* II, 207. Furthermore, though Tieck was fond of cats (Hewett-Thayer, *op. cit.,* p. 153), Schlegel stated in this fragment that he disliked them.

[62] Schindler-MacArdle, *op. cit.,* p. 378.

[63] Ihab H. Hassan, "The Problem of Influence in Literary History: Notes Toward a Definition," *Journal of Aesthetics and Art Criticism,* XIV (1955), 68-73.

NEW ROADS TO OLD IDEAS
IN BEETHOVEN'S *MISSA SOLEMNIS**

By WARREN KIRKENDALE

"FRAU v. Weissenthurn wishes to hear something about the ideas upon which you based your composition of the Mass." [1] This request was addressed to Beethoven in a conversation book of December, 1819, that is, at a time when his *Missa Solemnis* was not yet completed, but already much discussed. We do not know the reply. Later, writers have sought those "ideas" in the secularized religiosity of German Idealism, or simply in the realm of feeling. But did Beethoven himself conceive his ideas so indistinctly? Some of his older contemporaries had still known musical ideas as rational exposition of thought, musical formulations as carriers of meaning. Since the dawn of Humanism, music had appropriated, in both theory and practice, the entire sophisticated apparatus of rhetoric. As *ars bene dicendi* it had fulfilled with great refinement the tasks of *docere* and *movere* as well as *delectare;* it was to be not only enjoyed but also understood. However, by the time Beethoven arrived in Vienna this musical intelligibility had few advocates left among the musical public. Kant was no longer aware of it when he wrote that music

* This study was a contribution to the international symposium held in Vienna on the occasion of the bicentenary of Beethoven's birth. The original Latin, German, and French quotations and more complete documentation will appear in the German version, to be published in the *Sitzungsberichte der Österreichischen Akademie der Wissenschaften, philosophisch-historische Klasse,* 1971. I wish to thank Karla Langedijk for her assistance in obtaining the photograph for Plate III, Fred Blum for bibliographical help, and Paul Meyvaert for information on Ambrosius Autpertus.

[1] *Ludwig van Beethovens Konversationshefte,* ed. Georg Schünemann (Berlin, 1941-43), I, 167. The writer is Joseph Karl Bernard. Johanna Franul von Weissenthurn (1773-1847) is the actress, singer, and playwright to whom Beethoven dedicated the song WoO 120.

Throughout this article Beethoven's works without opus numbers are referred to by the numbers given in Georg Kinsky and Hans Halm, *Das Werk Beethovens: thematisch-bibliographisches Verzeichnis* (Leipzig, 1955). To indicate locations of manuscripts *RISM* abbreviations are used.

"speaks without concepts through nothing but feelings" and that it is
"more pleasure than culture." [2] The storm of Romanticism swept away
musical rhetoric, just as it broke up the iconographical traditions of the
visual arts and the *topos* stock of literature. Language, whether verbal,
pictorial, or musical, owes its effectiveness, indeed its very function as a
vehicle for the expression of ideas, to the conventional association of
certain modes of expression with certain meanings. But the romantic
"original genius" and those who built his cult despised what they regarded as the "dry rationalism" of such traditions, rejected that which
may be learned as "artificial" and "unnatural," and no longer understood the depth and wit of an art that had matured with the Enlightenment.

Beethoven — was he storm, or tree in the storm? Thirty years ago
Erich Schenk pointed to "Barock bei Beethoven," [3] and since then it has
become clear that in that great farewell to the "European memory"
(Curtius) the master was not merely the impetuous innovator who is
celebrated in popular literature. Today we see that he not only retained
traditional thought to an unexpected degree,[4] but even uncovered much
older, buried traditions, and formed musical "ideas" in the plain and
concrete sense of the century in which he was born — naturally with an
incomparably freer, personal vocabulary. And this perhaps nowhere so
profoundly as in his *Missa Solemnis,* the work which belongs to the oldest
musical tradition, the work which he believed to be his greatest.[5] Frau
von Weissenthurn may now, somewhat belatedly, be provided with a
partial answer.

The orchestra opens the Kyrie "assai sostenuto," with repeated tonic
chords and complete absence of melodic motion. The first Kyrie-invoca-
tion of the chorus follows with the same music (Ex. 1a). This motif
had opened countless orchestral Masses of the generation before Beethoven, typically in the form shown in Ex. 1b.[6] It is a *topos,* a traditional

---

[2] *Kritik der Urtheilskraft* (1790), par. 53. *Kants gesammelte Schriften* (Berlin,
1913), V, 328.

[3] *Beethoven und die Gegenwart. Festschrift Ludwig Schiedermair zum 60.
Geburtstag* (Berlin and Bonn, 1937), pp. 177-219.

[4] Warren Kirkendale, *Fuge und Fugato in der Kammermusik des Rokoko und
der Klassik* (Tutzing, 1966), pp. 241-306.

[5] *Beethovens sämmtliche Briefe,* ed. A. C. Kalischer (Berlin and Leipzig, 1906-
1908), IV, 136, 138.

[6] Leopold Hofmann, for example, begins nearly two-thirds of his thirty-two
Masses in this manner. Cf. Hermine Prohászka, "Leopold Hofmann und seine Messen," *Studien zur Musikwissenschaft,* XXVI (1964), thematic catalogue; and Beethoven's teacher Albrechtsberger employs it frequently in his orchestral Masses. Cf.

Ex. 1

formulation for this text, traceable in festive Masses via Biber's *Missa Sancti Henrici* (1701)[7] and Cavalli's *Missa concertata* (1656)[8] at least as far back as Benevoli's famous polychoral work of 1628 (Ex. 1c).[9] In nearly every case it announces a Missa solemnis, with trumpets and drums. Recent research has demonstrated that slow tempo and avoidance of melodic and harmonic movement belonged since the early Baroque era to the musical decorum of the King of Heaven.[10] The topos reflects the ancient conception of God as the one who possesses *apatheia,* is free from all passions and, as the first cause of being, is himself immovable — the concept taken over from the Stoics by the Greek Fathers into Western theology. Beethoven's formulation, unlike those of his predecessors, begins on a weak beat, thus removed still further from the dynamics of human passions. It is a borderline case of gesture in music: movement which is almost at a standstill. The invocation of Christ in the middle section shifts to the traditional triple time, andante, i. e., more human movement for Him who was also human.

In the Gloria, the prescribed gestures of the liturgy find their counterparts in the rhetorical figures of the music. The celebrant, when intoning

Andreas Weissenbäck, "Thematisches Verzeichnis der Kirchenkompositionen von Johann Georg Albrechtsberger," *Jahrbuch des Stiftes Klosterneuburg,* VI (1914), Nos. 3, 52, 66, 128, 145, 156. Karl Pfannhauser, "Zu Mozarts Kirchenwerken von 1768," *Mozart-Jahrbuch,* 1954, p. 162, gives examples by C. G. Reutter, Ferdinand Schmidt, and Johann Georg Zechner. Cf. also the Masses of Fux, K. 14, 15, 28, and Mozart, K. 139 and 258. The notorious "Schulmeistermesse" (US-Wc Ms. M2010A9 etc.) uses the formula satirically, and Cherubini's *Deuxième Messe solennelle* (Paris, chez l'auteur, n. d.; composed 1811) presents a characteristically French version with double dotting.

[7] *Denkmäler der Tonkunst in Österreich* (hereafter *DTÖ*): Vol. XLIX, *Messen von Heinrich Biber, Heinrich Schmeltzer, Johann Caspar Kerll* (Vienna, 1918) p. 1.

[8] London: Faber, 1966. Also Cavalli's setting of "Christe" to a falling third in long notes and repeated after a rest, is very similar to Beethoven's.

[9] *DTÖ*, Vol. XX: *Orazio Benevoli: Festmesse und Hymnus* (Vienna, 1903).

[10] Ursula Kirkendale, "The King of Heaven and the King of France: History of a Musical *Topos*," paper delivered at the annual meeting of the American Musicological Society, December, 1969; publication in preparation.

"Gloria in excelsis Deo," raises his arms to express joy,[11] and Beethoven, like so many of his predecessors, begins the movement with a rapidly rising melody, the rhetorical figure of the *anabasis* (Ex. 2). At the word "adoramus," where the priest bows his head,[12] composers suddenly lower the pitch and dynamics.[13] With a plunge from fortissimo to pianissimo Beethoven intensifies this gesture to a musical *proskynesis* (measures 80ff, 100ff.).

Ex. 2

a. Beethoven

Glo - ri - a   in ex - cel - sis   De - - - o

b. Albrechtsberger, 1785 (Weissenbäck No. 88)

Glo - ri - a   in ex - cel - sis De - - o

Glo - ri - a   in ex - cel   -   sis   De - - o

c. Albrechtsberger, 1802 (Weissenback No. 141)

Glo - ri - a   in ex - cel   - -   sis

Glo - ri - a   in ex -

At the invocation of the "Pater omnipotens" God is again depicted in music. We are not surprised that Beethoven realizes the omnipotence much more vehemently than his predecessors do. The familiar down-

[11] Cf. Pierre Le Brun, *Explication litérale, historique et dogmatique des cérémonies de la Messe* (Paris, 1716), p. 175. Cf. also Lamentations of Jeremiah, 3:41: "Let us lift up our heart with our hands unto God in the heavens." Beethoven's motif is rhythmically interesting in that it is actually duple meter in a context of 3/4 time; cf. the undesignated shift to 3/2 for the Gratias, measure 45. It was probably in connection with one of these passages that Beethoven noted in a sketch: "den Rithmus von 3 Täkte im Gloria anzeigen" (Gustav Nottebohm, *Zweite Beethoveniana* [Leipzig, 1887], p. 121), intending a designation such as he made in the string quartet Opus 131.

[12] Cf. Le Brun, *Explication... de la Messe*, p. 185, note 4.

[13] E. g., Leopold Hofmann (Prohászka, p. 94), Haydn's *Heiligmesse* (1796), Paisiello's First Mass (1803, "per la Cappella del Primo Console," US-Wc Ms. ML96 P212), Beethoven's First Mass (1807), Schubert's First Mass (1814), Seyfried's Third Mass (Leipzig, Hofmeister, pl. no. 1044 [= ca. 1824-25]), Preindl's Sixth Mass (Opus 12, US-Wc Ms. M2010 P92). Ignaz Schnabel's *Grande Messe* in F differentiated these two words by setting them a cappella in whole-notes (US-Wc Ms. M2010 A2 S34).

ward leap of an octave on "omnipotens" [14] is stretched here to a twelfth — a huge, powerful gesture akin to the style of the heroic opera of the time. Beethoven also reserved the first entry of the trombones for the one word "omnipotens," *fff* (measures 185ff.). Only after the Mass was completed did he add these instruments,[15] having carefully calculated their effect and noted in his sketches "omnipotens ganze Orgel posaun im Pedal." [16] A reviewer writing in 1828 finds that "A better indication of the correct use of trombones could not easily be found." [17]

Also the setting of "judicare" in the Credo (measures 221ff.) uses the trombones "correctly" to symbolize divine power.[18] The Old Testament associated them with the voice of God (Exod. 19:16, Zach. 9:14),[19] and the New Testament could easily transfer them to His heralds, the angels. This instrumental language had become the musical

[14] It usually occurs in dotted rhythm ♩ ♪ ♪ — e. g., in Haydn's *Missa Sancti Nicolai* (1772) and *Missa in tempore belli* (1796), Cherubini's Second Mass, Schubert's Second Mass (1815), etc. The emphasis of "omnipotens" by a long, sustained note on the first syllable is likewise traditional; cf. Haydn's *Heiligmesse* (1796) and Tomaschek's Missa Solemnis Opus 46 (US-Wc Ms. M2010 T64).

[15] Nottebohm, *Zweite Beethoveniana*, p. 153; *Konversationshefte*, III, 342, 365 (June-July, 1823); *Sämtliche Briefe*, IV, 316 (letter to Schindler, July, 1823). It was common practice at this time to notate the brass instruments and timpani on a separate score; cf. the autograph of Mozart's *Don Giovanni*, Peter Winter's Sanctus in D major (US-Wc Ms. M2010 A2 W82), Danzi's Mass in E-flat (US-Wc Ms. M2010 A2 D2), Schnabel's Mass in F, etc.

[16] D-BNba; cf. the indication in the score, "Pieno Org. con Ped.," and Beethoven's entry in a conversation book of March, 1820, referring to the Credo: "ganzes orchester erst bei patrem omni potentem d.h. Pauke u. Trompete trombonen" (*Konversationshefte*, I, 371). Christoph Straus, in his *Missa Veni sponsa Christi*, introduced "Patrem omnipotentem" with a clarino fanfare — Guido Adler, ed., *Handbuch der Musikgeschichte* (Berlin, 1930), I, 513; cf. also Beethoven's First Mass.

[17] [Georg Christoph] Grossheim, *Caecilia*, IX, 23.

[18] Anglo-Saxons may wonder why Beethoven employs trombones rather than trumpets to announce the Last Judgment. This usage is understandable when we realize that the angels' instrument of the Vulgate, the "tuba" (St. Jerome's uniform Latin translation for the variety of Hebrew words designating horn-like instruments), translated throughout the English Bible as "trumpet," is always rendered in German as "Posaune," i.e., trombone. The scriptural instrument, of course, is not to be identified with either modern type. For centuries artists depicted it as a horn-shaped instrument (cf. Plate I) or as a straight busine, even after the introduction of the coiled trumpet and the slide trombone in the fifteenth century; cf. Reinhold Hammerstein, *Die Musik der Engel. Untersuchungen zur Musikanschauung des Mittelalters* (Bern, 1962), p. 213.

[19] Cf. Origen, *In Jeremiam Homilia V*, in J. P. Migne, *Patrologiae ... series Graeca* (Paris, 1857-1912), XIII, 319C, and Beethoven's "Pater omnipotens." Further instances of trumpets and trombones to symbolize divine presence in literature and music are given by Wilhelm Ehmann, *Tibilustrium. Das geistliche Blasen* (Kassel, 1950), pp. 51-57.

Plate I

The Last Judgment, Pericope Book of Emperor Henry II
(ca. 1022) : Munich, Bayerische Staatsbibliothek,
Codex Lat. 4452, folio 201 .

equivalent of Matthew 24:31: "And He shall send His angels with a great sound of a trumpet, and they shall gather together His elect from the four winds." [20] The Last Judgment from the Pericope Book of Emperor Henry II may serve as an example for the iconographical tradition (Plate I). The chord on which Beethoven's trombones enter was selected only after long deliberation: [21] A-flat minor, with seven flats, transcends normal tonal experience — an extreme harmonic setting for the *extremum judicium*.[22]

The "judicare" passage combines simultaneously two different rhythms: long notes and eighth-note tremolos (measures 223ff.). The declamation of "judicare" on long notes was standard practice, in both orchestral and a cappella Masses.[23] Also this simplest of rhythms reflects the ancient ethical concept which we recognized in the Kyrie-topos. Not only the Stoics, but also the Old Testament knew that, as the prototype of the just judge, God is immovable: "Tu autem, dominator virtutis, cum tranquillitate judicas" (Book of Wisdom, 12:18). The Christian treatises on virtues have transmitted this image to modern times without alteration.[24]

The other rhythmic component, the tremolo, likewise has its traditional role here, where it represents the trembling of those awaiting their judgment. Here we recall the lines of the Dies irae, "Quantus tremor est futurus, Quando judex est venturus," set to tremolos by composers such as Straus, Kerll, and Mozart.[25]

In the preceding Gloria Beethoven employed the tremolo in a nearly identical situation, namely, for the invocation of Christ enthroned in heaven, "qui sedes ad dexteram Patris" [26] (measure 271). The association

[20] Gounod, in attempting to achieve a similar effect in his St. Caecilia Mass, found that he needed no less than twenty-five trombones!

[21] Nottebohm, *Zweite Beethoveniana*, p. 155.

[22] Cf. Grossheim, *Caecilia*, IX, 25: "a highly original harmonic progression."

[23] E. g. Reutter's *Missa S. Caroli* (1734 *DTÖ*, Vol. LXXXVIII, p. 41), Jommelli's Missa a 4 voci (US-Wc Ms M2010 A2 J64), M. Haydn's *Missa in Dominica Palmarum* (1794, *DTÖ*, Vol. XLV, p. 118) and *Missa sub titulo St. Francisci* (1803, *DTÖ*, Vol. XLV, p. 71), Tomaschek's Missa Solemnis, etc. M. Haydn's *Missa Sanctae Crucis* (1762; Vienna, Doblinger, 1949, p. 18), without orchestral accompaniment, simulates a trumpet effect with a fanfare melody.

[24] Cf. Ursula Kirkendale (note 10, above).

[25] *DTÖ*, Vol. LIX: *Drei Requiem ... aus dem 17. Jahrhundert* (Vienna, 1923), pp. 13, 78f. Abbé Vogler, like Beethoven, combines tremolos for "tremor" with long notes for "judex" (Requiem [Mainz: Schott, 1822]).

[26] Biber's *Missa Alleluia* employs six trumpets for this text; see Guido Adler, "Zur Geschichte der Wiener Messenkomposition in der zweiten Hälfte des XVII. Jahrhunderts," *Studien zur Musikwissenschaft,* IV (1916), 26.

of the throne with the judge's chair is clear from the same text in the
Credo ("sedet ad dexteram Patris. Et iterum venturus est cum gloria,
judicare vivos et mortuos"), and it was visible to Christians since the
early Middle Ages through the iconographical grouping of *Majestas* and
Last Judgment. Beethoven accompanies the tremolo with the majestic
dotted rhythm,[27] the musical emblem of the Sun King, which during the
eighteenth century had become the topos for majesty *par excellence*.

Tremolos also appear, a few pages earlier, for the word "peccata"
(measure 256). And in the Sanctus there is an extraordinary array of
them (measures 30-33). It surely has a theological basis. Caesarius, sixth-
century bishop of Arles, writes: ". . . cum tremore simul et gaudio clama-
bunt: 'Sanctus, sanctus, sanctus.' "[28] Indeed, the "tremor" of the tremolos [29] on the minor ninth chord is followed directly by the "gaudium"
of the festive violin figures for "pleni sunt coeli." The rhetoric of the Sanctus is further illuminated through the pianissimo tremolos on the identical
minor ninth chord for a passage of similar religious content in the Ninth
Symphony: "Über Sternen muss er wohnen" (measures 650-54).[30]

But the musical discourse on God is not exhausted with these more
or less traditional images. With the mention of the Trinity [31] in the Credo,
it is intensified to dogmatics, in a way which has few antecedents. The
text of the Credo, as formulated by the Councils of Nicaea and Constan-
tinople, had aimed particularly at affirming the divinity of Christ and of
the Holy Ghost, denied by the Arians and Macedonians, respectively.
Beethoven clearly underlines the ancient dogma when he not only heralds each of the three divine persons with an orchestral introduction, the

---

[27] Also in Cherubini's Second Mass.

[28] No. CCLXXXI of the sermons falsely attributed to Augustine; see J. P. Migne,
Patrologia . . . series Latina (hereafter *PL;* Paris, 1844-64), XXXIX, 2277.

[29] A much less marked use of tremolo in the Sanctus is found in Beethoven's
First Mass, Cherubini's *Messe à trois voix* in F (1808; Paris, Conservatoire, pl. no.
657 [= 1810]), Schubert's First Mass (1814), Cherubini's Quatrième Messe solennelle (1816; Paris, chez l'auteur, n. d.), Seyfried's Fourth Mass (Vienna, Haslinger,
pl. no. 5084 [= 1827/28]), and Hummel's Third Mass, Opus 111 (*ibid.,* pl. no.
5495 [= 1830]).

[30] Another clue to the meaning of Beethoven's trombones is the note in the
sketches for this movement: "auf Welt Sternenzelt [i. e., "Ahnest du den Schöpfer,
Welt? Such' ihn über'm Sternenzelt"] forte Posaunenstösse" (Nottebohm, *Zweite
Beethoveniana,* p. 186).

[31] Rudolf Gerber, "Aufbaugesetze in Beethovens 'Missa solemnis,' " *Das Musik-
leben,* V (1952), 317-21, hypothesized that the quasi-ternary proportions between the
various sections of the Gloria and Credo may have been intended to symbolize the
Trinity. I regard such an intention as unlikely with composers later than J. S. Bach.

prerogative of gods and kings in opera, but even uses the same orchestral ritornello and Credo motif to introduce the "unum Deum" (measures 1-4), the "unum Dominum Jesum Christum" (measures 34-36), and the "Spiritum Sanctum" (measures 265-67, with a slight distinction, mentioned below). With this thematic unity he applies the century-old technique of the "Credo Mass," which repeats the word "credo" before various articles of the Creed.[32] But he reduces the usual number of repetitions, reserving the second and third appearances of the motif for the second and third holy person. This usage might well be compared with the long-lived iconographical type which portrayed Father, Son, and Holy Ghost as three similar figures.[33] Perhaps the best-known representative of this type, which was cultivated from the tenth until at least the sixteenth century, is the elder Holbein's Coronation of the Virgin, in Augsburg. One which Beethoven may very well have known is the famous Töpfer altar of ca. 1515, in the church of St. Helen in Baden near Vienna (Plate II), a town frequently visited by him in his later years.[34] The altar had originally stood in Vienna's cathedral. It was sold to Baden after Benedict XIV, in 1745, forbade such portrayals because of their implication of tritheism.[35] Particularly objectionable from the theological point of view was the representation of the Holy Ghost in human form. Beethoven, however, makes a fine distinction. He makes only the first two orchestral ritornellos perfectly identical (measures 1-4, 34-36); the third is abbreviated and in a different key (measures 265-67). In setting the texts which immediately follow the ritornellos, he then uses identical music only for "in unum Deum" (measures 5ff.) and "in unum Dominum" (measures 37ff.), different music for "in Spiritum Sanctum" (measures 267ff.). This use of the same music for Father and Son is

[32] Cf. Georg Reichert, *Zur Geschichte der Wiener Messenkomposition in der ersten Hälfte des 18. Jahrhunderts* (Ph.D. diss., Vienna, 1935), pp. 27-57; *idem,* "Mozarts 'Credo-Messen' und ihre Vorläufer," *Mozart-Jahrbuch,* 1955, pp. 117-44.

[33] Others united three heads on one body or three faces on one head; cf. Karl Künstle, *Ikonographie der christlichen Kunst* (Freiburg, 1926-28), I, 221-33; Alfred Hackel, *Die Trinität in der Kunst. Eine ikonographische Untersuchung* (Berlin, 1931), chap. 3; Adelheid Heimann, "Trinitas Creator Mundi," *Journal of the Warburg Institute,* II (1938-39), 46; J. J. M. Timmers, *Symboliek en Iconographie der Christelijke Kunst* (Roermond, 1947), pp. 64f.; Ernst H. Kantorowicz, "The Quinity of Winchester," *Art Bulletin,* XXIX (1947), 73-85, especially fig. 8 and note 69; Wolfgang Braunfels, *Die Heilige Dreifaltigkeit* (Düsseldorf, 1954), pp. IX, LI.

[34] In 1817, 1821, 1822, 1824, and 1825.

[35] Brief of October 1 to the Bishop of Augsburg, in *Benedicti XIV. Pont. Opt. Max. . . . Bullarium, tom. I* (Prato, 1845), pp. 570-80. The Töpfer altar probably originated, like Holbein's painting, in Augsburg.

Plate II
"Töpfer" Altar (ca. 1515) in the Church of St. Helena,
Baden near Vienna.

extremely rare in Credo settings,[36] and therefore was probably calculated consciously by the composer, to express the concept "I and my Father are one" (John 10:30).[37] By deriving the ritornello of the Holy Ghost thematically from that of the Father and Son, Beethoven achieves a perfect musical equivalent of the words that follow: "in Spiritum Sanctum qui ex Patre Filioque procedit."

"Et incarnatus est," the words which proclaim the greatest mystery of the Christian doctrine and commemorate, as it were, the beginning of the Christian era, had, for centuries, been set off from their context in the Mass by a marked change of style. Composers of the mid-eighteenth century, such as Wagenseil, Richter, and the so-called Neapolitan school, tended to employ here the modern concertante style, with solo voices and often elaborate virtuosity.[38] The non plus ultra of this Incarnatus type is in Mozart's C minor Mass, K. 427. In the early romantic era the trend was reversed: the stile antico now gives the text a nimbus of awe and solemnity. This solution is only natural for the generation of Wackenroder, Tieck, E. T. A. Hoffmann, and Thibaut, which extolled the "Palestrina style" as the true ideal of sacred music. Thus composers such as Salieri,[39] Danzi,[40] and Witt[41] set the Incarnatus of their orchestral Masses as an a cappella insert, a musical correspondence to the genuflection of the priest at this point. Beethoven composed here a quasi-Gregorian melody; it was recognized already by the reviewer of the first performance as a kind of plainchant.[42] Gregorian melodies, of course, continued to be used in the Mass throughout the eighteenth century; but by Beethoven's time they were relatively rare, especially in orchestral Masses. The one composer who still used them extensively is Michael Haydn, in his a cappella Masses for Advent and Lent. It is significant that in some of these he limits the borrowed melody to the Incarnatus and expressly

[36] It occurs in Cherubini's Second Mass, in Hummel's First Mass, Opus 77 (Vienna, Haslinger, pl. no. 2751 [= 1818]) and, for "Domine Deus" and "Domine Fili," in the Gloria of Cavalli's Mass.

[37] The Scriptures always differentiate between the Father-Son on the one hand, and the Holy Ghost, on the other; cf. Le Brun, *Explication ... de la Messe,* p. 266.

[38] Cf. Karl Gustav Fellerer, *Der Palestrinastil und seine Bedeutung in der vokalen Kirchenmusik des achtzehnten Jahrhunderts* (Augsburg, 1929), p. 315; Ernst Tittel, *Österreichische Kirchenmusik* (Vienna, 1961), p. 145.

[39] Cf. Rudolf Nützlader, "Salieri als Kirchenmusiker," *Studien zur Musikwissenschaft,* XIV (1927), 161.

[40] Mass in E-flat (note 15, above).

[41] "Missa par Vitt organiste à Würstburg" [*sic*], US-Wc Ms. M2010 W83.

[42] Anonymous, *Allgemeine Musikalische Zeitung,* XXVI (Leipzig, 1824), 439: "von schauervoller Wirkung ist der pathetische, eintönige Choral auf die Glaubensworte: *et incarnatus est.*"

labels it "Corale." [43] In the *Missa dolorum B. M. V.* (1762) [44] it is set in
the style of a harmonized chorale, in the *Missa tempore Quadragesima*
of 1794 [45] note against note, with the Gregorian melody (Credo IV of
the *Liber Usualis*) appearing in the soprano. [46] I have little doubt that
Beethoven knew such works of Michael Haydn, at that time the most
popular composer of sacred music in Austria.

In sketches from the beginning and end of his career we find harmonizations of Gregorian melodies: the Lamentations of Jeremiah and
the *Pange lingua*. [47] When he began work on the *Missa Solemnis,* he noted
his intention: "In order to write true church music — look for all the
plainchants of the monks." [48] From such studies, not to mention his exercises in modal counterpoint for Haydn and Albrechtsberger, he learned
to write the Dorian melody for "Et incarnatus est." From his notes and
sketches it is evident that he regarded the "Gregorian" modes primarily
as a means of religious expression. In 1809 he wrote: "In the old church
modes the devotion is divine, I exclaimed, and God let me express it
someday." [49] And in 1818, when he first thought of writing a choral symphony: "A pious song in a symphony, in the old modes, Lord God we
praise Thee—alleluja." [50] The mode used here in the Incarnatus appears in
sketches of 1816, where he notes the authentic and plagal forms of the
Dorian scale; and the designation "dor" among the earliest sketches

[43] It will be remembered that in Italian this means "plainsong," and that in
German both Gregorian chant and Protestant hymn are designated as "Choral."

[44] Düsseldorf: Schwann, 1962, p. 13.

[45] *DTÖ*, Vol. XLV, p. 130.

[46] Other instances of Gregorian melodies in Masses of the late eighteenth and
early nineteenth centuries include the *tonus peregrinus* in Mozart's Requiem (for "Te
decet") and the eighth psalm tone for "Et in Spiritum Sanctum..." in Diabelli's
Pastoral Mass, Opus 147 (1830; Augsburg: Böhm, n. d.). Some composers used
archaistic headings when they, like Beethoven, wrote in a neo-Gregorian or neo-
Palestrina style. Thus, Anton André, in his (orchestral) Mass Opus 43 (Offenbach,
André, pl. no. 3894 [= 1819]) introduces the second Osanna with four measures
note-against-note, a cappella, in "Tempo di canto Gregoriano"; and Seyfried labels
the recurring whole-note cantus-firmus motif in the Credo of his Fourth Mass as
"Chorale."

[47] Joseph Schmidt-Görg, "Ein neuer Fund in den Skizzenbüchern Beethovens: die
Lamentationen des Propheten Jeremias," *Beethoven-Jahrbuch,* 1957-58, pp. 107-110;
idem, "Das gregorianische Pangue-lingua bei Beethoven," Johner-Festschrift: *Der
kultische Gesang der abendländischen Kirche* (Cologne, 1950), pp. 109-11.

[48] Beethoven's journal of 1818, quoted in Alexander Wheelock Thayer, *Ludwig
van Beethovens Leben* (Leipzig, 1908-17), IV, 130.

[49] Georg Kinsky, *Briefe, Dokumente. Von Scarlatti bis Stravinsky. Katalog der
Musikautographen-Sammlung Louis Koch* (Stuttgart, 1953), p. 57.

[50] Nottebohm, *Zweite Beethoveniana,* p. 163.

for the Kyrie may also refer to this mode.[51] However, these jottings did not influence his choice of mode for the Incarnatus. Did he have a particular reason for using the Dorian? No one has ever asked. We can now show that he arrived at his decision by a circuitous, speculative route, with the help of Zarlino's *Istitutioni harmoniche* of 1558. Conversation books of December, 1819, and January, 1820, document his search for this work. In December Joseph Czerny wrote, "We have some old Italians — Zarlino," and the following month Karl Peters, Lobkowitz's administrator, communicated: "We have Zarlino" (i. e., in the prince's library).[52] In Zarlino's chapter "Della natura, o prop[r]ietà delli modi" we learn about the Dorian mode: "Cassiodorus says, that it is the donor of modesty and the preserver of chastity." [53] Zarlino is relying on the letter of Cassiodorus to Boethius ca. 508 A.D.[54] And he can further lean on the authority of Agamemnon, who, "before departing from his homeland to go to the Trojan War, put his wife Clytemnestra in custody of a Dorian musician."[55] Is further proof needed for Beethoven's intelligent choice of the Dorian, the "chaste" mode, when he wanted to allude to the mystery of the Immaculate Conception? [56] We can add that in his only other modal composition, the slow movement of the string quartet Opus 132, he again followed these authors in matching the mode with the idea to be expressed.[57] This "Sacred song of thanksgiving of a convalescent to the Divinity in the Lydian mode" surely owes its mode to Zarlino's communication: "Cassiodorus believes . . . that the Lydian mode is a remedy for fatigue of the soul, and similarly for that of the body." [58] Finally, we may adduce that the first sketches of the Incarnatus have been accurately dated as December-January, 1819-20,[59] i. e., the same two months in which the notes on

[51] GB-Lbm Ms. Add. 29997, fol. 13^r; *Konversationshefte,* I, 27 (February-March, 1818).

[52] *Konversationshefte,* I, 100, 193.

[53] Pp. 301f.

[54] Migne, *PL,* LXIX, 571B. As part of his autodidactic program Beethoven had abstracts from Boethius made for him by his friend Karl Pinterics; cf. Anton Schindler, *Biographie von Ludwig van Beethoven* (Münster, 1860), II, 163.

[55] Zarlino, *Istitutioni harmoniche,* p. 302.

[56] It has not yet been determined whether Beethoven took a particular chant as his model. Two Dorian melodies with Marian texts begin with the same three or four notes, respectively, as his melody: the hymn *Ave maris stella* (LU 1259) and Perotin's monophonic conductus *Beata viscera Mariae Virginis* (I-Fl *Ms. Plut.* 29.1, fol. 422^r; D-W Ms. 1206, fol. 156^v, etc.).

[57] W. Kirkendale, *Fuge und Fugato.* . . . p. 288.

[58] P. 303. Cf. Cassiodorus in Migne, *PL,* LXIX, 571C.

[59] *Ludwig van Beethoven, Skizzen und Entwürfe: Drei Skizzenbücher zur Missa Solemnis. I: Ein Skizzenbuch aus den Jahren 1819/20* (Bonn, 1952), pp. 11-17 of the Preface, and the Dorian theme on p. 17 of the sketchbook.

Ioan. Collaert sculp.

QVI CONCEPTVS EST DE SPIRITV SANCTO, NATVS EX MARIA VIRGINE.

M. de Vos inuent.

Plate III

Annunciation from a Credo Cycle by Marten de Vos
(1532-1603), engraved by Joannes Collaert (1566-1628).

Zarlino were made in the conversation books.

One of the most prominent features of the Incarnatus is the long, slow trill in the high register of the flute. Also the very few eighteenth-century Masses which include this instrument [60] tend to employ it for the Incarnatus, just as Diabelli's Pastoral Mass does later. Haydn's *Schöpfungsmesse* achieves a similar effect with the flute register of the obbligato organ. There can be little doubt that the flute was chosen because of its pastoral associations. But in some cases, including Beethoven's *Missa Solemnis,* the rhetoric goes still further. Ignaz Seyfried, in his review of the first edition, already suspected that the "fluttering" figures of the flute depict the Holy Ghost in the traditional form of a dove, hovering above the Virgin ("scheint . . . auf den in Tauben-Gestalt flatternden Himmelsboten anzuspielen").[61] This interpretation appears bold at first sight. It has often been repeated, but never justified. But a few modest witnesses may be summoned. Fluttering thirty-second-note figures appear also in the first of Biber's "Rosary" Sonatas, together with the dove in the miniature Annunciation which adorns the music.[62] Beethoven makes his intention very clear by having the flute enter exactly on the words "de Spiritu Sancto" (measure 134). Like the trombones for "omnipotens," the flute trill was a calculated afterthought, added to the finished score.[63]

In portraying the Holy Ghost in the form of a dove, artists since the second century followed the evangelists' description of the baptism of Christ. In Annunciation scenes they often painted rays emanating from the dove and reaching the Virgin's ear, in accord with the idea of early Christian and medieval mystics that Mary conceived through the ear — thus the illustration of the Incarnatus in a sixteenth-century Credo cycle by Marten de Vos (Plate III). Of the many literary formulations, I cite only pseudo-Augustine: "virgo auribus impregnabatur";[64] the widely diffused song "Gaude, Virgo, Mater Christi / Quae per aurem concepisti";[65] and Walther von der Vogelweide: "Durch ir ôre enpfienc si

[60] E. g., fifteen of the 243 orchestral Masses in D-MÜs; Heinrich Stute, *Studien über den Gebrauch der Instrumente in dem italienischen Kirchenorchester des 18. Jahrhunderts* (Quakenbrück, 1929), p. 16.

[61] *Caecilia,* IX (1828), 226.

[62] *DTÖ,* Vol. XXV, *Heinrich Franz Biber: Sechzehn Violinsonaten* (Vienna, 1905), p. 3.

[63] Nottebohm, *Zweite Beethoveniana,* p. 153. The autograph of Beethoven's correction was at one time in the possession of Johannes Brahms.

[64] Migne, *PL,* XXXIX, 1988: *Sermo CXXI, in Natali Domini,* attributed to Ambrosius Autpertus.

[65] Ulysse Chevalier, *Repertorium hymnologicum* (Louvain, 1892-1921), I, 420,

den vil süezen." [66] So literally did the medieval mind understand the pre-incarnate Christ as *logos* — the word enters the body through the ear. (Also the closely related notion of fertilization by breath or sound, widely diffused in both Christian and Oriental cultures, may be remembered in this connection.) Although we cannot know whether Beethoven was aware of these long-lived theological and iconographical traditions, and although we must admit that all music is heard through the ear, I am tempted to point out that the prominent sound of the flute not only corresponds to the light colors of the dove in paintings, but also, emanating as it does from a reedless wind instrument, renders the fertilizing breath of the Holy Ghost much more directly than the painted rays could do. At the end of the Incarnatus the flute becomes silent, and with the words "Et homo factus est" we leave the mystic sphere of the medieval modes and return with an emphatic gesture to major-minor tonality, the realm of man.

The Crucifixus is a paradigm of rhetorical figures traditional for this text: tmesis, tremolo, syncopation, diminished seventh chords, "crossed" melodic intervals (tenor, measure 158), etc. Rather than list the parallels which can be found in almost any eighteenth-century Mass, I refer again to a passage from Biber's "Rosary" Sonatas, this time one depicting the crucifixion.[67] Here is the same combination of tmesis and tremolo as used by Beethoven. Three notations in the sketchbooks further illuminate the rhetoric of the Crucifixus. First, for the slow movement of the string quartet Opus 18 No. 1, allegedly inspired by the grave scene from *Romeo and Juliet*,[68] we find sketches combining tremolos and the tmesis rhythm, with the heading "les derniers soupirs." [69] Second, in a sketchbook for the *Missa Solemnis* the note "Crucifixus in ♯ Ton" [70] shows

---

III, 251f., IV, 147, locates this incipit in thirteen sources from the fourteenth to sixteenth centuries. ("Rejoice, Virgin, mother of Christ, who conceived through the ear.")

[66] *Die Gedichte Walthers von der Vogelweide* (Berlin, 1950), p. 49 ("Through her ear she conceived the very sweet one"). Further literary and pictorial examples are given by Rudolph Hugo Hofmann, *Das Leben Jesu nach den Apokryphen im Zusammenhange aus den Quellen erzählt und wissenschaftlich untersucht* (Leipzig, 1851), pp. 77f.; Yrjö Hirn, *The Sacred Shrine. A study of the poetry and art of the Catholic Church* (London, 1912), pp. 296-300; and Ernest Jones, "Die Empfängnis der Jungfrau Maria durch das Ohr. Ein Beitrag zu der Beziehung zwischen Kunst und Religion," *Jahrbuch der Psychoanalyse*, VI (1914), 137-39.

[67] *DTÖ*, Vol. XXV, p. 48.

[68] Thayer, *Beethovens Leben*, II, 186.

[69] Nottebohm, *Zweite Beethoveniana*, p. 485.

[70] D-Bds Ms. Artaria 180. ("Crucifixus in sharp key," "Kreuz" meaning both "sharp" and "cross").

Beethoven's interest in notational symbolism, even though this was not employed in the finished work. Third, among sketches for the death of Clärchen in *Egmont* there is the remark "Death could be expressed by a rest."[71] In the Mass, death comes with the long rests in the orchestra, on "sepultus est," and with the "morendo" of the few remaining voices.[72] But the section ends with a fermata on a bare fourth, i.e., a chord which lacks finality (measure 187). Could there be a more subtle indication that Christ's entombment is not an end but a transition? The message of the resurrection is then proclaimed by the tenor. Throughout the Mass it is this voice which introduces new events [73] — a usage which can be related to the traditional role of the tenor voice as *testo,* as well as to the more recent operatic function of the heroic tenor as leader (cf. the "Held" in the Ninth Symphony). The words "secundum scripturas" in the sentence on the resurrection reflect the concern of the early Christian apologists to reconcile the doctrines of the New Testament with those of the Old. Musically, the "old" scriptures are rendered by one of the few a cappella passages in the Mass, and by archaic harmonies, in sixteenth-century style.

Some more details in the Credo are worth noting. The word "mortuos" is set not only to the usual piano subito and long, low notes, but also to "dead" chords, without a third. And the idea of expectation is translated literally into music with the prominent anticipations in the orchestra simultaneous with "et exspecto" (measures 289-92). The repetition of "exspecto" is a less ingenious, more conventional procedure of musical rhetoric.[74] Another conventional repetition is that of the word "non" in the phrase "cujus regni non erit finis" (measures 262-64). However, other composers invariably complete the phrase by following the repetitions of "non" with "erit finis." Beethoven's terminal repetition of "non," in the form "non erit finis, non, non, non," has a precedent only in the satirical "Schulmeistermesse," which parodies the "Non mi lasciare, no, no, no" of the Italian secular cantata, with an intention which we would not want to attribute to Beethoven (Ex. 3). That we must ascribe this passage to his Promethean will to overcome mortality

---

[71] Nottebohm, *Zweite Beethoveniana,* pp. 277, 527.

[72] Cf. also Cherubini's Second Mass.

[73] Cf. also Beethoven's First Mass, Gloria, measures 75-135.

[74] "Expectation" was usually heightened by rests between the repetitions — e. g., Jommelli's *Messa a 4* (US-Wc Ms. M2010 A2 J65), Naumann's *Missa Solenne* (Vienna, Bureau des Arts et d'Industrie, pl. no. 167 [= 1803]), Beethoven's First Mass, Jean Martini's *Messe solennelle* (Paris, 1808), etc.

goes without saying,[75] but it is also apparent that at this point he has come dangerously close to the ridiculous.

Ex. 3   "Schulmeister-Messe"

non e - rit fi - nis, non, non, non, non.

The fact that Beethoven sets the articles of faith beginning with "Credo in Spiritum Sanctum" (Ex. 4a) rapidly in monotone declamation has frequently been interpreted as proof of indifference towards Catholic dogma.[76] However, this section of the text is not one which lends itself to extensive musical exegesis. Its length, its short, uniform phrases, and its abstract content demand a declamatory setting. Indeed, such settings were usual in Masses at least from the seventeenth to the early nineteenth century.[77] Diabelli even employed here the recitation formula of a psalm tone (see footnote 46, above). We may relate Beethoven's treatment of dogma to his well-known statement that religion and figured bass are "closed subjects, on which there should be no further dispute." [78] Declamation on a quasi monotone often serves for affirmative statements which reject contradiction. Similarly in the Gellert song *Bitten*, Opus 48, No. 1, Beethoven had employed six measures of repeated notes for the words "Lord! My fortress, my rock, my refuge. . . ." [79] (See Ex. 4b.) The relation of this idea to the Credo is confirmed through his later use of the Credo motif for a canon with the text "Gott ist eine feste Burg," WoO 188 (Ex. 4c). Here in the *Missa Solemnis* the monotone declamation of dogma combines simultaneously with the determined Credo motif to form a most forceful expression of faith.[80] Earlier in the Credo,

[75] Otto Weinreich, "Trigemination als sakrale Stilform," *Studie e Materiali*, 4 (1928), 198-206, demonstrates the wealth of emphatic ternary repetitions in cult, rite, and magic.

[76] E. g., by Otto Schilling Trygophorus, *Beethovens Missa solemnis* (Darmstadt, 1923), p. 68, who attempts to make Beethoven a Lutheran.

[77] E. g., Cavalli's *Missa concertata* (note 8, above), Lotti's Mass for three voices (from the library of Archduke Rudolph, published as "Studentenmesse," [Vienna: Universal Edition, 1913]), Jommelli's *Missa a 4 voci* (note 23, above); Haydn's *Missa Cellensis*, *Missa in tempore belli*, *Heiligmesse*, Tomaschek, *Missa Solemnis*; Weber's *2.ème Messe solennelle* (1818; Paris: Richault, n. d.), Cherubini's Fourth Mass.

[78] Schindler, *Biographie*, II, 162.

[79] C. P. E. Bach, in his setting of this text, also used repeated notes; cf. Ernst Bücken, "Die Lieder Beethovens. Eine stilkritische Studie," *Neues Beethoven-Jahrbuch*, II (1925), 36.

[80] Not only the employment, but also the shape of Beethoven's Credo motif grew out of the eighteenth-century tradition of the Credo-Mass. Such Masses form their

Ex. 4

a. Credo, mm. 268-75

b. Bitten, Opus 48, No. 1

c. "Gott ist eine feste Burg," WoO 188

four-note Credo motives by using the word twice in succession, frequently beginning with a falling minor third, as in the *Missa Solemnis;* cf. Reichert, "Mozarts 'Credo-Messen,'" p. 125. In sketches Beethoven noted: "es kann durchaus überall 2 mal Credo Credo"; see Joseph Schmidt-Görg, *Missa solemnis* (Bonn, 1948), p. 14.

at "Deum de Deo" (measures 61-64) and "Deo vero" (measure 67), Beethoven used the notes of the solid major triad, the alpha and omega of music, for unshakable dogma, as composers long before him had done and Baroque theorists had expounded.[81] With "Deo vero" this expression is intensified by unison; with "lumen de lumine" it is in C major, which had a tradition as key of "light."

Also in the subject of the final fugue "Et vitam venturi saeculi" (measures 309ff.) the major triad retains its old symbolism of perfection and fulfillment,[82] now for the life after death. The leisurely tempo — incomprehensible to the first reviewers [83] — the subdued dynamics, and the mild turn to the subdominant are not common in fugues.[84] (Beethoven employed them for similar effect in the string quartet Opus 131.) Thus life everlasting is envisioned not in the traditional manner as a vigorous physical existence, but as peace, removed from the bustle and noise of life on earth. It is perhaps the longest of all vocal fugues,[85] on the solitary height of the "Hammerklavier" Sonata and the *Grosse Fuge*. The sovereign mastery of compositional technique exhibited here may justify the suggestion that Beethoven was contemplating his own "vitam venturi saeculi," his immortality as an artist. Such an idea was not foreign to him in these years.[86]

At the beginning of the Sanctus a short but significant passage attracts our attention: four measures for brass ensemble (measures 9-12). If we recall that the Sanctus in the Book of Isaiah (6:3) was the hymn of the seraphim above the temple of Jerusalem, and that trumpets were

[81] Cf. Rolf Dammann, *Das Musikbegriff im deutschen Barock* (Cologne, 1967), pp. 40ff., 439-44.

[82] *Ibid.*

[83] Seyfried, *Caecilia,* IX, 230: "matt und schleppend." Anonymous, *Allgemeine Musikalische Zeitung,* XXVI (1824), 439: ". . . so könnte auch nicht geleugnet werden, dass gerade dieser zögernde, ängstlich erwartete Schluss die früheren Eindrucke schwächt, weil sich eben gar kein denkbarer Grund dazu auffinden lässt, als der Wille, einen eigenen Weg zu wandeln. In manchen Fällen ist es doch angemessener, den hergebrachten Formen treu zu bleiben. Wer fühlt sich bey einer feurigen Prachtfuge von Naumann, Haydn, Mozart nicht hoch begeistert . . .?" However, this particular departure from tradition is an intelligent one; cf. p. 195, below.

[84] W. Kirkendale, *Fuge und Fugato . . . ,* p. 305.

[85] The only rival for this title may be the "Et vitam" fugue in Cherubini's Credo of 1806. In the fugues of both composers, the length matches the idea of eternity, as does, on a smaller scale, Beethoven's sixfold (!) sequence on "saeculi," measures 351-56.

[86] In March and April, 1823 we find the following entries about the Mass in *Konversationshefte,* III, 112, 160: "It is a work of eternity." / "Even if you don't believe it, you are [will be] glorified, because your music [is] religion. . . . You will rise with me from the dead — because you must."

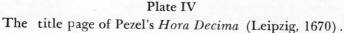

Plate IV
The title page of Pezel's *Hora Decima* (Leipzig, 1670) .

the instruments of both the angels and the temple priests, then we can recognize the appropriateness of the instrumentation. However, we have here also a more recent musical tradition, namely that of the German "Turmmusik" of the Renaissance and Baroque. This too was associated with the music of the angels. Thus the Stadtpfeifer Hornbock in Kuhnau's *Musicalischer Quack-Salber* testified: "We know from experience, that when our city pipers in the festive season play a religious song with nothing but trombones from the tower, then we are greatly moved, and imagine that we hear the angels singing."[87] And in the depiction of tower music on the title page of Pezel's *Hora Decima* (Leipzig, 1670; Plate IV) we see players in angelic form. Beethoven's miniature tower sonata is therefore a very fitting introduction for the Sanctus, the song of the heavenly host.

The repertoires of the tower and the liturgy were not unrelated. Since the sixteenth century at least, the tower musicians joined the church choirs when polyphonic music was performed.[88] Much of the music played from the towers consisted of harmonizations of the same popular religious songs which were sung in the services — in Catholic countries especially — after the Josephine reforms promoted the use of the vernacular. Among the most widely sung texts were the various "Heilig-Lieder," paraphrases of our Sanctus text.[89] One of their melodies found its way into Masses of Joseph and Michael Haydn and into Joseph Preindl's collection of *Melodien aller deutschen Kirchenlieder, welche im St. Stephansdom in Wien gesungen werden.*[90] Catholic communities, such as Vienna[91] and Salzburg,[92] cultivated tower music hardly less than the Lutheran,[93] some even in Beethoven's time. His connection with the long and honorable tradition is certain: in 1812 he made a late contribution to the vanishing repertoire, composing three trombone equales, WoO

[87] Dresden, 1700, p. 435.

[88] Walter Serauky, *Musikgeschichte der Stadt Halle,* Vol. I (Halle and Berlin, 1935), p. 289; Ehmann, *Tibilustrium,* p. 41.

[89] Cf. those published from 1808 on, listed in Wilhelm Bäumker, *Das katholische deutsche Kirchenlied in seinen Singweisen* (Freiburg, 1883-1911), IV, 740-43.

[90] Carl Maria Brand, *Die Messen von Joseph Haydn* (Würzburg, 1941), pp. 298f.

[91] A German *Stadtpfeifer* wrote: ". . . hab Ich der Stadt Wien damals [ca. 1570] 1 Jahr auf S. Stephans Thurm für einen gesellen gedient"; see Hans Engel, "Spielleute und Hofmusiker im alten Stettin zu Anfang des 17. Jahrhunderts," *Musik in Pommern,* I (1932), offprint, p. 4.

[92] Well into the eighteenth century, at least; see Hermann Spies, "Die Tonkunst in Salzburg in der Regierungszeit des Fürsten und Erzbischofs Wolf Dietrich von Raitenau (1587-1612)," *Mitteilungen der Gesellschaft für Salzburger Landeskunde,* LXXII (1932), 78-81.

[93] In Leipzig until 1806 (Ehmann, *Tibilustrium,* p. 35).

30, for the towermaster Franz Xaver Glöggl in Linz.[94]

The independent orchestral movement inserted between the Sanctus and Benedictus, entitled "Praeludium," seems to be unique among orchestral Masses, yet it makes perfect sense in the light of earlier liturgical practice. When polyphonic composition extended the length of the Sanctus, it became necessary to have the Consecration precede, rather than follow the Benedictus, in order not to delay the celebrant. In pontifical Masses since the sixteenth century the Consecration and Elevation of the Host were accompanied by improvised or composed organ music. Such Elevation music, marking the climax of the entire liturgy, is described in the *Caeremoniale episcoporum* of 1600, folio 52[r]: "In the Solemn Mass [the organ] is played with a rather grave and sweet sound while the most sacred Sacrament is raised." Similarly Adriano Banchieri, in his *Organo suonarino* (1611; page 99), says: "at the Elevation played gravely and softly, which moves to devotion." (It is quite possible that this frequently reprinted and widely diffused book was among the "old Italians" mentioned in the conversation book of December, 1819.) In composing music which fits these descriptions, Beethoven was evidently cognizant of the practice and took care to conceive his work in every detail as a Missa solemnis. This explains the musical style of the movement, that of a polyphonic organ improvisation: sostenuto, with sonorous harmonies, suspensions, and pedal point. It is played with "sweet sound," not rising above the piano dynamic indicated by Banchieri. There and in the *Caeremoniale* "grave" implies both the slow tempo and the low register — Beethoven omits the violins and subdivides the violas and cellos. A parallel passage in the Ninth Symphony further illuminates his intention: the shorter but very similar orchestral interlude for low woodwinds and divided violas and cellos, marked "divoto" (cf. Banchieri's "devotion"), introducing the words "Ihr stürzt nieder, Millionen" (measures 627ff.); this text completes the analogy, for the congregation kneels during the Consecration.

By the late eighteenth century the orchestra frequently replaced the organ for instrumental interludes of the Mass,[95] so that the Elevation and

---

[94] Cf. Othmar Wessely's valuable contribution "Zur Geschichte des Equals," *Beethoven-Studien. Festgabe der Österreichischen Akademie der Wissenschaften zum 200. Geburtstag von Ludwig van Beethoven* (Vienna, 1970), pp. 341-60, which became available after completion of this article.

[95] W. Kirkendale, *Fuge und Fugato...*, p. 86; Stephan Bonta, "The Uses of the Sonata da Chiesa," *Journal of the American Musicological Society,* XXII (1969), 72f. The function of Beethoven's movement was easily recognized by Seyfried in his review of 1828: "Anstatt des während der Consecration vorgeschriebenen Orgelspiels, hat unser Componist eigens ein Präludium ... gesetzt" (p. 227).

various items of the Proper were represented by movements of symphonies,[96] by virtuoso concertos,[97] and even by military fanfares.[98] Although Beethoven too employs the orchestra for the Elevation, his quasi-organ style is close to the legitimate tradition of organ music. He was familiar with this tradition from his youth, when he himself supplied the improvised organ interludes for the Rhenish service: a manuscript from Siegburg contains the rubric "Moderato, wird vor dem Alleluja gespielt von L. von Pethoven." [99] In composing his own Elevation music for the *Missa Solemnis,* he removes it from the unreliable hands of an improvising organist and likewise prevents the arbitrary insertion of a foreign orchestral movement — just as he and later nineteenth-century composers wrote out the cadenzas for their concertos.[100] The title "Praeludium" of this movement has often been construed as designating a "prelude" to the Benedictus. However, in Beethoven's time the verb "präludieren" was the normal expression for improvising organ music during the church service.[101] There can, then, be no doubt that with the word "Praeludium" Beethoven intended an allusion to the tradition and style of organ improvisation.

A striking and significant effect is achieved in the last measure of the Praeludium (measure 110), where a link with the Benedictus is established by the entry of the solo violin. At this moment the Consecration of the Host is completed and Christ becomes present on the altar. The effect of the sudden entry of the high, bright solo violin (g''') into the very dark, low orchestral background can not only be characterized by, but even identified with, the words "lux in tenebris," for it is thus that

---

[96]Cf. Joseph Heer, "Zur Kirchenmusik und ihrer Praxis während der Beethovenzeit in Bonn," *Kirchenmusikalisches Jahrbuch,* XXVIII (1933), 138f.

[97] E. g., by Dittersdorf in Bologna, 1763; see Karl Ditters von Dittersdorf, *Lebensbeschreibung* (Leipzig, 1801), p. 117.

[98] Cf. Charles Burney, *The Present State of Music in Germany, the Netherlands, and United Provinces* (London, 1773), pp. 115f.: [in Augsburg] "there was a rude and barbarous flourish of drums and trumpets at the elevation of the Host, which was what I had never heard before, except at Antwerp." At a Mass for the installation of a bishop in Paris 1802, a military band played such pieces as "Ah! le bel oiseau, maman" during the Elevation; see Michel Brenet, *La Musique militaire* (Paris, n. d.), pp. 87f.

[99] Heer, in *Kirchenmusikalisches Jahrbuch,* XXVIII, 132.

[100] Apparently he thought of supplying such pieces also for his First Mass; among sketches for the "Hammerklaviersonate" we find the note "Preludien zu meiner Messe" (Nottebohm, *Zweite Beethoveniana,* p. 353).

[101] Cf. Beethoven's note in a conversation book of March-May, 1819: "preludiren des Kyrie vom organisten stark u. abnehmend bis vor dem Kyrie piano" (*Konversationshefte,* I, 33).

St. John referred to the coming of the Saviour (1:5), the "lux vera" (1:9), the "lumen de lumine" which dispels the darkness of sin. Again the interpretation is strengthened by liturgical parallels: the "Wandlungskerze," the candle lighted at the altar at the moment of Transsubstantiation — the candle too is a symbol of Christ, since it consumes itself in giving light — and the "Elevation bell," with its bright sound.[102]

The Benedictus then brings to perfection the late-eighteenth-century type of mild, ecstatic movement heard while the Host is exhibited on the altar. Such movements very often achieve their effect with subdominant tonality, predominantly solo voices, and obbligato solo instruments,[103] most commonly the organ, as the traditional instrument of Elevation music.[104] Beethoven originally considered a concertino of four obbligato instruments [105] — violin, horn, bassoon, and cello — as in André's Mass of 1819 (Opus 43). He finally chose the solo violin to accompany Him "qui venit in nomine Domini," as J. S. Bach did in the Advent cantata BWV 132. The extended orchestral introduction continues to serve as Elevation music, as it does in the Masses of Haydn and his contemporaries. With verbal expression temporarily exhausted by the presence of Christ, Beethoven comes into his purely symphonic element. However, in order to make the meaning of this long orchestral section absolutely clear, he prefixes it with a single presentation of the text "Benedictus, qui venit in nomine Domini" (measures 114-17), in the manner of the old "motto aria." It is declaimed on a monotone, since it is to serve merely as a heading for the movement.

Whoever has followed the rhetoric thus far will recognize the initial long, slow *katabasis* in the flutes and solo violin as the descent of Christ upon the altar. Is it the analogy to the Nativity that leads so naturally to the style of the pastoral Mass, with its gently rocking trochaic melodies in 12/8 meter? Beethoven was doubtless familiar with at least some of

[102] Cf. Le Brun, *Explication . . . de la Messe,* pp. 480, 400; Peter Browe, "Die Elevation in der Messe," *Jahrbuch für Liturgiewissenschaft,* IX (1929), 37-43; Ludwig Eisenhofer, *Handbuch der katholischen Liturgik* (Freiburg, 1933), II, 163.

[103] E. g., the flute in Leopold Mozart's Mass in C (New York: Fox, 1963) and in Albrechtsberger's *Missa in C pro coronatione Francisci II Budae peragenda* (1792, Weissenbäck no. 97); the viola in Michael Haydn's Missa solemnis in G (Klafsky no. I, 38, *DTÖ,* Vol. LXII, p. VI); and the violin and cello in Salieri's Mass in D (see Nützlader, in *Studien zur Musikwissenschaft,* XIV, p. 161.)

[104] E. g., the "Orgelmessen" of J. Haydn (1766 and ca. 1775), Mozart K. 259 (1776), M. Haydn (1805, Klafsky no. I, 24), and Albrechtsberger (1796 and 1801, Weissenbäck nos. 111 and 134).

[105] Alexander Wheelock Thayer, *Chronologisches Verzeichniss der Werke Ludwig van Beethovens* (Berlin, 1865), p. 142; Nottebohm, *Zweite Beethoveniana,* p. 149.

the more recent representatives of this large musical progeny of St. Luke.[106] Yet his direct model was not a pastoral Mass, but another Christmas composition: Handel's *Messiah*. We know from the sketches that Beethoven studied this work while working on the Mass.[107] Here he is clearly indebted to the aria "He shall feed his flock," [108] and thus we may see very concretely in his *katabasis* the coming of the Good Shepherd.

The Benedictus has a close relative: the slow movement of the string quartet Opus 59, No. 2. In both works there is a single violin soaring high above its accompaniment in long, smooth triplets (Ex. 5), with occasional steep descents to the lowest register (Ex. 6). I do not regard this similarity as entirely accidental. According to Czerny, the slow movement of the quartet was conceived by Beethoven while looking at the starry heavens and thinking of the music of the spheres.[109] Its ethereal, seraphic style must have appeared to be the most suitable one to express the presence of the heavenly visitor in the Mass.

The setting of the Agnus Dei is unusual in that it has three rather than two complete presentations of the sentence "Agnus Dei, qui tollis peccata mundi, miserere nobis" before the Dona nobis pacem.[110] However, the harmonic plan adheres to the normal eighteenth-century practice of beginning in the relative or tonic minor and returning to the tonic only with the Dona nobis pacem, which is thus conceived as an independent movement. From the Miserere section it may suffice to mention a single rhetorical moment. The minor key is the one which Beethoven

---

[106] The earliest Missa pastoritia is probably that by Francesco Sale in Tyrol, 1589 (*Missarum solemniorum . . . Primus tomus*). In the eighteenth and early nineteenth centuries the genre was cultivated in Italy, Austria, and southern Germany by many composers. Vast quantities of pastoral music were also produced in Bohemia, but they rarely made use of the familiar quasi-siciliano idiom preferred in the Austro-Italian settings of the Incarnatus and Benedictus. Cf. Camillo Schoenbaum, "Harmonia pastoralis Bohemica," *Festschrift für Walter Wiora zum 30. Dezember 1966* (Kassel, 1967), pp. 348-56.

[107] W. Kirkendale, *Fuge und Fugato . . .* , p. 256.

[108] This seems to have been recognized already by Grossheim in 1828 (*Caecilia, IX, 25f.*).

[109] Thayer, *Beethovens Leben*, II, 532. Cf. *Konversationsheft*, I, 230, III, 128, and V, 164, on Beethoven's interest in astronomy.

[110] A departure which I have seen again only in Hummel's Second Mass, Opus 80 (Vienna, Haslinger, pl. no. 3019 [= c. 1820]). Beethoven could hardly have known that this threefold literal repetition was the earlier form of the Agnus Dei, as it was sung in the ninth and tenth centuries (and to this day in the Lateran church), and that only in the eleventh and twelfth centuries, during times of stress, did the Dona nobis pacem replace the "miserere nobis" of the third sentence.

Ex. 5

a. Opus 59, No. 2, second mvt., mm. 37ff., 42ff.

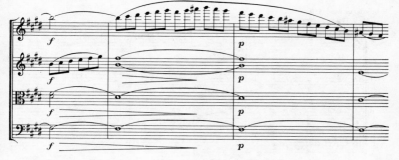

b. Benedictus, mm. 200ff.

once designated in his sketches as "h moll schwarze Tonart." [111] Operas

[111] Among B minor sketches to Opus 102, No. 2 (see Nottebohm, *Zweite Beethoveniana*, p. 326). This characteristic was not assigned to the B minor key by authors which Beethoven might have known, such as Schubart.

Ex. 6

a. Opus 59, No. 2, second mvt., mm. 69ff.

b. Benedictus, mm. 155ff.

and oratorios of the eighteenth century had reserved it for the expression of distress. Here it is intensified by bassoon and bass solo, which add "depth" to "blackness," characterizing the plea for mercy as a humble call "de profundis" — for centuries melodies creeping in the depths had been a topos for humility.

We have arrived at the final movement, the Dona nobis pacem, which for intellectual density has hardly a rival in the history of the Mass and therefore deserves a detailed scrutiny. The pastoral idiom of the Italian Baroque returns — peace is again Arcadian happiness. However, not content merely to depict peace, Beethoven contrasts it with its opposite, war — just as he introduces violent discord and the words "nicht diese Töne" into the "Ode to Joy." Though such a dramatic procedure is most unusual in a Mass,[112] it was intelligible and, alas, justified

---

[112] Also Beethoven's First Mass and Cherubini's *Messe à trois voix* in F interrupt the peaceful mood of the Dona with troubled episodes on the "Agnus Dei" text.

then as now.

More than any other passage in the *Missa Solemnis,* it is the military episodes which have puzzled commentators.[113] One other work, and only one, is invariably mentioned in this connection: Haydn's *Missa in tempore belli,* which also includes trumpet fanfares and drum rolls in the Dona. While there can be little doubt that the *Missa Solemnis* was influenced directly by this Mass and others by Haydn, I should like to point out its place in a much more ancient tradition. The oldest collection of prayers for the Mass, the so-called Leonine Sacramentary,[114] already contained *Missae tempore hostili,* motivated by the siege of Rome by the barbarians in the fifth and sixth centuries. From occasional prayers in time of war (cf. LU 1867) a fixed votive liturgy eventually developed (*Missa pro Pace, LU* 1285-87).[115] Also musical military idioms had invaded the Mass long before Haydn and Beethoven. When Renaissance composers based their parody Masses on French chansons, they did not exclude the ever popular battle chanson from their models. Thus Jannequin used his famous chanson *La Guerre* (ca. 1528), the prototype of all battle pieces, for his Mass *La Bataille,* published in 1532.[116] This was followed by a long series of battle Masses.[117]

"Battaglia" music had an uninterrupted existence until far into the nineteenth century, and Beethoven himself contributed his "Battle Symphony" for Wellington's victory, a work frequently underestimated when considered apart from its genre. And as early as 1809, when the French

[113] Anonymous, *Allgemeine Musikalische Zeitung,* XXVI (1824), 440: "Was der Tonsetzer mit dieser Phrase eigentlich beabsichtigt habe, möge schwer zu entziffern seyn." Seyfried, *Caecilia,* IX, 230: "Was übrigens die wunderliche Trompeten-Fanfarre, das eingemengte Recitativ, der fugirte, den Ideenfluss nur störende Instrumental-Satz ... eigentlich sagen will, — was die dumpfen, unrhythmischen, bizarren Pauken-Schläge im Grund bedeuten sollen, mag der liebe Himmel wissen." Schindler even recommends that these passages be omitted in performance (II, 79). Cf. also Thayer, IV, 352.

[114] Migne, *PL,* LV, 21-156.

[115] Cf. Anton Baumstark, "Friede und Krieg in altkirchlicher Liturgie," *Hochland,* XIII/1 (1915-16), 257-70.

[116] *Liber decem missarum,* a collection published by Jacques Moderne, Lyon, 1532 and 1540.

[117] To name only Victoria's *Missa pro victoria,* G. Anerio's immensely popular *Missa de la battaglia,* Lappi's *Missa sopra la battaglia,* Banchieri's *Missa victoria,* Straus's Masses *ad modum tubarum* and *cum tympanis ac 5 tubis campestribus,* C. Grossi's Mass *Capriccio guerriero,* and Foggia's *Missa detta la battaglia.* Not all of these were parodies. Cf. also Rudolf Gläsel, *Zur Geschichte der Battaglia* (Leipzig, 1931), pp. 44, 86.

troops invaded Austria, he had made sketches for a battle piece.[118] Considering the great impact of the march music of post-revolutionary France upon Beethoven's *oeuvre,* we are not surprised to find notations for a march as part of the earliest sketches for the Agnus Dei.[119]

Fanfare melodies for trumpets or *clarini* are not uncommon in orchestral Masses of the eighteenth century,[120] not to mention the field Masses of the military camps, which used trumpets in place of bells (for Introit, Elevation, etc.). However, in the orchestral Masses these instruments merely reinforce the tuttis, and the character of their fanfares is usually joyous and festive. Beethoven's Mass is unique in its extended solo passage for trumpets and timpani in the unmistakable and menacing form of a battle fanfare (measures 170ff.). For full understanding of this passage, it would be of interest to know whether Beethoven used an actual military signal of his time and, if so, what it signified. Unfortunately there is little hope of making such a discovery, for the signals had long been not only a strict secret of the trumpeters' guild, but also a military secret and therefore seldom committed to writing. Thus Johann Ernst Altenburg, in his *Versuch einer Anleitung zur heroisch-musikalischen Trompeter- und Pauker Kunst* of 1795, did not print a single military signal.[121]

[118] Nottebohm, *Zweite Beethoveniana,* p. 262. Cherubini, whose First Requiem was highly admired by Beethoven, ended his Coronation Mass of 1825 (Paris, chez l'auteur) with a "Marche religieuse, executée, après la messe, le jour du sacre de Charles X pendant la Communion du Roi."

[119] Nottebohm, *Zweite Beethoveniana,* p. 150; Johannes Wolf, "Beethoven Kirchenmusiker?" *Beethoven-Zentenarfeier* (Vienna, 1927), p. 125.

[120] Cf. Stute, *Studien über den Gebrauch der Instrumenten . . . ,* pp. 21f. A characteristic example is Fux's *Missa corporis Christi* of 1713, *Sämtliche Werke,* Ser. I, Bd. 1 (Kassel and Graz, 1959). A Mass of Antonio Burroni, D-MÜs Ms. B45, contains an indication for an unwritten vocal "cadenza col clarino" on the word "miserere."

[121] The only extant examples before the nineteenth century are those written in two manuscripts ca. 1600 and published in *Das Erbe Deutscher Musik, Reichsdenkmale, Bd. 7: Trompetenfanfaren, Sonaten, und Feldstücke* (Kassel, 1936). These pieces have little in common with Beethoven's fanfares. Only the signals "Aufs Pferd (Montacawalla)" and especially "Wache (Auged = Guet)" resemble the trumpet parts in the second episode (measure 326). They are published also in Georg Schünemann, "Sonaten und Feldstücke der Hoftrompeter," *Zeitschrift für Musikwissenschaft,* XVII (1935), 161. Leopold Nowak, "Beethovens 'Fidelio' und die österreichischen Militärsignale," *Österreichische Musikzeitschrift,* X (1955), 373, demonstrates a close relationship between the fanfare of Beethoven's opera and those of the Austrian army. However, the only source quoted for the latter, Archduke Karl's *Dienst-Reglement für die kaiserlich-königliche Infanterie* (Vienna, 1807-1808), contains, in the copies which I consulted, only drum rolls, no trumpet signals. The Austrian trumpet signals have been attributed, without the slightest evi-

Trumpets and drums formed, of course, a normal part of the Missae solemnes for the most festive occasions.[122] But Beethoven's prominent use of a military fanfare may be regarded as particularly appropriate for a Mass dedicated to a member of the imperial family, Archduke Rudolph. Altenburg emphasized that Emperor Joseph II, Rudolph's grandfather, had introduced trumpets and drums to his dragoons in 1774; that the highest paid trumpeters in Europe were those in imperial service; and that the patron of the trumpeters' guild, the archangel Gabriel, was at the same time the protector of the imperial residence. Rudolph had been much in need of such protection in 1809 when Napoleon's troops had forced him to leave Vienna and Beethoven wrote the sonata *Les Adieux* for him. Indeed, the passage in the Mass may be regarded as a product of Beethoven's personal experience in that year. Ferdinand Ries relates how the composer spent the night of May 11 with great fear in his brother's cellar, as the city was bombarded by French artillery.[123] Beethoven must have known what Altenburg knew: "But frightful and terrible is the sound of the trumpet when it announces the near advance of the enemy." Only if we imagine ourselves in such a situation will we feel the full impact of the first military episode, ominous in its initial piano dynamic, terrifying in its slow crescendo (measures 164-88), the "naher Anmarsch." [124] Such extraordinary, paralyzing tension demands drastic expression in the next vocal entry. And this appears: *recitativo accompagnato* (measure 174). This style is not entirely unknown to the Ordinary of the Mass, as Adler believed, but it is, nevertheless, extremely rare.[125] The opera composer Cavalli used it, likewise for an emphatic invocation, on "Domine Deus," [126] and Haydn, in his only cantata-Mass — which honors the patron saint of music — employs it before the Incarnatus aria. In his songs, Beethoven had already turned to

---

dence, to Michael Haydn. More relevant would be the French military signals of the early nineteenth century, but an examination of such material has thus far yielded no results.

[122] Listed in the *Diarium cantus figuralis aliarumque functionum musicae totius anni* from Herzogenburg, 1751, quoted by Reichert, *Zur Geschichte der Wiener Messenkomposition,* p. 2. Cf. Fr[anz Xaver] Glöggl, *Kirchenmusik-Ordnung. Erklärendes Handbuch des musikalischen Gottesdienst* (Vienna, 1828), par. 16: "Vom Gebrauch der Trompeten und Pauken in der Kirche:" "nur an doppelten Festen erster und zweiter Klasse" (p. 36).

[123] Franz Wegeler and Ferdinand Ries, *Biographische Notizen über Ludwig van Beethoven* (Coblenz, 1845), p. 121.

[124] Altenburg, *Versuch,* p. 24. Cf. Nottebohm, *Zweite Beethoveniana,* pp. 464, 151: "piano . . . pauken in h und fis nur von weitem, agnus dei hiermit gleich anfang."

[125] Adler, "Zur Geschichte . . ." p. 33.

[126] *Missa Concertata* (see note 8, above).

recitative in exceptional moments of great psychological tension. The plea for mercy in the Mass, marked "ängstlich," reveals the same intention as the song *Der Wachtelschlag*, WoO 129 (1803), which breaks momentarily into recitative at the words "Schreckt dich im Wetter der Herr der Natur, bitte Gott, bitte Gott!" [127]

Peace is eventually restored and the pastoral music returns. It leads into a fugato (measures 216 ff.) on a subject from Handel's Hallelujah chorus. I have no doubt that Beethoven borrowed it consciously. We have seen that he studied *Messiah* while composing the Mass. Why does he quote Handel at this point? It is clear that this triumphant theme, which everyone could associate with the "hallelujah" text, is very appropriate after the danger of war has been averted. There is, however, a deeper reason. Just as Napoleon and the French were for Beethoven representatives of war, Wellington and the English were the restorers of peace. And Handel's oratorios, then as now, were regarded as English music, their enthusiastic performances in Germany and Austria during the Wars of Liberation had been tantamount to political propaganda. As in the "Battle Symphony" the patriotic song of the French succumbs to that of the English, so in the Mass the military fanfares cede to the most popular piece in the repertoire of English sacred music.

A clue for the understanding of the second troubled episode in this rondo-like movement (*ABACA*) is provided by Beethoven's subtitle: "Bitte um innern und äussern Frieden" ("Plea for inner and outer peace"). That the first episode, with its battaglia language, represents the disturbance of "outer" peace is not to be contested. May we then interpret the second, with its extended and restless orchestral fugato, presto (measures 266ff.), as the disturbance of inner peace? [128] The "inner" struggle is distinguished from the external strife by the intellectual device of the fugato, and by an "inner," thematic relationship between one of the fugato subjects and the "peace" motif of the principal section (measures 107f.). The first episode had no such connection with the rest of the movement; it remained an external interpolation.

The episodes can be best understood in relation to a much older practice. They are tropes, inserted into the liturgical text and expanding

---

[127] "If the Lord of nature frightens you in a storm, pray to God, pray to God." In sketches for the Dona Beethoven notes "durchaus simple Bitte Bitte Bitte" (Nottebohm, *Zweite Beethoveniana*, p. 465).

[128] Only this sequence, not that of the heading, could be artistically justified. In a sketch, Beethoven first wrote "darstellend äusseren Frieden," then added the words "u. inneren"; cf. Harry Goldschmidt, "Zwei Skizzenblätter — ein Beitrage zur Programmatik Beethovens," *Musik und Gesellschaft*, III (1953), 55-57.

its ideas. Until well into the sixteenth century, the Agnus Dei was a favored text for the troping process, and its tropes occasionally reflect, as Beethoven's do, the strife of the times.[129] Edmund Martène's *De antiquis ecclesiae ritibus* of 1702, reprinted in 1736, still states that the Agnus Dei was recited "not continuously, but interpolated and mixed with private prayer," a formulation which can be traced back at least to the twelfth century. The outburst of recitative in Beethoven's first episode, with its strongly subjective style of dramatic monody, comes indeed close to a "private prayer."

It has not yet been recognized that the reference to inner and outer peace in Beethoven's heading is not a subjective invention of the composer,[130] but is deeply rooted in ancient theological concepts. Prayers for inner and outer peace had formed an essential part of the liturgy from the earliest centuries of the Christian era.[131] Beethoven's dual concept is fully developed in twelfth- and thirteenth-century commentaries on the Dona nobis pacem. Alain de Lille, in his *Summa de arte praedicatoria,* distinguishes "pax temporis, pax pectoris, et pax aeternitatis." [132] This threefold distinction embraces the dualistic interpretation of the Agnus Dei, for the third kind of peace, "pax aeternitatis," is accessible only to the dead, and it therefore has its place in the Requiem Mass, where the Dona nobis pacem is altered to "dona eis requiem sempiternam." (Cf. also above, the discussion of the "Et vitam" fugue.) Alain's great contemporary, Pope Innocent III, assigns inner and outer peace to the first and second "miserere," respectively, of the Agnus Dei; then both species combined, to the Dona.[133] The dichotomy of "pax interna — pax externa" still belongs to the topos fund of Baroque treatises on virtues, such as Wilhelm Friedrich von Efferen's *Manuale politicum de ratione status* of 1630. That Beethoven attached particular importance to the peace of mind is revealed by the note in his sketches for the Agnus Dei: "Strength of the sentiments

[129] For example: "Agnus Dei, Defensor noster, adveni. . . ," or "fer opem tribulatis, dona nobis pacem," among the "Tropi ad Agnus Dei" in *Analecta Hymnica Medii Aevi,* ed. Clemens Blume and Guido M. Dreves, Vol. XLVII: *Tropi Graduales* (Leipzig, 1905), pp. 383, 387.

[130] E. g., Paul Nettl, *Beethoven-Handbook* (New York, 1956), p. 145: "These words show the subjectiveness of Beethoven's work."

[131] Cf. Baumstark (note 115, above).

[132] Migne, *PL,* CCX, 156A. Similarly Guillaume Durand (d. 1296), *Rationale Divinorum Officiorum* (Venice, 1491), fol. 62^r.

[133] *De Sacro Altaris Mysterio, PL,* CCXVII, 908D. "We therefore say 'miserere nobis' for the soul, likewise 'miserere nobis' for the body; 'dona nobis pacem' for both: so that we have spiritual peace of mind and temporal peace of body." These words are taken over almost literally by Durand, *Rationale,* fol. 61^r.

of inner peace above all ... Victory!"[134] Does the word "victory" in this context allude to the familiar image of the Lamb of God carrying the flag of victory?

We have arrived at the end of our path through the score. Since I have been speaking of a heading, I may look back on the other singular inscription in this Mass, the famous "Von Herzen — Möge es wieder — zu Herzen gehen!" ("From the heart — may it go again to the heart"). This too is hardly, as hitherto believed, a romantic effusion of the composer's overflowing heart. Again we hear an echo of older theological parlance. The motto stands not at the head of the entire Mass, but at the beginning of the Kyrie only. And did not Jacques Bossuet, the great theologian of Louis XIV, call the Kyrie text "the language of the heart"?[135]

"I believe that I have treated the text as it has seldom been treated." When Beethoven wrote these words about his First Mass to Breitkopf & Härtel (June 8, 1808; *Briefe*, I, 229), he was surely aware that he had taken unusual care of musical exegesis. But how much more does his statement apply to the *Missa Solemnis*, where every textual concept, indeed almost every word is musically interpreted![136] (Nowhere did Richard Wagner exhibit his insensitivity towards older music so blatantly as when he said of this work, "The text is not comprehended by us according to its conceptual significance, but it serves merely as material for the voices.")[137] But ever since the times of Galilei and Doni theorists had warned against undue concentration on single words.[138] And indeed, in the long chain of images in the Gloria and Credo, Beethoven indulges in such an endless, reckless, monumental wealth of mosaics, that his contemporaries were dismayed. The accepted balance between form and content was distorted; an avalanche buried moderation and convention. The complete freedom, the maturity of a late style could not easily be

---

[134] Nottebohm, *Zweite Beethoveniana*, p. 151.

[135] Undocumented reference by Wilhelm Weber, *Beethovens Missa solemnis* (Leipzig, 1908), p. 49, who strangely enough, does not connect it with Beethoven's motto. I have not yet located the passage in Bossuet's voluminous writings.

[136] Cf. [Joseph] Fröhlich's review in *Caecilia*, IX (1828), 42f.: "Jedes Instrument, jede Figur, jedes p., pp., for., cresc., jedes Schleifen und Stossen ist berechnet, und muss nach dem Character der Stelle wie dieser durch die Worte und die in denselben enthaltenen Bilder bestimmt ist, immer anders gegeben werden. Auf diese Weise bekömmt manche Figur, die dem ersten Anblicke nach nichtssagend, gemein, ja dem Texte widersprechend erscheint, eine grosse, herrliche Bedeutung."

[137] *Gesammelte Schriften und Dichtungen* (Leipzig, n. d.), IX, 103.

[138] *Dialogo di Vincentio Galilei Nobile Fiorentino della Musica Antica, et della Moderna* (Florence, 1581), p. 88f.; Giovanni Battista Doni, *Lyra Barberina* (Florence, 1763), II, 73: "L'errore consiste in questo, che in vece di esprimere, o imitare tutto il concetto ... si mettono ad esprimere le parole separate...."

comprehended. Timidly the first reviewers voiced their discomfort at the fragmentation, the too rapid changes of key, tempo, and dynamics, the transitions too abrupt to be followed by the listener.[139] And Goethe, who in these years expressed his dislike of "überfüllte Musik," [140] would probably have felt no differently. However, we must recognize that Beethoven does achieve unity in the Gloria and Credo by linking contrasting episodes with short orchestral ritornellos and by using recurring motives for different or identical texts. This structural coherence is not, as has been suggested, an innovation of the great symphonist, but is found in the Gloria and Credo movements of orchestral Masses since the mid-seventeenth century.

Frau von Weissenthurn's question could not have been more apposite. What distinguishes the *Missa Solemnis* from the vast contemporary production is above all the intense concern with ideas. This led the composer to undertake extensive preparatory studies, from the translation, declension, or conjugation of single words of the text with the help of a dictionary,[141] to the collection of plainchants, the examination of sacred music in Archduke Rudolph's library,[142] and the occupation with musical ethos in ancient treatises. And it is clear that, much more than has been hitherto suspected, the master occupied himself with theology and liturgics, isolated as he was in his deafness and withdrawing more and more into a world of images and speculation. He obviously wished to say the last word on the subject.[143] We begin to understand the unusually long gestation period of four and a half years.

Beethoven's acquaintance with the various musical, literary, iconographical, theological, and liturgical traditions is sometimes more, some-

---

[139] Anonymous, *Allegmeine Musikalische Zeitung,* XXVI (1824), 439: "Die Behandlung des *Credo* ist in der That ungewöhnlich und höchst originell; sowohl die Grundtonart, B dur, als das Zeitmaass wird oft, vielleicht etwas gar zu oft gewechselt, und das Ohr ist beynahe kaum vermögend, den raschen Wechsel aufzufassen." Seyfried, *Caecilia,* IX, p. 229 (on the Gloria and Credo): "Der oftmalige, doch wohl gar zu häufige, unmotivierte Wechsel des Zeitmaasses, der Ton- und Tactarten, gibt ein zerstücktes Bild . . . und erzeugt gewissermasen jenes beengende Gefühl, so aus Mangel an Einheit, aus der gleichsam blos rhapsodischen Behandlungs-Weise zu entspringen pflegt. . . ."

[140] Letter to Zelter, June 6, 1825.

[141] Even to the extent of deriving "Pilatus" from "pilo": "pilato — pilo berauben, plündern, mit Wurfspiess versehen pilatus"; manuscript in D-Bds. quoted by Thayer, *Beethovens Leben,* IV, 334, and Wolf, *Beethoven-Zentenarfeier,* p. 124.

[142] See Beethoven's letter of July 29, 1819 (*Briefe,* IV, 27).

[143] He pursued a similar intention in other late works, especially in the *Grosse Fuge;* cf. W. Kirkendale, "The 'Great Fugue' Op. 133: Beethoven's 'Art of Fugue,' " *Acta musicologica,* XXXV (1963), 14-24.

times less demonstrable. The evidences of it are incontestable for the trombone chords and flute trills to symbolize the power of God and the dove of the Holy Ghost, for the authority of Zarlino on the character of the Dorian mode, for the traditions of the pastoral Mass, tower and Elevation music, and for the quotation from *Messiah*. That he knew the Töpfer altar or Michael Haydn's use of Gregorian melodies for the Incarnatus is probable. Still within the realm of possibility is his acquaintance with Biber's "Rosary" Sonatas, with battaglia Masses, with the passages on Elevation music in the *Caeremoniale episcoporum* and in Banchieri's treatise, and with the account of military music in Altenburg's book. It is less likely that he knew firsthand the works of the Church Fathers.[144] However, the patristic writings were so consistently copied by later authors, and famous theological formulations were so well preserved in popular pious literature, that a knowledge of them could be derived from any number of sources. A few links in the chain are sufficient to demonstrate the continuity in the history of ideas and to show the appropriateness of Beethoven's formulations.

The century in which Beethoven was born had already brought not only the antiliturgical reforms of Joseph II, but also such thorough studies of historical sources as Lodovico Muratori's *Liturgia Romana Vetus* (1748) and Martin Gerbert's *De cantu et musica sacra* (1774).[145] In theological and liturgical matters Beethoven must have enlisted the advice of learned specialists for his *opus magnum,* just as painters used to do in working out an iconographical program. We find a clue to the identity of a helper in a conversation book early in 1820: "Kanné has just produced a history of the Mass. It is still in the censorship office." [146] August Friedrich Kanne was the most talented, original, and alcoholic of Beethoven's intimate companions, a human encyclopedia,[147] a former student of theology, and composer of a Mass himself. He had become

[144] The manuscript mentioned above in footnote 141 contains a general reference in Beethoven's own hand: he translates the Latin words as they were used "bey Kirchenvätern"! See Thayer, *Beethovens Leben,* IV, 334.

[145] Cf. also Anton L. Mayer, "Liturgie, Aufklärung und Klassizismus," *Jahrbuch für Liturgiewissenschaft,* IX (1929), 67-127.

[146] *Konversationshefte,* I, 242. The writer is Janitschek. On Kanne cf. Schindler, *Biographie,* I, 72, 227f.; II, 165-68; Constant von Wurzbach, *Biographisches Lexikon des Kaiserthums Österreich,* X (Vienna, 1863), 438-43; Thayer, *Beethovens Leben,* IV, 5; V, 281, 325; Theodor Frimmel, *Beethoven-Handbuch* (Leipzig, 1926), I 247f; Wilhelm Hitzig, "Ein Brief Friedrich August Kannes," *Der Bär,* 1927, pp. 42-52.

[147] Heinrich Laube's *Reisenovelle* "Beethoven und Kanne" (1833): "ein Atlas von Gelehrsamkeit" (*Gesammelte Werke* [Leipzig, 1908], VI, 76). Cf. Schindler, *Biographie,* II, 165: "ein Mann von universeller Bildung."

Vienna's most perceptive music critic and protagonist of Beethoven's music, and finally was to serve him as torchbearer at his funeral and as necrologist. Beethoven esteemed him highly and consulted him repeatedly on artistic questions. Unfortunately, the history of the Mass does not seem to have survived the censorship. At least it was never published.[148] (Kanne is known to have destroyed some of his manuscripts.) If it could someday be found, I venture to predict that it would throw further light on Beethoven's composition. But even if Beethoven did not read it, he very probably benefited from it through Kanne's advice, and he surely read his friend's "Beytrag zur Musik-Geschichte des Mittelalters" [149] and his essays "Über die musikalische Malerey" [150] and "Über die Harmonie in der Tonkunst in Beziehung auf ihre Verwandtschaft mit der Malerey, Plastik und Dichtkunst." [151]

ADDENDUM: Two further notations in sketches for the *Missa Solemnis* support the interpretations given here. That the transition from the Dorian mode to D major for "Et homo factus est" was intended to express the departure from the realm of mystery and the return to that of humanity is confirmed by Beethoven's note on this passage: "hier menschlich" (quoted by J. Schmidt-Görg in a paper at the congress of the Gesellschaft für Musikforschung, Bonn, Sept. 9, 1970). And Beethoven wrote on sketches for the "Et vitam" fugue the motto "Plaudite amici" — an anticipation of his famous last words "Plaudite, amici, finita est comoedia" (Heinrich Lindlar, "Marginalien zu Beethovens Missa solemnis," *Schweizerische Musikzeitschrift* 110 [1970] 71); herewith is secured the association of the "Et vitam venturi saeculi" with his own life and afterlife (see above, p. 182).

[148] I wish to thank Theophil Antonicek for kindly searching for Kanne's manuscript for me in the major Viennese libraries, including the remains of the Zensurarchiv.

[149] *Allgemeine Musikalische Zeitung*, I (Vienna, 1817), cols. 209-11, 213-15, 221-33.

[150] *Ibid.*, II (1818), cols. 373-80, 385-91, 393-95, 401-5. His remark on the "adoramus" accords with Beethoven: a composer "wird einen desto schöneren Contrast zu bilden im Stande seyn, wenn er die Stelle 'adoramus te' mit dem Schauder heiliger Andacht ausdrückt." His subsequent words on the setting of the Mass recall the attitude of Galilei and Doni: "Wir meinen, man soll den Sinn des aus Worten bestehenden ganzen Satzes zu einer Richtschnur nehmen, & darnach seine Musik componieren, also nicht einzelne Worte." He looks with disfavor on composers "die . . . alles ausdrücken . . . und jedes einzelne auszudrücken suchen" (col. 402).

[151] *Conversationsblatt. Zeitschrift für wissenschaftliche Unterhaltung*, III (Vienna, 1821), 769-71, 787-90, 801-3, 811-13, 821-23, 833-37. The sentence "Ja selbst der von einer Krankheit Genesende fängt an zu singen, sobald er sich wieder seiner Kraft bewusst wird" (p. 836), may have influenced Beethoven's formulations "Heiliger Dankgesang eines Genesenen," and "Neue Kraft fühlend" in Opus 132 (1825).

BEETHOVEN'S BIRTH YEAR

By MAYNARD SOLOMON

"I lived for a while without knowing how old I was."
— Beethoven to Wegeler, May 2, 1810 [1]

FOR many years of his life, and especially in his last two decades, Beethoven believed that he had been born in December of 1772 rather than in December, 1770. Thayer claims that the incorrect birth year, 1772, is the one which is ". . . given in all the old biographical notices, and which corresponds to the dates affixed to many of his first works, and indeed to nearly all allusions to his age in the early years." [2] Beethoven's father is blamed for the alleged discrepancy. Some biographers accuse him of deliberate falsification. Thayer (whose opinion on this subject has been most influential) finds the "conclusion irresistible" that the boy's age was "purposely falsified" by his father in order to promote his possibilities as a *Wunderkind* along the lines of the Mozart children: "There is, unfortunately," he writes, "nothing known of Johann van Beethoven's character which renders such a trick improbable." [3] Schiedermair — whose more lenient approach is adopted by several of the more recent biographers, including Riezler,[4] Hess,[5] Forbes [6] and Schmidt-Görg [7] — gives Johann the benefit of the doubt, stressing the

[1] Emily Anderson, ed. and trans., *The Letters of Beethoven* (London, 1961), I, 270-71 (Letter 256).

[2] Alexander Wheelock Thayer, *Thayer's Life of Beethoven,* ed. Elliot Forbes (Princeton, N. J., 1964), I, 54.

[3] Thayer, *The Life of Ludwig van Beethoven,* ed. Henry E. Krehbiel (New York, 1921), I, 54-55. Thayer's assumptions about Johann's desire to create a *Wunderkind* along Mozartean lines are anticipated by Ludwig Nohl, *Beethovens Leben* (Leipzig, 1867 [Vienna, 1864]), I, 79 and 370.

[4] Walter Riezler, *Beethoven* (London, 1938), p. 21.

[5] Willy Hess, *Beethoven* (Zürich, 1956), p. 21.

[6] Thayer-Forbes, *loc. cit.*

[7] Joseph Schmidt-Görg, *Beethoven, die Geschichte seiner Familie* (Bonn, 1964), p. 16; cf. also the entry "Beethoven" in *Die Musik in Geschichte und Gegenwart,* I (Kassel, 1949-51), cols. 1513-14.

widespread laxity in keeping family records at that time, and wondering whether the alcoholic father might not have simply made a mistake: "It is more obvious and natural to assume that father Johann even as early as 1778 no longer knew precisely the birth year of his son." [8] In either case, there is no disagreement among the biographers as to the existence of a two-year discrepancy during the Bonn period, and Beethoven's false beliefs about his age are universally attributed to either the father's falsification of his age or to the errors on the first editions or autographs of his earliest works.

However, Thayer is not accurate in stating that all the old biographical notices gave 1772 as Beethoven's birth year or in his assertion that 1772 corresponded to the dates of many of his first works. Nor can it be shown that Johann van Beethoven ever deducted two years from his son's age. Close scrutiny reveals not a single confirmable instance of a discrepancy exceeding one year during the Bonn period and only one biographical notice with a 1772 birth year. We find a consistent pattern of deductions of one year, which leads to the conclusion that Beethoven, his family and associates all believed during those years that he had been born in December, 1771. The deduction of two (and on occasion even more than two) years was made by Beethoven himself, and this evidently took place only at some time after his arrival in Vienna.

On March 26, 1778, Johann presented Ludwig at a concert in Cologne and announced him in the *Avertissement* as being "his little son of six years." [9] Beethoven was then a few months past seven; therefore it is clear that Johann — deliberately or by miscalculation — deducted one year. There is no further reference in the documentary evidence which connects Johann with the subject of the birth year.

There are other documents showing an understatement of Beethoven's age during this period. On October 14, 1783, he submitted a dedicatory letter to Elector Maximilian Friedrich, accompanying his dedication of the three sonatas for pianoforte WoO 47, in which he writes: "I have now reached my eleventh year. . . . Eleven years old. . . ." The title page of the sonatas reads: ". . . verfertigt von Ludwig van Beethoven, alt eilf Jahr," and the publisher announced the works in *Cramer's Magazine* of October 14, 1783, as compositions "of a young genius of 11 years." [10] Here again, only one year has been deducted, since Beethoven was

[8] Ludwig Schiedermair, *Der junge Beethoven* (Leipzig, 1925), p. 132.

[9] Thayer-Forbes, I, 57-58.

[10] Thayer, *Ludwig van Beethovens Leben,* ed. Hermann Deiters, 2nd ed. (Leipzig, 1901), I, 147-48.

then twelve. Because of the unquestioned assumption that there was a two-year discrepancy during the Bonn period, many scholars have made simple arithmetical errors regarding this dedication and other documents of the period, and these errors have perpetuated the myth of the two year differential.[11] Thayer, although his generalizations are incorrect, commits no such arithmetical errors, and he notes that "at first, the falsification rarely extends beyond one year . . ."[12]

Other works which tend to confirm a consistent pattern of one year deductions are the Variations on a March by Dressler [WoO 63] ("composed . . . by a young amateur Louis van Beethoven aged ten"), published in 1782 or at the latest in early 1783, and the song, "Schilderung eines Mädchens" [WoO 107] ("11 years old") published in 1783. When a work composed in these years bears a notation on the score as to Beethoven's age but is published only many years later, there is clearly some difficulty in dating it. Such are the Fugue in D major for Organ [WoO 31] ("at the age of 11 years") the Concerto in E-flat major for Pianoforte and Orchestra [WoO 4] ("composed by Louis van Beethoven aged twelve"), the Minuet for Pianoforte in E-flat major [WoO 82] (a copy seen by Nottebohm, now lost, stated: "at the age of 13"),[13] and the Prelude for Pianoforte in F minor [WoO 55] (again, according to Nottebohm, "at the age of 15 years").[14] Some Beethoven scholars have dated these works by circular reasoning, using an assumed birthday of December, 1772, as the point of departure and adding the designated number of years. In 1868 Nottebohm arrived at an incorrect (1780) dating of the Variations on a March by Dressler via the same method, but using

[11] A few examples: Kinsky writes that the dedication shows Beethoven as "two years younger than he truly was." (Georg Kinsky and Hans Halm, *Das Werk Beethovens* [Munich, 1955], p. 493); Miss Anderson makes the same error: "He was then 13" (Anderson, III, 1410, note 3) as does Kalischer (A. C. Kalischer, ed., *Beethoven's Letters,* trans. J. S. Shedlock [London, 1909], I, 2) and numerous others. Schiedermair (pp. 130-31) makes many errors in both directions: he refers to the concert of March, 1778, as having been given when Beethoven was eight, to the dedication to the elector as diminishing Beethoven's age by two years, and to Neefe's biographical notice of 1783 as giving the "age of the boy as two years younger," when in fact all of these assertions are incorrect. For several other examples, cf. Theodor Frimmel, *Beethoven Jahrbuch* (Munich and Leipzig, 1909), II, 345; J.-G. Prod'homme, *La Jeunesse de Beethoven* (Paris, 1927), p. 61; Joseph Schmidt-Görg, "Stand und Aufgaben der Beethoven-Genealogie," in *Beethoven und die Gegenwart,* ed. Arnold Schmitz (Berlin, 1937), p. 306.

[12] Thayer-Krehbiel, I, 55.

[13] Gustav Nottebohm, *Thematisches Verzeichniss . . . von Ludwig van Beethoven,* 2nd ed. (Leipzig, 1868), p. 149.

[14] *Ibid.*

the date of December, 1770, as his reference point.[15] Kinsky dates these works by analogy to the Electoral Sonatas, thereby arriving at a one-year difference even though he (as we saw above) assumes a two-year deduction from Beethoven's age in this period.

As for the older biographical notices to which Thayer refers, the first of these in print is Christian Gottlob Neefe's famous paragraph of March 2, 1783, in *Cramer's Magazine*:

Louis van Betthoven, son of the tenor singer mentioned, a boy of eleven years and of the most promising talent. He plays the clavier very skillfully and with power, reads at sight very well, and . . . he plays chiefly *The Well-Tempered Clavier* of Sebastian Bach, which Herr Neefe put into his hands . . . So far as his duties permitted, Herr Neefe has also given him instruction in thorough-bass. He is now training him in composition and for his encouragement has had nine variations for the pianoforte, written by him on a march . . . engraved at Mannheim. This youthful genius is deserving of help to enable him to travel. He would surely become a second Wolfgang Amadeus Mozart were he to continue as he has begun.[16]

Neefe was probably the prime mover in arranging for publication of many of the works cited earlier; here, as well as in those instances, it is evident that he consistently believed his pupil to have been one year younger than his actual age.

Another early biographical notice is that of Carl Ludwig Junker, in Bossler's *Musikalische Correspondenz* of November 23, 1791:

I heard also one of the greatest of pianists — the dear, good Bethofen, some compositions by whom appeared in the Speier Blumenlese in 1783, written in his eleventh year. . . . Three sonatas for pianoforte by him were also printed around that time by Bossler's publishing house. . . .[17]

Junker provides no new information on our subject. The ambiguity of his phrase "in his eleventh year" (rather than "at the age of eleven") should not lead us to assume that he believed Beethoven to have been born in 1772.

There is a significant biographical reference in the *Allgemeine Musikalische Zeitung* in 1799, which refers to ". . . the worthy pianist Beethoven, who in his thirteenth year had already published sonatas of his own. . . ."[18] If we read "in his thirteenth year" to mean that he was

[15] *Ibid.*, p. 154. Here, Nottebohm appears to have forgotten Beethoven's birth date, for he was really only nine for all but the last two weeks of 1780.

[16] Thayer-Forbes, p. 66.

[17] Emerich Kastner and Theodor Frimmel, *Bibliotheca Beethoveniana* (Leipzig, 1925), p. 3

[18] "S" (Nicolaus Simrock?), letter on the state of music in the Rhineland, dated "end of July, 1799," *Allgemeine Musikalische Zeitung*, I (1799), col. 880.

twelve, then this is a correct statement of Beethoven's age by someone who was probably a fellow Rhinelander.

There is only one notice before 1800 which specifies a 1772 birth year, and it appears to have been widely copied by early nineteenth-century dictionary and encyclopedia authors. This is Ernst Ludwig Gerber's *Historisch-biographisches Lexikon der Tonkünstler* (Leipzig, 1790):

Beethoven (Louis van). Son of a tenor in the Electoral Court at Bonn; born there 1772, a student of Neefe; in his 11th year he was already playing Sebastian Bach's *Well-Tempered Clavier*. Also in the same year he had already published at Speier and Mannheim his earliest attempts at composition — 9 Variations on a March, 3 Clavier Sonatas and several Lieder.[19]

This notice derives primarily from Neefe's of March 2, 1783. Gerber's errors are easily attributable to hasty research and to the same simple arithmetical error which has plagued so many biographers and scholars — the miscalculation which stems from overlooking the month in which Beethoven was born. In this case, Gerber probably deducted eleven (the age given on Beethoven's first publications) from 1783 (the year of the first publications) and thereby arrived at a birth year of 1772. I am not aware of any early biographical notice which gives both the month and the year of Beethoven's birth.

Apart from Gerber's secondhand entry, the fact is that at no point during his stay in Bonn can it be confirmed that Beethoven's age was understated by two years. Moreover, his age was in almost every case clearly understated by one year. We may, therefore, safely date those Bonn compositions which bear an age reference by assuming a consistent birth date of December, 1771. We may discard the notions that Beethoven's father deducted two years from Beethoven's age and that the first publications and biographical notices understate his age by two years. Beethoven's persistent belief that he was born in December, 1772 (or later), originated in his own mind, and this belief arose at a later date, after his childhood had ended.

The first indication of Beethoven's own confusion about his age dates from 1785. In that year he wrote on the autograph of his three quartets for piano and strings WoO 36: "trois quatuors pur le clave[c]in, violino, viola e Basso, 1785, compose par luis van Beethoven, agè 13 ans." This would be congruent with the December 1771 birth date, but Thayer notes: "The figure indicating the composer's age was first writ-

19 Kastner-Frimmel, p. 2.

ten '14' and then changed." [20] Fourteen, of course, was his correct age. Perhaps there is some connection between this indecision and an official report to Elector Maximilian Franz in mid-1784 which states Beethoven's age correctly: "Ludwig van Beethoven, age 13, born at Bonn, has served two years, no salary." [21] Clearly the court itself was under no misapprehension about Beethoven's age, and it is possible that the information in the report was brought to the young composer's attention, perhaps by some court official who may have noted the discrepancy. Whatever the cause, in 1785, far from believing that he was two years younger, we have, in Beethoven's own hand, evidence that, if anything, he then regarded himself as having been born either in 1770 or 1771, and was undecided about his real age.

The next written reference by Beethoven to his age occurs in the Heiligenstadt Testament of October 6, 1802, as follows: "Perhaps I shall get better, perhaps not, I am ready. — Forced to become a philosopher already in my 28th year [*schon in meinem 28. jahr gezwungen Philosoph zu werden*], oh, it is not easy." [22] Whether at this time Beethoven believed that he had been born in 1773 (or later) we cannot tell for certain, but it certainly appears so. In any event, he soon was to fix on 1772 as the "real" year of his birth.

* * *

In 1806, Ferdinand Ries, seeking to find out Beethoven's exact date

[20] Thayer-Forbes, I, 82, note 9; Kinsky-Halm, p. 478. To compound the confusion, Schiedermair (p. 179) and Nottebohm (p. 143) mistakenly write that Beethoven's correct age at this time was fifteen!

[21] Thayer-Forbes, I, 79. Thayer, seeing in this report a possible refutation of his theory about Johann's falsification of Ludwig's age, speculated that in this case "an untruth could not be risked, nor be of advantage if it had been . . ." (Thayer-Krehbiel, I, 55). Forbes, following Schiedermair, asks pointedly "whether the falsification of age could be purposely any the more risked in a dedication to the Elector . . ." (Thayer-Forbes, I, 54). The risk or embarrassment involved in such a false dedication (as was the case in the Electoral Sonatas of 1783) makes it more than likely that Johann, too, believed Ludwig to have been born in 1771.

[22] Translation from Thayer-Forbes, I, 305. Miss Anderson (III, 1352-53) transposes the reference into the past: "At the early age of 28 I was obliged to become a philosopher, though this was not easy." Kalischer-Shedlock (I, 60) and Nohl-Wallace (*Beethoven's Letters* [Boston, n.d.], I, 47) do not screen the difficulty, and both note the great discrepancy between this reference and Beethoven's real age, Kalischer-Shedlock suggesting a four-year gap and Nohl-Wallace a five-year error. This lends substance to Nohl's conjecture — based on a close reading of several items in the Fischoff manuscript — that Beethoven celebrated his twenty-fifth birthday in 1799, and that he on more than one occasion "regarded himself as at least four years younger than he actually was." (Nohl, *Beethovens Leben* [Leipzig, 1867], II, 464.)

of birth, obtained a copy of his certificate of baptism, which was dated December 17, 1770, and sent it to Beethoven in Vienna, succeeding only in arousing the composer's anger. The subject remained a matter of friction between them until as late as 1809, when Beethoven wrote to Ries:

> ... your friends have given you bad advice — But I know all about these friends, for they are the same people to whom you also sent those nice reports from Paris about me — the very same people who enquired *about my age,* about which you were able to provide them with such reliable information — the very same people who have already lowered my good opinion of you on several occasions and have now done so for good.[23]

Ries explains the events in Paris without specifying who his questioners were:

> Some friends of Beethoven wanted to know with certitude the day of his birth. With much effort, in 1806, when I was in Bonn, I looked up his baptismal certificate which I finally located and sent to Vienna. Beethoven never wanted to speak about his age.[24]

Despite the heavy irony and anger of Beethoven's reply, his mind was not set at rest concerning the discrepancy between the evidence of the baptismal certificate and his own belief that he was younger. On May 2, 1810, he wrote an urgent letter to Wegeler in Coblenz, asking that he obtain another "correct" certificate of baptism:

> I ask you to obtain for me *my certificate of baptism* — ... take note of the fact that I had a brother *born before me,* who was also called Ludwig, but with the additional name of 'Maria,' and who died. In order to determine my true age, you should, therefore, first find this Ludwig. For I know that other people, by giving out that I am older than I really am, have been responsible for this error — Unfortunately I lived for a while without knowing how old I was — I had a family book but it was lost, Heaven knows how — So please do not be annoyed at my earnestly requesting you to find out all about Ludwig Maria and the present Ludwig who was born after him — The sooner you send me the certificate of baptism, the greater will be my gratitude. — ...[25]

Wegeler's response was a confirmation of Ries's evidence. He sent Beethoven a copy of his baptismal certificate dated June 2, 1810, duly signed by the "Mayor's office of Bonn," which sets forth 1770 as his birth year. Beethoven still would not accept the document as valid.

[23] Anderson, I, 253 (Letter 236).

[24] Franz Wegeler and Ferdinand Ries, *Biographische Notizen über Ludwig van Beethoven* (Coblenz, 1838), p. 136.

[25] Anderson, I, 270-71 (Letter 256).

He wrote on the back of it:

1722   The baptismal certificate seems to be incorrect, since there was a Ludwig born
before me. A Baumgarten was my sponsor, I believe.

Ludwig van Beethoven [26]

Uncertainty lingered, and is confirmed by Bettina Brentano's letter to
Anton Bihler of July 9, 1810: ". . . he does not know his age himself but
believes he is thirty-five." [27]

The subject was to recur in later years. The *Tagebuch* of 1818 has
the following notation: "Frau Baumgarten vom ersten und zweiten Ludwig." [28] And a conversation book entry dating from February, 1820, reveals Beethoven still speculating about the identity of his sponsor, which
might serve as a means of proving that he had indeed been born in
1772: "Bongard must have been the name of the woman who was my
godmother — or Baumgarten." [29] Actually, her name was Frau Baum,
clearly set forth in the baptismal certificates which he had received first
from Ries, then from Wegeler, and now from another well-wisher, Wilhelm Christian Müller.

In a letter to an unknown correspondent dated April 22, 1827, Müller
describes his experiences with Beethoven concerning the birth-year question:

We wanted to know from him when his birthday was, in order to celebrate it —
actually we wanted to send him a ring. He replied that he didn't know precisely
either the day or the year. My daughter wrote to Professor Arnd in Bonn and
asked him to obtain and send us a birth certificate from the Church Register. This
designated the date as December 17, 1770. Through us he came to know the truth,
and we spoke with him about it as recently as 1820, and he jestingly said that he
would not have believed that he was such an old bloke. . . .[30]

It is nice to learn that Beethoven had reached the point where he could
joke about his age, but Müller's evidence did not settle the question
either. In the conversation book for December 15, 1823, his nephew

[26] Thayer-Forbes, I, 54.

[27] Ludwig Nohl, *Beethoven nach den Schilderungen seiner Zeitgenossen* (Stuttgart, 1877), p. 63. O. G. Sonneck, *Beethoven, Impressions of Contemporaries* (New
York, 1926), mistakenly renders "fünfunddreissig" as "fifty-three." Curiously, Bettina
also remained for many years under the illusion that she was younger than her actual
age, believing that she was born in 1788 rather than 1785.

[28] Nohl, *Die Beethoven-Feier und die Kunst der Gegenwart* (Vienna, 1871), p.
72; Albert Leitzmann, *Beethovens persönliche Aufzeichnungen* (Leipzig, n. d.), p. 36.

[29] Georg Schünemann, ed., *Ludwig van Beethovens Konversationshefte* (Berlin,
1941-43), I, 232. Cf. also I, 221.

[30] Frimmel, *Beethoven-Forschung, Lose Blätter, No. 1* (Vienna, 1911), p. 27.

writes: "Today is the 15th of December, the day of your birth, but I am not sure whether it is the 15th or 17th, inasmuch as we can not depend on the certificate of baptism and I read it only once when I was still with you in January." [31] Clearly, Beethoven had not yet, nor would he ever come to terms with the facts so simply set forth on the certificate.

Beethoven manifestly had all the facts available to convince him of his real birth year: at least three copies of the baptismal certificate; the independent researches of Ferdinand Ries, Franz Gerhard Wegeler, and the Müllers; the name of his sponsor clearly given as Frau Baum — obviously the "Frau Baumgarten" or "Bongard" he had been seeking; the fact that the baptismal certificate gave his correct baptismal day. It would have been an inconceivable coincidence that the Ludwig Maria born before him had been baptized on precisely the same date of a different year. It is also improbable that Beethoven could imagine that he was only one year and four months older than his brother Caspar Carl, who was born in April of 1774.[32] And the vivid memories which he retained of his grandfather (who died on December 24, 1773) would have been impossible if he had been only one year old when the Kapellmeister died.

In view of these unmistakable ways by which Beethoven could have tested and confirmed the accuracy of the baptismal certificates, we must conclude that he was unwilling or unable to subject the issue of his birth year to rational consideration. The birth-year delusion can no longer be described as rising from a deliberate falsification by Johann van Beethoven of his son's age. The delusion was Beethoven's own. We may surmise that Beethoven was unable or unwilling to reconstruct or remember some portion of his childhood which had been eradicated from his memory. Schindler tells us that "Beethoven himself as a rule did not speak of his early youth, and when he did he seemed uncertain and confused." [33] That the erasure involved Beethoven's memory of events or relationships of his early life is more than probable. What was being erased is not equally clear.

---

[31] Thayer-Krehbiel, I, 53.

[32] There is some difficulty with Caspar Carl's age as well. Upon his death, the *Wiener Zeitung* carried a notice: "Died on November 16, Hr. Karl van Beethoven ... aged 38 years..." (Thayer-Krehbiel, II, 321), an understatement of his age by three years.

[33] Anton Schindler, *Beethoven as I Knew Him* (*Biographie von Ludwig van Beethoven,* 3rd ed.), ed. Donald W. MacArdle (Chapel Hill, N. C., 1966), p. 46.

BEETHOVEN'S CONTRAPUNTAL
STUDIES WITH HAYDN

By ALFRED MANN

I T is one of the ironies of music history that the association of Haydn and Beethoven as teacher and student appears to have been unsuccessful. To begin with, Haydn was Beethoven's second choice, and a patently awkward pedagogical situation was outlined in Count Waldstein's farewell message to Beethoven at his second departure for Vienna in November, 1792: "By working assiduously you will receive Mozart's spirit from Haydn's hands." It was, in fact, the very industry of the pupil that was not satisfied by Haydn's lessons, which before long were discreetly supplemented through sessions with Johann Schenk. Though known to later generations primarily as the composer of *Der Dorfbarbier,* the Viennese Singspiel master was well qualified for this teaching task. He was intimately acquainted with the work upon which Haydn based his instruction, Johann Josef Fux's *Gradus ad Parnassum,* for he had studied the text with one of Fux's own students, Georg Christoph Wagenseil.

While Schenk's account of the events, contained in his autobiographical sketch,[1] may not be totally reliable (his date for the beginning of the meetings with Beethoven precedes that of Beethoven's arrival in Vienna by three months), the clandestine arrangement between Schenk and Beethoven doubtless took place, and Beethoven's genuine gratitude is documented in a remark from a later meeting with Schenk which was recorded by Schindler. Haydn's second journey to England, barely a year after Beethoven's arrival, provided the occasion for a definite change. Beethoven took up contrapuntal studies with Albrechtsberger; in matters of vocal style and Italian prosody he turned to Salieri for advice.

The "failure" of Haydn's teaching has intrigued critical scholarship. Beethoven's studies bearing Haydn's corrections were preserved with the manuscripts of his works and acquired by his publisher Tobias Haslinger

---

[1] Published in *Studien zur Musikwissenschaft,* XI (1924), 75ff.

after Beethoven's death. Haslinger turned them over to Seyfried, Beethoven's fellow student under Albrechtsberger, for editing, and Seyfried prepared an account of Beethoven's studies that was published under Haslinger's imprint in 1832. Seyfried's book aroused much divided opinion. On the one hand, his opening statement was accepted on face value: "These studies of the unforgettable master represent so invaluable a legacy to the entire world of the arts that it would have been preposterous to make even the slightest changes." On the other hand, his editorship was categorically challenged and the whole work considered fictitious. (Seyfried's role was the harder to appraise since Albrechtsberger's *Gründliche Anweisung zur Komposition,* on which Beethoven's studies with Albrechtsberger had been based, had been reissued in Seyfried's *J. G. Albrechtsbergers Sämtliche Schriften,* also published by Haslinger — the second edition of 1837 containing a detailed explanation of the rather competent editorial procedure.) It was left to Gustav Nottebohm to show that Seyfried's edition of Beethoven's studies was "neither authentic nor fictitious but forged." [2]

Nottebohm had found out that the original manuscript was still in the possession of Haslinger's daughter-in-law, in fact, that the entire body of Beethoven's theoretical writings, designated as *Contrapunktische Aufsätze, 5 Pakete,* at the sale of 1827, was still contained in the five folders described in the sales catalogue. By the brilliant analysis presented in his *Beethoveniana,* Nottebohm distinguished five groups of manuscripts (not corresponding to the five *Pakete*), all of which Seyfried had freely mingled and altered, ascribing them to the Albrechtsberger period so that the "herrliche Kunstbruder" was portrayed within the confines of Seyfried's own instruction. The five groups identified by Nottebohm are (1) Beethoven's studies with Haydn, (2) Beethoven's studies with Albrechtsberger, (3) a compilation of *Materialien zum Generalbass* and *Materialien zum Kontrapunkt* paraphrased by Beethoven, evidently in 1809, from various theoretical works for his own teaching purposes, (4) Beethoven's copies of works by other composers, and his notes dealing mostly with fugal studies and dating from different periods, and (5) a spurious set of contrapuntal studies, written by another Albrechtsberger student (Seyfried himself?) with Albrechtsberger's corrections and comments. A sixth group, representing Beethoven's studies with Salieri, was entirely excluded from Seyfried's edition.

Returning to the sources, Nottebohm obtained an insight into the course of Beethoven's training not afforded any one observer before. His

[2] *Beethoveniana* (Leipzig 1872), p. 203.

findings were presented a year later in a comprehensive discussion of Beethoven's studies: *Beethovens Studien* (Leipzig and Winterthur, 1873; a second volume, planned to be devoted to Beethoven's teaching, did not appear.) In it he gives a searching interpretation of Haydn's contrapuntal lessons, quoting forty-two excerpts from Beethoven's studies for which Haydn's corrections exist. On the basis of this investigation Nottebohm judges that Haydn was hasty, careless, and inconsistent in his teaching and that he was, in fact, not thoroughly familiar with the rules and principles of strict counterpoint.

The fact that Nottebohm's work was one of the outstanding contributions towards the rising literature of objective and documentary studies that marked the time of the Beethoven centennial has lent his verdict special weight. Nevertheless, his writing lacks a decisive perspective: he does not take into account the complexity of the two artistic personalities involved, or fully reckon with the awkwardness of the didactic situation. Now that another century has passed, there is an obvious need for reviewing the evidence and subjecting Beethoven's studies with Haydn to fresh appraisal.

The original form of the manuscript, though restored through Nottebohm's description from Seyfried's unrecognizable presentation, is still unpublished. Nottebohm quotes forty-eight of 245 extant examples (his selection includes six uncorrected, in addition to forty-two corrected, examples), and he suggests that the total number of exercises initially contained in the manuscript was closer to 300 than 245, While he does not specify where the suspected gaps are, their places can be rather easily assigned to two spots in the manuscript. More important is the fact that — as Nottebohm himself conjectures — we would probably have an incomplete picture of the studies Beethoven wrote for Haydn even if these gaps were closed.

The manuscript consists of fifty-four pages containing sixteen staves each and measuring $12\frac{1}{2} \times 9\frac{1}{4}$ inches in oblong. Evidently still in the state in which it was when Nottebohm had examined it, the manuscript became part of the collection of the Gesellschaft der Musikfreunde in Wien through a bequest of J. Standhartner, one of its members, in 1891. At one time the pages must have been sewn together, as is shown by stitching holes lined up roughly with the second and last staves of each page. There is no original pagination; page numbers, entered lightly in pencil, were added by Hedwig Krauss, into whose care the collection passed at the death of Eusebius Mandyczewski in 1929. The proper sequence of pages is easily verified, for the manuscript is made up largely of double leaves which are still connected and at times gathered in groups, and the exercises are arranged according to the order of the contrapuntal species and of a set of cantus firmi in the six authentic modes.

A rather consistent plan for the number of examples Beethoven compiled in this book can be seen from the following table:

	Modes:	D	E	F	G	A	C	pages
Examples of two-part counterpoint	1st species	4	2	2	2	2	2	2-3
	2nd species	2	2	2	2	2	2	3-4
	3rd species	2	2	2	2	2	2	4-5
	4th species	2	2	2	2	2	—	6
	5th species	—	—	—	—	—	—	
Examples of three-part counterpoint	1st species	2	4	3	3	3	3	7-10
	2nd species	3	3	4	3	3	4	10-14
	3rd species	3	3	3	3	3	3	15-19
	4th species	3	3	3	4	1	—	19-22
	5th species	—	—	—	—	3	3	23-24
Examples of four-part counterpoint	1st species	4	4	4(5)[3]	4	4	4	24-30
	2nd species	4	4	4	4	4	4	30-36
	3rd species	4	4	4	4	4	3	36-42
	4th species	4	5	4	4	4	5	42-48
	5th species	4	4	4	4	4	4	49-54

Separate headings for the various species appear throughout the two- and three-part exercises, the four-part exercises being grouped under the single heading *4 stimmiger Contrapunkt*. Page 1 is set aside for a title written with, for Beethoven, unusual care. The relatively small number of pages used for the two-part exercises is explained by the fact that here a single cantus firmus melody serves both as a lower and an upper part of a two-part setting, systems of three staves representing in each case a pair of examples. Pages 3-6 form one double leaf, and pages 7-14 form a gathering of two double leaves. Two additional exercises for the fourth species and twelve for the fifth (a pair for each cantus firmus) were most likely contained on two pages which, being a single leaf placed between the present pages 6 and 7, were lost. Pages 15-22 form a gathering of two double leaves and pages 23-26 again form one double leaf. In this case apparently six additional exercises for the fourth species and twelve exercises for the fifth, all contained on one double leaf, were lost. In three-part counterpoint Beethoven compiles groups of three

---

[3] An alternate version appearing immediately after one of the examples in this group and on the same four-stave system is not included in Nottebohm's total count.

exercises for each cantus firmus — corresponding to groups of two in two-part, and groups of four in four-part counterpoint — following a pattern by which each cantus firmus is placed in turn in each of the three parts; the first pair of three-part exercises, in which the Dorian cantus firmus is used only in treble and bass, forms an exception. Whenever a cantus firmus appears twice in the same register, Beethoven marks the examples involved *1*) and *2*), and in these cases four examples rather than the usual three are allotted to one cantus firmus. The last example on page 22 is marked *1*), so that we may assume that at least six additional examples for the fourth species — three for the Aeolian and three for the Ionian cantus firmus — would have followed on a succeeding page.

Thus the examples lost may amount to a total number of thirty-two rather than the fifty-five estimated by Nottebohm. But the general plan of the manuscript, its appearance and meticulously written title page, suggest that we are dealing with a fair copy, a methodical selection made from other manuscripts that may have contained a considerably larger amount of material. This is evident from an example (the last on page 33) in which Beethoven had written out an upper part in half-notes before beginning to enter the cantus firmus below, then discovered a missing measure and started afresh on the following page. It is evident also from a number of details, not listed by Nottebohm, in which Haydn corrects flaws that occurred in transcription and that show a certain carelessness on the part of the student rather than the teacher.

In one example (page 26) the cantus firmus is incorrectly copied, and the right notes are indicated by small letters added by Haydn. In two other examples (pages 24 and 47) Haydn changed a clef which Beethoven had entered incorrectly. The error occurred in both cases for the same reason: an unusual combination of four vocal registers was involved. Haydn had to change an alto clef used for a second part to a tenor clef, and a tenor clef used for a third part to an alto clef. He seems to have been especially aware of the spacing of registers. A four-part example written for two altos, tenor, and bass in which the tenor begins and ends above the second alto, bears his mark *NB* at the margin. (A similar concern can be gathered from corrections made by Mozart in Thomas Attwood's studies.)

The character of these slight emendations is indicative of the more important ones. While the argument of Haydn's haste in reviewing the manuscript cannot be dismissed — for he bypassed obvious errors in examples that he touched up in other spots — the argument of his

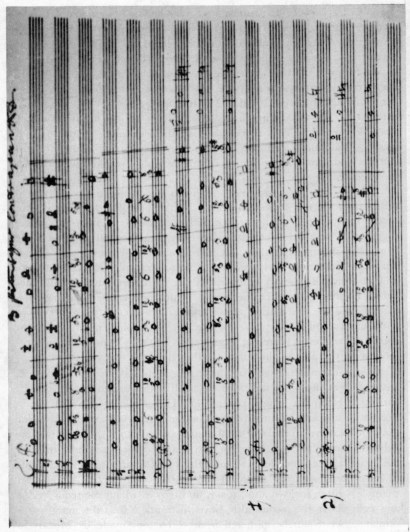

Plate I

Page 7 of Beethoven's contrapuntal studies with Haydn.

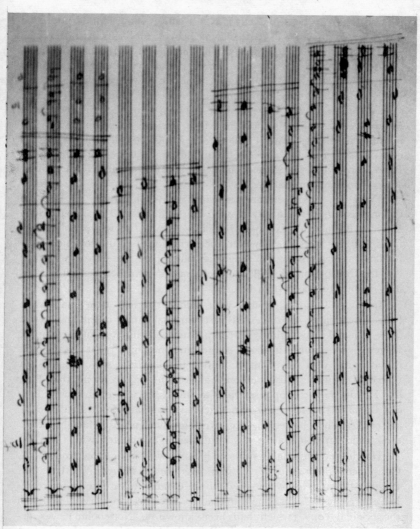

Plate II
Page 45 of Beethoven's contrapuntal studies with Haydn.

inconsistency can be disproved. Haydn's entries show that his attention was directed towards a particular choice of problems, but those he selected, he treated systematically. This manner of correction appears in a different light if we take into consideration that it may have taken place in two or three sessions during which a newly copied manuscript was examined and that assignments and corrections spaced over a greater span of time preceded these sessions. (Haydn's annotations are divided rather evenly between sections in which the entries are made in dark ink or in pencil; see Plates I and II.) How methodically Haydn took up certain issues can be gathered from the pencil corrections shown on Plate II by which he singled out every instance of an awkward dissonance resolution on that page.

There is a striking instance in which Nottebohm raises the question of inconsistent correction by Haydn. Here Haydn had changed hidden fifths in Beethoven's example, but, in so doing, he wrote hidden octaves. Without question, however, the correction is an improvement: the hidden parallels involve no longer an outer part but only inner parts, and the distribution of similar and contrary motion between all parts is more evenly balanced than before.

It is usually not a concern with hidden parallels alone that causes their correction by Haydn. As his first marginal entries in the manuscript show (Plate I), his writing, in comparison with his student's examples, suggests spaciousness in both sound and motion. What Nottebohm misses in Haydn's treatment of hidden parallels is a set of established rules. In discussing this question, however, he has to admit that Fux, like Haydn, fails to apply set rules to this aspect of counterpoint. It is also disconcerting to Nottebohm that Haydn departs from such rules as are consistently followed in Fux's writing, and from this fact he draws the conclusion that Haydn was insufficiently acquainted with them.

Haydn had thoroughly dealt with Fux's work. We know from G. A. Griesinger's *Biographische Notizen über Joseph Haydn* (1810) that Haydn's "thoroughly worn copy" of the *Gradus* was studied with ceaseless effort. Haydn's marginal annotations have been preserved, although the original copy (which had been known to Nottebohm) was destroyed in World War II. C. F. Pohl, the biographer of Haydn, had taken the precaution of transcribing all of Haydn's entries onto corresponding pages of another copy of the work which now also forms part of the collection of the Gesellschaft der Musikfreunde in Wien. This set of annotations is in many respects a remarkable document. It covers a space of at least twenty years — for, according to the biographical sources, Haydn was occupied with his study of the work in the early 1750s, but his annotations include references to Kirnberger, whose writings he could not have examined until the 1770s — and it represents perhaps the most detailed critique to which Fux's text has ever been subjected. Haydn's remarks, formulated, like the text of the book, in Latin, are concerned with corrections of errors and ambiguities as well as criticism of subject matter. There is almost no issue in the course of instruction for which Haydn has not given — and apparently handed down — exhaustive commentary.

The matter of hidden or delayed parallels is touched upon again and again, but invariably the point of departure is the ambiguous nature of the problem. In an example in which Fux discusses hidden fifths — accepting their use both in a passage occurring between an inner and an outer voice and one occurring between the two outer voices — Haydn notes next to the second passage "judged bad by other authors" and changes Fux's part-writing. It is the same spot upon which Beethoven, preparing a summary from the *Gradus* almost twenty years after his studies with Haydn, comments: "The last one, however, would never be acceptable to my ear."

How did Haydn acquaint Beethoven with Fux's text? Surely, in trying to reconstruct the teaching situation, we cannot disregard the wealth of Haydn's commentary upon this text. Haydn had had an abstract made from the *Gradus* in 1789, three years before the beginning of Beethoven's instruction. Entitled *Elementarbuch der vershiednen Gattungen des Contrapunkts aus den grösseren Werken des Kappm. Fux, von Joseph Haydn zusammengezogen,* this abstract is written and dated by Haydn's student F. C. Magnus, who, being taught without charge, apparently did some copying services for Haydn at the time. The manuscript, which passed in 1949 from the Esterházy Archives to the National Széchényi Library in Budapest, breaks off after seventeen pages, leaving the major part of the neatly bound book unused. Since the existing fragment is written with great care, it must represent a copy made from another manuscript either written by Haydn or taken down from his dictation. Several obvious mistakes suggest that Haydn did not check the Magnus copy. At the time Seyfried dealt with Beethoven's manuscripts, these must have included a copy Beethoven may have made from the same source that Magnus had used, for a major portion of the Magnus manuscript text appears mixed into Beethoven's text in Seyfried's book. At the time Nottebohm dealt with the material Beethoven's copy had been lost, but Nottebohm had an additional source at his disposal which has since disappeared.

We are left here without dependable guidance, because Nottebohm, who must have considered this phase of Beethoven's instruction unimportant, abandons scholarly accuracy, splicing two manuscripts in his presentation of the *Elementarbuch* "with the omission of certain superfluous portions and without considering the original wording." He mentions that, of the two manuscripts used, one was incomplete and the other unreliable, but does not identify either of them. That the incomplete manuscript was the Magnus copy is proved by the account given in Pohl's Haydn biography, the first volume of which was published in 1878, five years after Nottebohm's *Beethoveniana*. The source of the manuscript Nottebohm describes as unreliable remains unexplained, although the outline of its contents that can be surmised from Nottebohm's rendering suggests a connection with Beethoven's work that will be discussed in more detail below.

Even though the fragmentary Magnus manuscript offers merely a suggestion of how Beethoven's lessons with Haydn may have begun, what information it does contain conveys a rather clear impression of Haydn's general plan for this compendium. Haydn wished both to condense and supplement the explanations given by Fux. What he added, partly in his own formulation and partly drawn from Mattheson's *Vollkommener Capellmeister,* indeed reflects the same concern as the commentary in his *Gradus* copy. It is prompted by an interest in clarity and completeness, but it also carries Fux's work beyond its time. Here, of course, his stand parallels Fux's own vis-à-vis the Palestrina style.

The tendency towards exploration and reformulation of contrapuntal practice is most pronounced in the discussions concerning four notes against one. Fux's rule admitting a dissonance on the third beat in a linear succession of quarter-notes marks a departure from the sixteenth-century style. Haydn adds to this in his *Gradus* annotations the possibility of two dissonances in linear succession (fourth and diminished fifth), and in the *Elementarbuch* he discusses the use of three consonances and — in an obvious concession to a harmonically oriented style — four consonances in one measure.

These details again show a concurrence of Haydn's contrapuntal teaching with that of Mozart. It is likely that Haydn's annotated *Gradus* copy had gone through Mozart's hands, for Mozart's extensive presentation of the contrapuntal species in the Attwood studies shows a remarkable affinity with their interpretation by Haydn and a much more critical approach to Fux's text than could have been derived from lessons with his father and with Martini. (Of particular interest in this respect is a comparison of the marginal notes in the *Gradus* copies owned by Leopold Mozart, by Martini, and by Haydn.)[4] The Attwood studies precede the Magnus copy of Haydn's *Elementarbuch* by approximately three years. They date from the time of Mozart's close association with Haydn, and the mutual influences that pervade the works of the two masters during this period seem to have existed also in their didactic activity — in fact, their renewed interest in contrapuntal technique was an essential factor contributing to the rise of the classical Viennese style. The *Schulung im strengen Satz* upon which Beethoven entered in 1792 must be considered different in substance and spirit from the academic subject as taught in later periods.

* * *

When Beethoven published his piano sonatas Opus 2, dedicated to Haydn, he was twenty-six years old — the same age at which Mozart began the composition of his six quartets dedicated to Haydn. While the relationship of Beethoven to Haydn cannot be compared to that of Mozart to Haydn, we must not overlook the fact that Haydn's student was a composer of a certain measure of experience, whose Opus 1 was preceded by a number of other published works. Yet Beethoven's impatience at perfecting his technique was guided by more than the personal disposition of a brusque young artist of proven competence whose wish for undisturbed study had been all too long postponed. There was, both in Beethoven's own attitude and in that of his generation, a new sense of inquiry, a new orientation towards the past.

Among Beethoven's fellow students under Albrechtsberger was R. G. Kiesewetter, one of the first distinguished modern music historians. The influence of historical studies upon questions of music theory began to be felt, although it was slow to produce decisive results. It was at first the desire for a narrower formulation of principles rather than their broader exploration that guided theoretical thought. This bent towards strictness, which stands in curious contrast to Beethoven's independence, must have complicated his role as a student of Haydn, who, born before the youngest Bach son and serving as a choirboy under Fux, had assimilated the heritage of the Baroque with an ease no one after him was able to match.

It was probably Haydn himself who, before leaving on his second

[4] See the present writer's account in *J. J. Fux Sämtliche Werke,* Series VII, Vol. I.

journey to London, brought together Beethoven and Albrechtsberger, Haydn's "old and sincere friend." [5] Beethoven, still nominally on leave from his employment at the electoral court in Bonn, was to accompany Haydn according to the original plans. The elector, whose disapproval may have decided the situation, visited Vienna shortly before Haydn's departure, and in the new electoral budget for the year 1794 Beethoven's status appeared revised: "he remains in Vienna, without pay, until recalled to service."

A marginal annotation entered by Albrechtsberger in Beethoven's book of studies with Haydn (see Plate III) explains the point of departure for Albrechtsberger's instruction:

Bᴴ A
F — is a permissible *Mi contra Fa* in A minor and E plagal vi [reference to example 'Etwas aus A moll' at the bottom of the page]. In the transposèd minor keys this *Mi contra Fa* falls on the 6th tone of the lower voice.

On the basis of his particular contribution to music theory — the change from modal to tonal counterpoint — Albrechtsberger proposed a full review of the study of counterpoint, a review that was in fact twofold. He treated counterpoint as both *strenger Satz* and *freier Satz,* the latter being species counterpoint in which concessions towards modern practice, such as had occasionally been introduced in Mozart's and Haydn's examples, were admitted by a set of given rules. This course of studies was based upon Albrechtsberger's *Gründliche Anweisung zur Komposition,* which had appeared in print two years before Beethoven's arrival in Vienna. Though the contrapuntal studies with Albrechtsberger take considerably less space in Beethoven's extant manuscripts than his previous *Übungen im Contrapunkt,* they seem to have received his concentrated attention. But, as we shall see, Beethoven eventually discarded the system, reverting in his own teaching to Haydn's contrapuntal instructions.

A development somewhat parallel to this is indicated by Beethoven's studies in fugal writing. Haydn's *Elementarbuch* deals — as stated in its title — specifically with the contrapuntal species. That his teaching included no formal instruction in fugue may not have been due merely to the limitations of time. Teacher and student may in fact have commenced contrapuntal studies with an exchange of views similar to that which took place between Mozart and Attwood, according to a reminiscence recorded by Samuel Wesley:

Mr. Thomas Attwood, his Majesty's Organist, who studied in Germany under

[5] From Albrechtsberger's dedication in an exchange of canons with Haydn (1806).

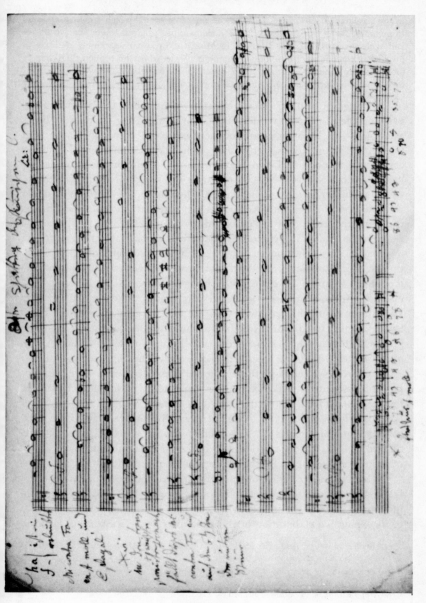

Plate III

ethoven exercises, Page 6, with marginal comment by Albrechtsberger.

Mozart, related to me many years ago an anecdote of his which frequently recurs to memory. Being naturally anxious to make a rapid progress under such a master and such a genius, he soon observed to Mozart, "Sir, I am extremely desirous to produce a good fugue from your instructions" — to which he replied, "Do not be too much in a hurry — study plain counterpoint for about twelve months, and then it will be quite time enough to talk about fugues." [6]

Although Haydn's *Gradus* annotations continue in the portion of the work devoted to fugue — including some illuminating changes in Fux's examples — it becomes clear that here he is concerned no longer with theoretical formulations but rather with the examination of another composer's work. To Haydn fugue assumed an importance compatible neither with systematic exercise nor with the image of the *stylus gravis*. In Albrechtsberger's teaching, on the other hand, fugue forms a direct continuation of strict and free species counterpoint, treated according to the respective rules and to certain additional precepts, so that even the *Fuge in der freien Schreibart* is subjected to considerable restriction.

At the outset Beethoven must have welcomed this methodical approach. His examples of two-part fugues, written under Albrechtsberger's guidance, seem to be done with the same care as the contrapuntal exercises. In writing three- and four-part fugues, however, he becomes less attentive, and his irritation with the "art of creating musical skeletons" [7] begins to appear. Nottebohm came to the conclusion that the lessons with Albrechtsberger were hastily brought to an end, with much of the material that was intended to be covered having been omitted.

Beethoven's interest in theory, nevertheless, remained alive. An important association developed, after his studies with Albrechtsberger, between Beethoven and Emanuel Aloys Förster (1748-1823), another composer from the Haydn circle, to whom Beethoven referred in later years as "my old master." [8] This relationship, in some respects comparable to that of Haydn and Mozart, forms an essential link in the chain of influences leading to Beethoven's mature contrapuntal style.

What makes the figure of this little-known Viennese master so interesting with regard to the continuation of Beethoven's studies is his prolific string quartet writing, heavily criticized by contemporaries because of its exhaustive elaboration of thematic material. His String Quartet in

[6] British Museum, Add. MS 35014, fol. 115, see *Neue Mozart-Ausgabe, Kritische Berichte,* Serie X, Werkgruppe 30, p. 48.

[7] A remark referring to Albrechtsberger's teaching in Beethoven's letter to B. Schott's Söhne, Mainz, of January, 1825; see Emily Anderson, ed. and trans., *The Letters of Beethoven* (London, 1961), III, 1169.

[8] Thayer, *Life of Beethoven,* see note 9, below.

F minor, Opus 16, No. 5 (reprinted in *Denkmäler der Tonkunst in Oesterreich,* Vol. 67), was obviously of direct influence on Beethoven's C minor Quartet, Opus 18, No. 4. Thayer presents convincing arguments in the first volume of his Beethoven biography for the conclusion that Beethoven "had studied quartet composition with him, as he had counterpoint with Albrechtsberger, and operatic writing with Salieri." [9] Thayer's information comes from Förster's son, who had received piano lessons from Beethoven in 1802 and again in 1804; he related to Thayer the fact that during those years Beethoven met with Förster twice a week for quartet sessions and that they spent many other evenings together "when the conversation usually turned upon musical theory and composition." At Beethoven's suggestion Förster published his *Anleitung zum Generalbass* in 1805. [10]

1809, the year of Haydn's death, is the year that Nottebohm established as the date for Beethoven's own *Materialien zum Generalbass* and *Materialien zum Kontrapunkt.* Beethoven had been called upon a number of times to teach composition, but he had always refused, sending even Count Razumovsky to Förster for instruction. In the case of Archduke Rudolph, Beethoven finally made an exception, and it is for him that Beethoven's notes seem to have been compiled.

Considering the range of Beethoven's own studies, the *Materialien zum Kontrapunkt* shows a remarkably direct orientation. The return to Haydn's teaching is so complete that every detail bears out parallels between Beethoven's and Haydn's attitudes toward the study of counterpoint. Like Haydn, Beethoven draws his material entirely from existing literature which he paraphrases and annotates. Like Haydn, Beethoven bases his contrapuntal instruction on an abstract of Fux's *Gradus* interspersed with quotations from other sources. Beethoven's abstract, forming the major portion of his *Materialien* and entitled *Einleitung zur Fuxischen Lehre vom Kontrapunkt,* contains a larger choice of supplementary sources than either Haydn's *Gradus* annotations or the Magnus manuscript of Haydn's *Elementarbuch.* The same sources, however, can be detected in Nottebohm's edited version of the *Elementarbuch.* For in-

[9] See Alexander Wheelock Thayer, *Life of Beethoven,* ed. Elliot Forbes (Princeton, N. J., 1964), I, 262.

[10] There are indications that Beethoven may have studied quartet writing with Haydn. Fritz Zobeley in his *Ludwig van Beethoven in Selbstzeugnissen und Bilddokumenten* (Reinbek bei Hamburg, 1965; p. 47), observing that Beethoven arranged his piano sonata Opus 14, No. 1, for string quartet, adds that "since he copied one of Haydn's quartets long before that, it is not impossible that Beethoven was introduced to four-part string writing by the great master of the quartet himself."

stance, the opening paragraph of Beethoven's *Einleitung,* derived from Türk's *Kurze Anweisung zum Generalbassspielen,* reappears in the beginning of Nottebohm's presentation of the *Elementarbuch* text. A passage whose wording suggests C. P. E. Bach's *Versuch* follows in both texts shortly thereafter. Thus the additional manuscript that Nottebohm used for his edition of the *Elementarbuch,* unidentified and now lost but at the time of Nottebohm's investigation evidently preserved with Beethoven's theoretical writings, may have contained notes, or a copy of notes, for Beethoven's own fashioning of an *Elementarbuch,* a draft for his *Einleitung.*

Nottebohm was puzzled by the compilation of excerpts from such a variety of authors who presented at times entirely conflicting precepts, and he raises the question of why Beethoven did not use a single manual of instruction, or, if more than one, a few written from the same point of view.[11] In presenting this argument, he disregards Beethoven's searching interest in theory — an interest that had accompanied the composer's growth from apprentice to master. The *Materialien zum Kontrapunkt* was written in the same year in which the Fifth Symphony was published and in which the Fifth Piano Concerto (dedicated, like the Fourth, to the archduke) was composed.

In similar manner Nottebohm takes issue with Beethoven's fugal writing in the conclusion of the variations Opus 35 and in the second and fourth movements of the *Eroica,* for he claims that Beethoven neglects the essential, in favor of unessential, aspects of fugal technique.[12] Studies in music theory and music history remained separate domains ruled by different standards in Nottebohm's work, and it is for this very reason that he does not grasp the full scope of Haydn's didactic influence. The counterpoint lessons with Haydn were Beethoven's first formal introduction to the world of polyphony, but Haydn's instruction guided the student far beyond the rudiments of the polyphonic language. To Beethoven applies in equal measure what Alfred Einstein wrote of Mozart: he "learned from Haydn to handle polyphony and counterpoint lightly, as a playful exercising of humor and wit, though also, to be sure, as an object of the greatest seriousness."[13]

[11] *Beethoveniana,* p. 202.

[12] *Beethoven's Studien,* pp. 197, 200.

[13] *Mozart, His Character, His Work* (New York, 1962), pp. 154f.

BEETHOVEN'S SEPTET, OPUS 20:
AN ARRANGEMENT FOR
MILITARY BAND

By MYRON SCHWAGER

THERE is a good deal of evidence that the septet Opus 20 was received with greater and more immediate public enthusiasm than most of Beethoven's works. Finished in the spring of 1800, it was offered on the following December 15 to the publisher Hoffmeister; already, the composer states in his letter, "this septet has been very popular." [1] Apparently sensing the commercial possibilities of the work, he then says, "For its more frequent use one could arrange the three wind instrument parts, i. e., the bassoon, clarinet, and horn, for another violin, viola, and violoncello." Another year and a half passed before publication actually took place (June, 1802), but during this period Beethoven wrote several more letters to the publisher. In some of them, we are able to find additional remarks which hint at the septet's popularity and market potential.

January 15, 1801: "And for the time being I am offering you the following compositions: a septet (about which I have already told you, and which could be arranged for the pianoforte also, with a view to its wider distribution and to our greater profit)...." [2]

April 22, 1801: "It would be nice if my dear brother, besides publishing the septet as it stands, were to arrange it too for a flute, for instance, and perhaps as a quintet. This would satisfy the *lovers of the flute* who have already entreated me to do this; and they would swarm around it and feed on it like insects." [3]

June 21, 1801: "I am so conscientious that I have refused to give the piano arrangement of the septet to *several publishers* who approached me about this. Yet I don't even know whether you are going to make use of the septet in that arrangement." [4]

[1] Emily Anderson, ed. and trans, *The Letters of Beethoven* (London, 1961), I, 42-43.

[2] *Ibid.,* I, 47.

[3] *Ibid.,* I, 51.

[4] *Ibid.,* I, 55.

From these extracts, all of which were written a year or more before the septet was even published, it appears that the work was destined for future arrangement. Upon publication, its popularity could have become only more widespread; the composer even refers to it in the *Wiener Zeitung* of October 20, 1802 (a mere three months after publication) as the "well-known septet of mine, Opus 20. . . ." [5] Right away, arrangements started to appear for all sorts of instrumental combinations, from wind sextet to guitar duet,[6] and it is probable that Beethoven was asked more than once to contribute to their growing number.

A personal concession to the demand for arrangements of his septet came when the composer transformed it into the piano trio Opus 38 (ca. 1802-1803); but in view of the extraordinary popularity of the parent work, it is pertinent to ask why Beethoven did not attempt to capitalize even further than he did upon its success. Why, for example, did he not make more arrangements of the work himself so as to share in the profits which were being made by numerous publishers who freely produced their own adaptations? One cannot be sure that he did not have this in the back of his mind; indeed, there exist manuscript fragments of an arrangement for eleven wind instruments, which are claimed to have been written by the composer. According to a report by Arthur Holde, this manuscript (sixteen pages) has been, at one time or another, in the hands of Prince Metternich, Napoleon III, Charles F. Tretbar, and Henry Ford.[7] It is now in the Beethovenhaus in Bonn.

The main information concerning this document is to be found in two paragraphs in Willy Hess's *Verzeichnis der nicht in der Gesamtausgabe veröffentlichten Werke Ludwig van Beethovens* (Wiesbaden, 1957), pp. 20-21. While much of the information there is useful, some of it is incorrect. The fragments, which are adapted from both the variation movement and the finale, are listed as *Fragment einer Bearbeitung des Andante con Variazioni aus dem Septett für 9-10 Instrumente.* Based upon the erroneous information (communicated to Hess by Donald MacArdle) that each of the movements has a different instrumentation, the assumption is made that "This group [of pages] is not one arrangement but two attempts." Since each of the fragments contains parts for

---

[5] *Ibid.,* III (Appendix H), 1434.

[6] For a list of these arrangements and information concerning them, see Georg Kinsky and Hans Halm, *Das Werk Beethovens* (Munich, 1955), p. 50.

[7] Arthur Holde, "Beethoven-Handschriften in Amerika," *Österreichische Musikzeitschrift,* VII (1952), 301-4.

eleven separate instruments,[8] however, it is probable that they belong to a single arrangement; it is unknown whether a complete one ever existed.

Another misleading statement, also communicated by MacArdle, maintains that the score "has been attested by several important musical authorities to be beyond a doubt in the early handwriting of Ludwig van Beethoven." Who the "musical authorities" are is not known; also unknown is whether the "early handwriting" is meant to apply to the music, to Beethoven's signature, or to the many expression marks one finds scattered throughout the score. At any event, any claim that the musical notation is unquestionably in Beethoven's hand is open to serious challenge. The reasons are as follows:

1. One of the most consistent features of the composer's manuscript notation from before 1800 until the end of his life is a pair of dots, placed after each expression mark (p:, cres:, sf:, etc.); even when the master was in an apparent hurry, at least one of the dots was clearly marked. In the manuscript under discussion, there are no such dots.

2. When forks are used by Beethoven to indicate crescendo or decrescendo, they are often extremely wide; those in this manuscript are rather narrow.

3. The abbreviation for crescendo (cres) in the fragments is written in a way unlike that found in any of the Beethoven manuscripts I have ever seen. First of all, it is not followed by the usual dots; secondly, the letter *c* has a characteristic hook at the top, used in this form by Beethoven only in the signs for common time and *alla breve*.

4. Whoever undertook this manuscript had an idiosyncratic way of writing a quarter-note on middle C without lifting the pen; there is no real head to the note, the ledger line standing for both the line and the note head. This practice is foreign to Beethoven's notation.

5. In writing a treble clef, Beethoven was not in the habit of bringing the stem completely through it, usually leaving it to some extent incomplete. In this manuscript, the stems are drawn straight through the clef.

6. There are numerous details which are less conclusive, but which add to the general weight of evidence that the composer did not write this copy himself. For example, when dots occur over notes, they are

[8] The error in determining the number of instruments appears to have been made in counting staves, rather than parts. In the variation movement, the horns occupy a single stave as do the bassoons. In the finale, only the horns share a single stave.

too carefully placed; Beethoven often wrote dots which look more like short, vertical lines. Also, he rarely made a fraction out of the time signature, such as found here (2/4).

7. Evidence that the manuscript was done by a copyist rather than the composer may be found in the fact that mistakes in copying were made, and later corrected. In the variation movement, for example, the part of the uppermost instrument (flute) used in presenting the second eight bars of the theme was mistakenly copied in the place where the first eight bars of variation I were to be written. It was crossed out after the mistake was realized. In the finale the horn part found in measure 141 was mistakenly copied in measure 142 and had to be crossed out.

Whether the signature, "L: Beethoven," written at the top of the first page is authentic, and, if so, from what period of the composer's life it might come, are matters I shall leave for others to determine. It is possible that the score was written by one of the composer's copyists and then signed by the master; but since it is neither clear who the copyist was nor whether the signature is unquestionably that of Beethoven, a sounder approach to the problem of authenticity appears to be offered by an investigation of the following two questions: (1) What does the work represent; in other words, what sort of group was it written for, and who might have influenced its composition? (2) Is there anything in the stylistic approach which indicates that Beethoven made the arrangement?

The first of these questions is the more difficult to answer, partly because the arrangement was made for an unusual number of instruments, the designations of which are, for the most part, absent or indecipherable in the manuscript. Also, the uppermost two parts, the first of which appears to be designated as "Fl" (flute?), are written for instruments whose basic pitch is E-flat; so far as is known, there is no other work by Beethoven which uses high E-flat instruments of this nature.

Helpful in determining the instrumentation is the listing of an arrangement of the septet in the ninth supplement (1825) of *Whistling's Handbook* as follows: "Grand Septetto . . . Arrangé en Harmonie pour Flute, Petite Clarinette, deux Clarinettes, 2 Cors, 2 Bassons, Trompette, Serpent et Trompone [*sic*] par Bern. Crusell." [9] As in the case of the Beethoven fragments, this publication of 1825 is a work for eleven instruments, and it is not unreasonable to assume that Beethoven's instrumentation is at

[9] Cf. Kinsky and Halm, *Das Werk Beethovens,* p. 50.

least similar to that of Crusell.[10] Considering the range and key of each instrument in the manuscript, they are hypothesized as follows: an E-flat flute, an E-flat clarinet, two B-flat clarinets, two E-flat horns, a B-flat trumpet (with an alternate E-flat trumpet),[11] two bassoons, a trombone, and a contrabassoon. The last instrument is deduced partly from the manuscript indication, which appears to be "F[a]g," and from the fact that it is frequently directed to play "col fagotto 2do." The next to the last instrument is thought to be a trombone because, as is the case of the trumpet, its notes are extremely sparse, and then mainly for support.

Why this particular combination? In the case of Crusell's version, one could say confidently that it was almost surely intended for military band, since the arranger, a clarinetist of considerable fame, was director of the Music Corps of the Royal Swedish Grenadier Regiments; the presence of three clarinet parts and a serpent would seem to support this supposition.[12] In all likelihood Beethoven's arrangement was intended for similar use, though the composer's connection with the market for military music is more tenuous than is that of Crusell. His total output of band music consists of several short marches, écossaises, and a polonaise, most of these composed around the years 1809-1810, according to Kinsky-Halm.[13] Although the F flute and the F clarinet are employed, there is no evidence of high E-flat instruments; but one march (WoO 18) requires three clarinets (one in F, two in C), giving it a clear-cut military connection. The latter was originally written for Archduke Anton (brother of the composer's well-known patron, Archduke Rudolf), probably for regimental use, but it is unknown whether for the *Hoch- und Deutschmeister-Regiment* or for the *Badener Curcapelle*.[14]

It is unfortunate that most of the research which has been done to

[10] Taking into consideration the outside possibility that the Crusell arrangement and that reportedly by Beethoven are closely related, I have made several attempts to locate an exemplar of the former work, but none has been successful.

[11] In the variation movement, a B-flat instrument is called for; in the finale, the part makes sense only if played on an E-flat instrument. This could have been achieved either by the use of a crook or of two separate instruments.

[12] In a letter to C. F. Peters, dated June 5, 1820, Crusell writes, "Seitdem ich die Direction der beyden Leib-Grenadier Regiments Musik übernommen, haben sich meine Geschäfte so vermehrt, dass ich, während den Dienst bei den Königl. Corps sehr wenig Zeit für die Composition übrig habe, die nicht der Militär-Musik gewidmet ist." For the complete letter, see Daniel Fryklund, "Några brev från Bernhard Crusell," *Svensk Tidskrift för Musikforskning,* XXXI (1949), 174.

[13] See Kinsky and Halm under WoO 18, WoO 20, WoO 21, WoO 22, WoO 23, WoO 24, and WoO 29.

[14] For further details, see Gustav Nottebohm, "Skizzen aus dem Jahre 1809," *Zweite Beethoveniana* (Leipzig, 1887), p. 259.

date on European military music in the eighteenth and nineteenth centuries is woefully superficial, and little or no emphasis has been placed upon the music itself, undoubtedly because so much of the repertoire consisted of unpublished arrangements made by various bandmasters from currently popular works. Thus our knowledge of the extent to which E-flat flutes and clarinets were used by these groups is scanty indeed. One revealing bit of information from Joseph Fröhlich's clarinet tutor, *Vollständige theoretisch-praktische Musik-schule* (Bonn, 1810), is that "the D, E-flat, and high F clarinets are usually used only for Janizary or Turkish music." [15]

However, regimental bands were not absolutely fixed as to instrumentation or to the number of personnel; thus, it is likely that Beethoven would have arranged the work for a particular regimental band which included high E-flat woodwinds among its instruments. What this group might have been is open to question, and much more research would have to be undertaken in the area of military music and regimental personnel before such a problem could be solved. Although E-flat wind parts are undeniably rare in published scores from the early nineteenth century, it is precisely that fact which strongly suggests that the arrangement was intended for military use.

We know that Beethoven had frequent contact with professional military personnel during many of his years in Vienna; how could he have avoided it at a time when Napoleon's armies were threatening most of Europe, not to mention his very doorstep? Several of his friends and acquaintances were involved in one way or another with the military. There were, for example: General Bernadotte, French ambassador to Vienna and, later, King of Sweden; Dorothea von Ertmann, wife of Captain Stefan von Ertmann and interpreter of Beethoven's piano works; Frederick Starke, military bandmaster, the Kapellmeister of an Austrian regiment during the Napoleonic wars — teacher, composer, arranger; Dr. Johann Schmidt, personal friend and doctor, who was Professor of Anatomy at the Academy of Military Medicine in Vienna; and many others. Dr. Schmidt had a direct connection with the septet, since the above-mentioned arrangement for piano trio, Opus 38, was dedicated to him. As was customary, the work was probably reserved for the exclusive use of the doctor and his family for a period of time prior to its publication (January, 1805); it is well within the realm of possibility that, while in possession of the trio arrangement, he performed it for friends,

---

[15] See Eugene E. Rousseau, *Clarinet instructional Materials from 1732 to ca. 1825* (diss., University of Iowa, 1962), p. 213.

some of whom may have been associated with the Military Academy. How attractive the idea of an arrangement of this work would have been to a regimental bandmaster, whose musicians were used to a daily fare of arrangements, among the most popular of which were some adapted from serenades.

Though the above discussion leaves us with no conclusive evidence that Beethoven made the arrangement in question, it does show that social influences were such that he could very well have been responsible for it. It is an investigation of the music itself which can give us the best clues as to whether the work is genuinely his. Unfortunately, we possess only twenty-seven bars, or about eleven percent, of the variation movement. Due to this paucity, as well as to the fact that a set of variations often involves a distribution of instruments which is not characteristic of a whole piece, my general remarks are confined to the finale, for which we have one hundred and four measures, or about fifty percent of the whole (bars 86-120 and 141-211). Missing are the entire exposition, twenty-four bars of the development, and twenty-one bars of the recapitulation; of the latter portion, we are fortunate in possessing both the second and final thematic groups, from which we can make a guess at how they might have been treated in the exposition. On the basis of what exists, and a comparison with the model, a fairly accurate reconstruction of the entire movement would not be difficult.

If there is one outstanding feature of this arrangement (hereafter referred to as the "band piece") which indicates that it might be by Beethoven, it is the surprisingly close relationship which its formative principles and many of its details bear to those of the trio Opus 38.[16] In the latter work, the piano (right hand) takes over the violin part, the clarinet includes virtually all of the notes given it in the original, and the cello is given the task of supplying those notes played by any of the instruments other than the violin and clarinet which happen to be of the greatest interest at any given time. The result suggests in reverse, Webern's orchestration of the second ricercar from Bach's *Musical Offering;* instead of breaking down melodic lines into motivic units through the application of a different timbre to each, Beethoven fashions a cello line from numerous separate melodic units which, on account of the specific instrumentation given them in the septet, originated with a varied

[16] It is taken for granted in all subsequent musical references that the reader will consult one of the available editions of the septet Opus 20 or its arrangement, the piano trio Opus 38. In some cases, a consultation of both versions will be necessary as indicated by the context of my discussion.

Ex. 1   Model: Septet, Opus 20

Arrangement: Piano Trio, Opus 38

assortment of timbres. The cello part of the introduction (adagio) to the first movement of the trio involves borrowings from the septet as follows:

instruments: horn bassoon viola   cello   viola
measures: 1-7 / 7-12 / 14 / 15-17 / 17-18

In the eighteenth and final measure of the introduction, an arpeggio figure is newly composed to sound in tenths with the violin (Ex. 1). Also, the viola part in bar 14 has been slightly altered to allow a smooth transition back to the cello part in bar 15.

In the band piece, the two high E-flat instruments become the vehicle of the violin part, the clarinet part is again preserved (this time it alternates between the two B-flat clarinets), and the other parts are distributed among the remaining instruments. Analogous to the retention of the original clarinet part by alternating it between two instruments, the horns collaborate to preserve, essentially unchanged, the original horn part; but, like most of the other instruments, they at times play a role similar to that of the cello in Opus 38. In measures 177-88, for example, the first horn adapts the following parts:

instrument: cello   bassoon   viola (8va↑)
measures: 177-82   /   182-84 /   185-88

If we did not know the trio and the extraordinary patchwork role which the cello plays there, we might be tempted to consider this band piece as having been arranged by some anonymous hack; but the approach is so similar to that of the trio that it makes Beethoven's authorship quite plausible.[17]

Likewise important to our understanding of the band piece is the fact that it incorporates details which are found in Opus 38, but which are absent in the septet. To list a few, there is the syncopation in measure 154 (cello = bassoon I), the octave leaps in measures 182-83 (piano = B-flat clarinet II), and the arpeggios which occur in measures 206-7 (piano = B-flat clarinets). The last two details give us a hint as to the sequence of composition, for they appear to have been conceived for the piano; but if one is skeptical of this contention, there is the following additional evidence.

It has been mentioned in connection with Opus 38 that the clarinet part reproduced virtually all of the clarinet notes of the original septet. This implies there are some places in that arrangement in which the

---

[17] The string version of Beethoven's Quintet for Piano and Winds, Opus 16, shows a similar approach. See especially the introduction to the first movement.

original part was not imitated exactly; two such places appear in the
finale (measures 144-47 and 176-182) where notes from the viola part
are given to the wind instrument. Thus, the septet has one clarinet part
in these particular measures and the trio has another. Surprisingly, both
versions appear in the band piece, one in each of the B-flat clarinets. In
the case of the first example (measures 144-47) the part from the trio
is notated an octave lower (B-flat clarinet II), but the syncopation
caused by the quarter-rest (measure 144) occurs in that part only in the
trio, not the septet.

Ex. 2

Septet, Op. 20, mm. 144-46

B♭ Cl.

Vla.

Trio, Op. 38

B♭ Cl.

Band Arrangement

B♭ Cl. I

B♭ Cl. II

Thus, one finds in the band piece certain details which occur otherwise only in the septet and certain other details which occur only in the
trio version; as in the case cited above, there is sometimes even a simultaneous occurrence of details from each of the earlier versions. From
these facts it appears that anyone other than the composer who might
have made the band arrangement would have been obliged to consult
both the septet and trio versions in the course of his work, making a
kind of composite; such a procedure would have been inordinately involved and probably feasible only after publication of the trio version,
which did not take place until 1805. If Beethoven made the arrangement
himself, it could have been done anytime after the trio's composition and
certainly without consulting the two extant versions; in this case, certain
of the details which had been devised specifically for the trio might have
suggested themselves, perhaps subconsciously, as the composer worked on
the band version.

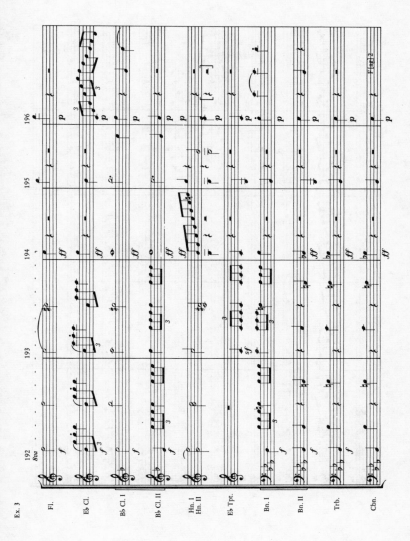

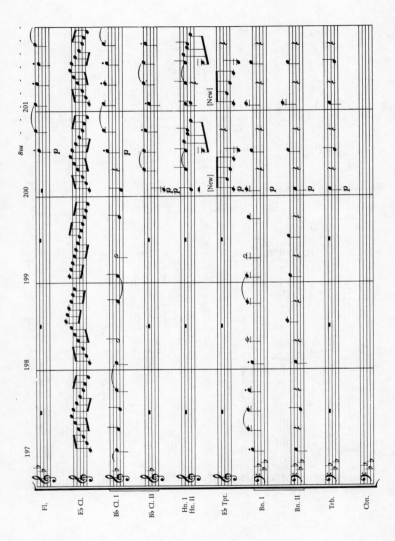

Courtesy of the Beethovenhaus, Bonn

Plate I

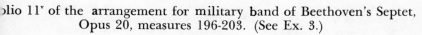

ɔlio 11ᵛ of the arrangement for military band of Beethoven's Septet, Opus 20, measures 196-203. (See Ex. 3.)

Another feature which one might expect in a genuine Beethoven arrangement is that of new musical details, whether introduced for idiomatic or for compositional reasons. Indeed, there are some of these. In the first half of measures 200 and 201, for example, one finds that the arranger has given the trumpet a new eighth-note figure which foreshadows that of the second horn in the latter half of each measure. (Ex. 3). While it is perfectly natural to want to bolster bars 200-204 as a contrast to the preceding four bars, which present essentially the same material, this specific choice is one which affects the momentum of the music as well as the total sound level. This sort of device is prevalent in all of Beethoven's chamber music arrangements.[18]

Also new is the arpeggio in measure 208 in which the trumpet supports the E-flat clarinet part, but foreshadows the descending quarter-note arpeggio in bar 209 of the septet (Ex. 4). Another change is found in measures 192-94 (Ex. 3) where the triplet rhythm alternates between the E-flat clarinet and two other instruments (B-flat clarinet II and bassoon I); though these few bars are understandably treated differently

Ex. 4

[18] The designation "chamber music arrangement" is meant to apply to those works which have been transcribed for chamber ensemble, regardless of the nature of the original medium. This genre includes such works as the string quartet Opus 14, No. 1, the string version of the piano quintet Opus 16, and the string quintet Opus 104.

in all three versions due to idiomatic considerations, the entrance of the trumpet in measure 193 adds a dimension (a kind of built-in crescendo) to the band piece which one finds in neither of the earlier versions.

Aside from the above-mentioned details, the trumpet plays a relatively minor role, as does the second horn; both are used mainly to support the other instruments, a customary practice at the time. The first horn, however, is given a more interesting part to play than in the septet, for it alternately supplies parts taken from the bassoon, viola, and cello as well as most of its own notes. In places where it plays notes other than its own, horn II usually takes over the first part, as in measures 164-65 (Ex. 5). These bars are particularly interesting for two reasons: (1) The repeated eighth-notes in horn I (and trumpet) occur at this point in neither the septet nor the trio; however, they do occur earlier in all three versions (measures 158-59). (2) The arpeggiated eighth-notes in horn II are present in the septet, but absent in the trio, affording another indication that some material came not directly from the original work but from ideas in the trio.

Ex. 5

From the foregoing, there is much to suggest that Beethoven was indeed the arranger of this band piece. Its close relationship with the piano trio Opus 38 in its formative principles and its seemingly random incorporation of ideas from that arrangement (as if done in a subconscious manner) argue in favor of it. Also, the new musical details appear to be very much in keeping with what we know of the composer's style of arranging; but if they seem to be fewer than one might expect, it is perhaps only because this work is already thrice removed from the earliest ideas upon which the piece is based (sketches — septet — trio — band piece). A flood of invention at such a late point in the cycle would be too much to ask, even of Beethoven.

BEETHOVEN AND THE
LONDON PIANOFORTE SCHOOL

By ALEXANDER L. RINGER

IN the spring of 1787, when Beethoven left Bonn on his first, abortive
trip to Vienna, the Josephine era was gaining its final momentum.
Reactionary forces eventually reversed many of the reforms instituted by
Marie-Antoinette's progressive brother, Joseph II. Still, in Mozart's days,
especially in the late seventeen-eighties, Austria in general and Vienna in
particular enjoyed the artistic and intellectual fruits of unprecedented
freedom.[1] In terms of subsequent events it is of relatively little importance
whether or not Beethoven actually succeeded in meeting Mozart, as
originally planned; far more significant historically is the fact that
Mozart's Vienna made a lasting impact on the sensitive teenager from
provincial Bonn, who returned five years later to receive, in Count
Waldstein's famous words, "the spirit of Mozart from the hands of
Haydn." By 1792 Mozart, whose artistic maturity had been so inextric-
ably tied to the liberating spirit of the Josephine era, was of course no
longer among the living. As for Haydn, who agreed to become Beethoven's Viennese mentor after examining his dramatic funeral cantata
written on the death of Joseph II in 1790, that musical stalwart of traditional eighteenth-century values never even tried to bridge the generation
gap. Before long Beethoven found it expedient to entrust himself to the
guidance of lesser but more accessible men like the popular tunesmith
Schenk and the solid but conventional craftsman Albrechtsberger.

In post-Josephine Vienna the true "spirit of Mozart" was hardly apt
to flourish, As so often in history, political and military threats from
abroad, both real and imagined, spawned political oppression at home.
Beethoven, a young idealist who believed in man's duty "to do good
whenever one can, to love liberty above all else, never to deny the

---

[1] Cf. Alexander L. Ringer, "Mozart and the Josephian Era: Some Socio-Economic Notes on Musical Change," *Current Musicology,* IX (1969), 161-63.

truth, even though it be before the throne," [2] reacted to this regressive atmosphere at times with, undisguised cynicism. "I believe," he wrote to Simrock in 1794, "that so long as an Austrian can get his brown ale and his little sausages, he is not likely to revolt." [3] What saved him from complete disillusionment were such steadfast personal friends as Franz Wegeler and Karl Amenda, slightly older companions of his youth in Bonn, and the von Breuning family, ever dedicated to his welfare. Moreover, as a fashionable pianist "on the make," young Beethoven enjoyed a vogue among some of Vienna's most beautiful and cultivated women. But on the musical scene, only the indestructible Haydn continued to create works of outstanding interest, though by this time mostly in the choral field. It was thus nothing less than a matter of artistic survival which forced a composer of Beethoven's progressive tendencies to seek creative models elsewhere. That he found them primarily in republican France and protodemocratic England was virtually inevitable in view of the historical circumstances.

With very few exceptions, the English composers who aroused Beethoven's curiosity were English by cultural adaptation rather than birth. Like other European capitals, including Paris and Vienna, eighteenth-century London attracted superior musicians irrespective of national origin because it offered economic and artistic opportunities unavailable elsewhere, in conformance with a historical rule that applies no less to Berlin between the two world wars or the court of Burgundy in the early fifteenth century. It was thanks to an unusually rich concert life, adventurous publishing houses, a pianoforte industry unmatched in quality and efficiency — in short, to the many novel opportunities offered by England's budding capitalistic society — that outstanding musicians of such diverse national backgrounds as the Italian-born Clementi, the Bohemian Dussek, the German Cramer, and the Irishman Field became part and parcel of the London musical scene in the seventeen-nineties. That the singular role of London in the development of instrumental music after Mozart has been ignored to the point where a leading contemporary scholar can still speak with impunity of an alleged *Komponistennot* in late-eighteenth-century England merely testifies to the stubborn persistence of the nationalistic fallacy in musical historiography. [4]

[2] Emily Anderson, ed. and trans., *The Letters of Beethoven* (London, 1961), I, 6.
[3] *Ibid.,* I. 18.
[4] Cf. Georg Knepler, *Musikgeschichte des 19. Jahrhunderts* (Berlin, 1961), I, 412. Knepler explains this alleged dearth of composers in Marxist terms as part of a "faulty circle of bad thoughts and good business" (*ibid.,* p. 413). On the "capitalistic" side William S. Newman relegates his discussion of "Dussek and other early

Increasingly dominated by the growing fortunes of a rapidly rising middle class, the British capital offered music, "the favorite art of the middle classes," [5] the art in which middle-class emotions find their most direct and unhampered expression, an entirely new market. The extent to which this middle class market motivated immediate and drastic musical changes is illustrated nowhere more dramatically than in the stylistic peculiarities of the "London Pianoforte School." Whereas continental Europe was ready for the pathos and sonorous splendor of Schumann or Chopin only in the wake of a whole series of socio-economic convulsions, the middle-class predilection for harmonic texture of the type characterized by Wagner half a century later as a sea into which "man dives to yield himself again, radiant and refreshed, to the light of day," [6] motivated "the prophecies of Dussek" in England well before 1800.[7] And in their own individual ways the melodic-rhythmic eccentricities of Clementi, the glittering passagework of Cramer, and the often self-indulging sentimental elegance of Field all satisfied the passion for novelty and built-in obsolescence, the gullibility and escapist mentality, of the new product-oriented society. On the whole, the English public, anticipating its Continental counterparts by more than a generation, favored a domesticated type of musical art catering to short-range emotional effects, often at the expense of structural solidity and logic. For music, not unlike the Gothic novel, was to provide an affective counterweight to the highly rationalized behavior that produced the urban middle classes' ever-increasing material affluence.

Dussek, Clementi, and their followers thus developed distinct stylistic characteristics no less unique than those associated with their far better known and justly famous Viennese contemporaries. This is not to say that these two schools of musical thought exerted no mutual influence. On the contrary, just as the London Pianoforte School could not have done without the pioneering work of Haydn and Mozart, the Viennese composers soon put to good use the textural innovations of their colleagues across the Channel. The very opening chords of Haydn's Sonata

---

Czech romantics" to the last quarter of *The Sonata Since Beethoven* (Chapel Hill, N. C., 1969) apparently convinced that "Czechoslovakia, Poland, and Hungary" occupied peripheral positions in European musical history in time as well as space.

[5] Arnold Hauser, *The Social History of Art* (New York, 1958), III, 82.

[6] Richard Wagner, *Das Kunstwerk der Zukunft,* trans. in Oliver Strunk, ed., *Source Readings in Music History* (New York, 1950), p. 884.

[7] Cf. Eric Blom, "The Prophecies of Dussek," in his *Classics: Major and Minor* (London, 1958), pp. 88-117 (originally published in installments in *Musical Opinion*, 1927-28).

in E-flat (No. 52), written after Dussek lent him his own piano of latest English manufacture, are proof that such direct influences were readily acknowledged. By the same token, Dussek assumes the stature of a prophet only in the eyes of those who think of European history in unilateral and evolutionistic terms, insensitive to the high degree of artistic diversification typical of sophisticated societies, separately and collectively, depending upon a variety of frequently incompatible socio-economic factors.

Even though Haydn's mature works reflect his eventual close links with the musical life of London in many unmistakable ways, it was Beethoven who produced the first, perhaps also the last, synthesis of stylistic-aesthetic elements associated with revolutionary Paris as well as the Vienna-London axis. If Paris left its traces primarily in his dramatic output, both symphonic and operatic, London made decisive contributions toward the great choral compositions and, above all, the thirty-two piano sonatas. The Ninth Symphony, which was written explicitly for the London Philharmonic Society, bears eloquent witness to what struck his visitor Johann Andreas Stumpff in 1824 as Beethoven's "exaggerated opinion of London and its highly cultured inhabitants." [8] The sonorities of the last piano sonatas, in turn, would be unthinkable without the remarkable qualities of the Broadwood piano that he received from England in 1818. By then, however, Beethoven looked back to a quarter of a century of intimate acquaintance with music especially written for instruments of English manufacture. The contributor to the *Encyclopaedia Britannica,* who in 1797 claimed the pianoforte as "a national instrument, . . . an English contrivance," [9] surely exaggerated in ascribing its invention to William Mason. But he did have a point when he praised the English pianoforte for "its superior force of tone, its adequate sweetness, and the great variety of voice of which our artists have made it susceptible." [10] Beethoven, for one, was highly appreciative of that "great variety of voice," especially as promoted by Muzio Clementi, the London Pianoforte School's titular head. His by no means extensive musical library contained nearly all of Clementi's sonatas, "the most beautiful, the most pianistic of works." [11] And it was mainly because of a manifest

[8] Cf. Alexander Wheelock Thayer, *Life of Beethoven,* ed. Elliot Forbes (Princeton, N. J., 1964), II, 919.

[9] Edwin M. Ripin, "A Scottish Encyclopedist and the Pianoforte," *The Musical Quarterly,* LV (1969), 496.

[10] *Ibid.*

[11] Cf. Anton Felix Schindler, *Beethoven As I Knew Him,* ed. Donald W. MacArdle (Chapel Hill, N. C., 1966), p. 379.

lack of enthusiasm for Clementi that Carl Czerny, Beethoven's star pupil, was eventually dismissed as his nephew's piano teacher. The high regard in which he held Cramer, on the other hand, speaks with particular persuasion from the marginal comments he inserted in his nephew's copy of the Cramer Etudes.[12]

While the importance of Clementi as a "forerunner of Beethoven" has not gone unrecognized,[13] the general assumption seems to have been that his direct influence remained limited to "first period" Beethoven. Actually, Clementi never disappeared from the master's constantly expanding musical horizons. If the beginning of Opus 7 betrays his knowledge of Clementi's Opus 12, No. 4 (Ex. 1), and its finale recalls Clementi's Opus 24, No. 2, the conclusion of the *Sonata appassionata* is even more clearly indebted to that of Clementi's Opus 36, No. 3 (Ex. 2).

Ex. 1   Clementi, Op. 12, No. 4, first mvt., mm. 1-4

Beethoven, Op. 7, first mvt., mm. 1-6

Ex. 2   Clementi, Op. 36, No. 3, third mvt., conclusion

[12] *The Beethoven Cramer Studies,* ed. John S. Shedlock (London, 1893).

[13] See among others, J. S. Shedlock, *The Pianoforte Sonata* (London, 1895), pp. 131-39; Adolf Stauch, *Muzio Clementis Klavier-Sonaten im Verhältnis zu den Sonaten von Haydn, Mozart u. Beethoven* (Oberkassel bei Bonn, 1930); Georges de Saint Foix, "Clementi, Forerunner of Beethoven," *The Musical Quarterly,* XVII (1931), 84-92.

Beethoven, Op. 57, third mvt., conclusion

In 1823, about to conclude his life's work as a keyboard composer, Beethoven paid Clementi a last characteristic homage by parodying numbers 16 and 17 of the 1817 edition of the *Gradus ad Parnassum* in his Diabelli Variations. Retaining Clementi's general idea and structural outline he substituted broken octaves for Clementi's simple scale patterns and, as an added touch, employed the same numbers but in reverse order (Ex. 3).

Ex. 3   Clementi, *Gradus ad Parnassum,* No. 17, mm. 1-2

Clementi, *Gradus ad Parnassum,* No. 16, mm. 1-2

Beethoven, *Diabelli Variations,* No. 16, mm. 1-2

Beethoven, *Diabelli Variations,* No. 17, mm. 1-2

According to his pupil Ludwig Berger, Clementi conceived both of the sonatas in his Opus 34 orchestrally, the first as a piano concerto, the second as a symphony.[14] No doubt several others published in the seventeen-eighties, especially those with slow introductions, were at least indirect fruits of this symphonic preoccupation sparked by Haydn's phenomenal London successes.[15] Whatever their exact motivation, however, the best of his works from that period display the aesthetic intensity and corresponding tight motivic organization as well as the exterior dimensions that typify the mature eighteenth-century symphony rather than its keyboard counterpart. The G minor Sonata, Opus 34, No. 2, with its thematically pregnant opening largo offers a brilliant demonstration of the kind of symphonically inspired structure that must have been on the mind of the critic J. B. Schaul who wrote in 1809: "All passages . . . are a direct outgrowth of the dominating idea which is never lost sight of." [16] Indeed, no eighteenth-century keyboard composer anticipated Beethoven's concept of the "underlying idea" more explicitly. As C. M. Girdlestone put it with specific reference to Opus 34, No. 2, "Clementi alone could teach Beethoven to satisfy that craving for unity which he, too, brought with him into music." [17]

Unlike Clementi's, Dussek's contributions to Beethoven's stylistic arsenal have been virtually ignored. His solitary champion, Eric Blom, extolled Dussek primarily for his "prophecies" of romantic keyboard idioms. While none would wish to deny Dussek's often amazing anticipations of stylistic traits identified with nineteenth-century composers from Schumann to Brahms, one wonders how Blom could have failed to notice the extent to which, for example, Dussek's sonata Opus 9, No. 1, influenced Beethoven's Opus 22 in matters of texture and patterning as well as structure (Ex. 4).[18]

[14] Max Unger, *Muzio Clementis Leben* (Langensalza, 1914), pp. 72-73.

[15] Cf. Georges de Saint-Foix, "Les Symphonies de Clementi," *Revue de musicologie,* VIII (1924), 2.

[16] Quoted in Adolf Stauch, *op. cit.,* p. 49.

[17] C. M. Girdlestone, "Muzio Clementi," *Music and Letters,* XIII (1932), 290. Cf. also Alexander L. Ringer, "Clementi and the *Eroica*," *The Musical Quarterly,* XLVII (1961), 454-55.

[18] Donald Francis Tovey, *Beethoven,* ed. Hubert J. Foss (London, 1965), p. 106, calls Opus 22 "the most conventional of all Beethoven's works" and characterizes the main subject of its first movement as a *"locus classicus* for masterful perfunctoriness."

J. Racek and V. J. Sýkora in their three-volume edition of the Dussek sonatas (Prague, 1960) refer to both Opus 9 and Opus 10 as "compositions for piano solo." The original Sieber editions, however, suggest violin accompaniment. While it is, of course, possible that the French publisher simply followed established tradition in this respect, the fact remains that the violin was dropped from all editions published after

Ex. 4   Dussek, Op. 9, No. 1, second mvt., mm. 49-51

Beethoven, Op. 22, first mvt., mm. 22-23

A complete accounting of the many stylistic parallels and, on occasion, outright borrowings attesting to Beethoven's sustained interest in Dussek is quite beyond the scope of the present study. But even a relatively small sampling suggests why Dussek was so quickly forgotten after his death in 1812. There was simply no further need for the works of an admittedly very talented composer whose most distinctive contributions had been fully absorbed and raised to far higher aesthetic levels by Beethoven, the traumatic hero of the Romantic era. As Eric Blom pointed out in his critical appraisal of the collective achievement of Clementi, Dussek and Field, "the triumvirate tactfully went with the evolution step by step, now offering a suggestion, now taking a hint," in contrast to Beethoven who tended to force the issues.[19] How Beethoven reacted to such "suggestions" can be seen from a comparison of his Opus 10, No. 3, with Dussek's Opus 31, No. 2, an accompanied keyboard sonata published ca. 1795. Neither the melodic-rhythmic characteristics of Beethoven's materials nor their phrasing and dynamics, leave any doubt as to their origins (Ex. 5). Moreover, since Beethoven rarely, if ever, limited his sources to a single work, his Opus 10, No. 3, also draws heavily on Dussek's Opus 35, No. 2. That Dussek set the pace not only rhythmically, harmonically, and dynamically, but also structurally follows from the obvious similarities in the preparation and initiation of

---

Dussek left France for England. Mr. Jerald Graue, who is currently working on a University of Illinois dissertation exploring the achievements of the London Pianoforte School as a whole, agrees that the so-called complete edition of Breitkopf & Härtel (1813-17) and the later Dussek publications by Litolff, the Czech editors' primary sources, are quite unreliable in matters of titles as well as musical texts of the earlier sonatas.

[19] Eric Blom, "John Field," in *op. cit.,* p. 125.

the recapitulation in the respective first movements (Ex. 6). At least at
that relatively early stage of his career, it would seem, Beethoven was
ready to go to great lengths to enhance his growing reputation as a
sparkling young virtuoso, even if this meant copying the manners and
mannerisms of established colleagues.[20]

Ex. 5   Dussek, Op. 31, No. 2, first mvt., mm. 142-47

Beethoven, Op. 10, No. 3, first mvt., mm. 74-79

Ex. 6   Dussek, Op. 35, No. 2, first mvt., mm. 156-59

Beethoven, Op. 10, No. 3, first mvt., mm. 131-34

Historically, the issue is, of course, much less one of "influence," let
alone plagiarism, than of musical conditioning and outlook. The case of

[20] Tovey in *op. cit.*, p. 92, wondered whether Beethoven's Opus 10, No. 3, "can
have been acceptable to orthodox musicians in 1798." While it is difficult to know
exactly what is meant here by "orthodox," no well-informed musician was unaware
of Clementi by that time. And it was precisely Clementi who had made the most of
the "rhetorical gestures and pauses" to which Tovey refers. Cf. Schindler, *op. cit.*,
p. 417.

Dussek's Opus 39, No. 3, may serve to illustrate this crucial point. Eric Blom dismissed that particular sonata with the remark that "a study of the first movement is almost profitless." [21] Had he been less single-minded about the supposed nature of his hero's "prophecies," he surely would not have missed the uncanny resemblance of its beginning to that of Beethoven's Opus 10, No. 1 (Ex. 7). Since the two works appeared almost simultaneously, it would be difficult to furnish proof positive for the generative primacy of either. Even so, one is hard put to believe that Beethoven was totally unfamiliar with the Dussek piece at the time he composed his own. For all we know, he may have seen it in manuscript or, more likely, heard it performed by one of the many itinerant emissaries of the London Pianoforte School.

Ex. 7   Dussek, Op. 39, No. 3, first mvt., mm. 1-4

Beethoven, Op. 10, No. 1, first mvt., mm. 1-5

Dussek's Opus 35, dedicated to Clementi, must have made a very special impression on Beethoven. For its impact can be traced from Opus 10 through Opus 28, Opus 53, and Opus 57, to Opus 101, whose fugal development section Dussek anticipated in the finale of the first of the three sonatas in his set. Once again, historians taking for granted that the climactic figure in the "Viennese Classical School" merely brought to fruition seeds planted by Haydn and Mozart could hardly be expected to turn to Dussek's Opus 35 for antecedents of some of Beethoven's most original "middle period" pieces. And yet, the G major Sonata, Opus 35, No. 2, left easily recognizable traces in Beethoven's Opus 53 (Ex. 8) as well as in his earlier Opus 28 (Ex. 9). The stormy C minor Sonata, Opus 35, No. 3, on the other hand, affected the *Appassionata* especially with respect to the motivic significance of dynamic accents.

[21] Eric Blom, "The Prophecies of Dussek," in *op. cit.*, p. 106.

Ex. 8   Dussek, Op. 35, No. 2, first mvt., mm. 131ff.

a.   Beethoven, Op. 53, third mvt., mm. 183ff.   b.

Ex. 9   Dussek, Op. 35, No. 2, second mvt., mm. 1-2

Beethoven, Op. 28, fourth mvt., mm. 2-4

Paul Bekker remarked well over half a century ago that Beethoven's Opus 81a, *The Farewell,* is saddled with a programmatic outline as un-original in conception as its musical realization is unique.[22] But Bekker failed to note that both the program and the realization owed a great deal to Dussek's *The Farewell,* Opus 44. As usual, Beethoven took motivic and textural cues from Dussek without the slightest compunc-tion, adopting freely some of Dussek's most characteristic sonorities (Ex. 10). Years earlier, in Opus 27, No. 1, such a direct transfer (from Dus-sek's sonata Opus 9, No. 2) had produced those typically "Beethoven-

[22] Paul Bekker, *Beethoven* (Berlin, 1921), p. 175. Beethoven resented the French title *Les Adieux,* which the publishers, Breitkopf und Härtel, had printed without his permission. Farewell, he wrote to them in October, 1811, is "something quite different from 'Les Adieux.' The first is said in a warm-hearted manner to one person, the other to a whole assembly, to entire towns." Cf. *The Letters of Beethoven,* I, 338.

ian" exchanges of clearly defined thematic material and decorative figurations between the two hands. As can be seen in Ex. 11, both Dussek
and Beethoven add sonorous "fillers" whenever the thematic material

Ex. 10   Dussek, Op. 44, second mvt., mm. 38-40

Beethoven, Op. 81a, second mvt., mm. 15-17

Ex. 11   Dussek, Op. 9, No. 2, first mvt., mm. 39-41

mm. 43-45

Beethoven, Op. 27, No. 1, third mvt., mm. 106-9

mm. 112-15

appears in the treble range. But, somehow, Dussek sounds even more Beethovenian in this instance than Beethoven himself.

Opus 81a belongs with the Choral Fantasy and the keyboard fantasy Opus 77, the *Pastoral Symphony,* the Mignon songs, the cello sonata Opus 69, the two trios Opus 70, and the piano sonata Opus 78 to Beethoven's most "romantic" period. Its contribution toward the unprecedented structural freedom of his later years can hardly be exaggerated, if only because it was one of the first works in which the formally dialectical treatment of his celebrated "two principles" gave way to subtler shadings and gradations. The pairing of entire, expressively complementary, compositions like the loosely knit "Harp" Quartet and the tersely organized F minor Quartet represented a final attempt to stay nominally within the limits of the classical matrix. Thereafter, traditional devices, though by no means rejected out of hand, had to yield, whenever necessary, to the intrinsic requirements of Beethoven's truly revolutionary conception of musical form as psychological process. Interestingly enough, this radical reappraisal of traditional patterns of freedom and restraint found its first artistic realization in the final group of keyboard sonatas, written after the arrival of the Broadwood piano from England and after music by Clementi's prize pupil, John Field, had become readily available.[23] Whether Beethoven had occasion to acquaint himself with the work of the quickly forgotten George Frederick Pinto as well is imposible to ascertain. But to judge by the stunning parallels between Pinto's Sonata in E-flat minor and the first movement of Beethoven's Opus 110, one would be inclined to think so.[24]

Though born of an Italian mother whose maiden name he assumed, Pinto was the only native English member of the London Pianoforte School. Tragically short lived — he died in 1806 at the age of twenty — he was also its most daring representative. At a time when Beethoven had barely moved into his "second period" young Pinto, together with his but slightly older friend Field, went a long way toward the transformation of

---

[23] Field's first three nocturnes were published by Peters in 1814 and may well be responsible for some of the nocturne-like passages in Beethoven's later sonatas, for example the first variation in the final movement of Opus 109. It may not be entirely without interest in this connection that his nephew Karl was playing a Dussek sonata while Beethoven was working on that particular composition. Cf. Joseph Czerny's remark in *Ludwig van Beethovens Konversationshefte,* ed. Georg Schünemann (Berlin, 1942), II, 144.

[24] The Pinto sonata has been made available in a modern edition by Nicholas Temperley (London, Stainer and Bell: 1963). Current awareness of Pinto is due almost entirely to Dr. Temperley's efforts. Cf. "George Frederick Pinto," *Musical Times,* CVI (1965), 265-70.

Dussek's rich keyboard idiom into the fully developed musical language of nineteenth-century Continental Romanticism. Pinto may or may not have enjoyed Dussek's formal guidance for a while. It hardly matters, for by 1803, when Pinto's sonatas were published well ahead of Dussek's most "romantic" works, the aesthetic die was solidly cast.

Circumstantial evidence suggests at least the possibility that Beethoven was not unaware of what his young English colleague was trying to accomplish. Johann Peter Salomon, with whom Pinto studied violin and who referred to his protégé as "the English Mozart," had known Beethoven since his early Bonn days and stayed in touch with him until his death in 1815. Shortly after the turn of the century Beethoven, eager to be represented on one of Salomon's programs, sent him a copy of his Septet "purely out of friendship." Among Salomon's close associates in London was Ferdinand Ries, Beethoven's one-time pupil and lifelong correspondent. Above all, Clementi passed through Vienna in 1804, the year after the publication of Pinto's two piano sonatas Opus 3, which, though "printed for the author," list Clementi and Company among the principal sales agents.[25] It may also be worth recalling in this context that Beethoven received numerous visitors from London while working on his last keyboard works. In 1818, the year of the "Hammerklavier" Sonata, Beethoven repeatedly saw Cipriani Potter as well as Johann Andreas Stumpff and Sir Julius Benedict.

As a "prophet" of keyboard things to come Pinto is virtually without peers. In contrast to Clementi, whose idiom retained certain orchestral affinities throughout, Pinto thought "pianistically" in the nineteenth-century sense from the very outset. To cite but one persuasive instance, the middle section of the slow movement in Opus 3, No. 2, could easily pass for early Chopin (Ex. 12).[26] The corresponding movement in the

Ex. 12   Pinto, Op. 3, No. 2, second mvt., mm. 37-41

[Poco adagio affetuoso]

[25] In 1807 Clementi and Beethoven met again and concluded their first publication accord. Two years later they dined together at the house of Henikstein, the Viennese banker. Cf. *The Letters of Beethoven*, I, 252.

[26] The author is indebted to Nicholas Temperley for a photostatic copy of this most unusual excerpt.

E-flat minor Sonata, on the other hand, adds further support to the contention that Beethoven, far from rejecting convention, never ceased to make careful selective use of a broadly based repertory of generalized ideas representing a great variety of stylistic strains. That his illustrious Viennese predecessors assumed less and less significance in that enduring process was an inevitable function of his ever keen alertness to the swiftly changing times in which he lived.

Essentially monothematic, the sonata Opus 110 ranks, of course, among the most sublime studies in thematic expansion and integration. Pinto's sonata, too, thrives on a minimum of motivic substance, though inevitably at a much lower level of sophistication. The more striking similarities between the two sonatas are, however, not of a structural nature. They pertain rather to melodic, harmonic, and textural details, going well beyond the uncanny thematic resemblances between Beethoven's opening movement and Pinto's adagio in the same meter and key (Ex. 13). Thus, Pinto's measures 34-37 read almost like a blueprint of Beethoven's measures 18-19: nearly identical chordal descents after a wide skip in the bass, nearly identical figurational patterns in the treble, identical points of harmonic arrival (Ex. 14). And both composers vary

Ex. 13   Pinto, Op. 3, No. 1, second mvt., mm. 1-4

Beethoven, Op. 110, first mvt., mm. 1-5

Ex. 14   Pinto, mm. 34-37

Beethoven, mm. 18-19

their recapitulations through arpeggiation in the left hand, a device of which Pinto was particularly fond. Pinto similarly anticipated the melodic contour as well as the repeated chord accompaniment of a particularly beautiful passage in the third movement of Opus 110 (Ex. 15).

Ex. 15   Beethoven, third mvt., mm. 17-19

Pinto, second mvt., mm. 24-28

Like Beethoven, Pinto makes abundant use of counterpoint in his finale, but his simple points of imitation are clearly no match for Beethoven's fugal technique. There is indeed a curious affinity between Pinto's end product and the skeletal ideas found in so many of Beethoven's sketches. By the same token the Englishman's music does not even hint at anything like the seamless unfolding of organic movement that typifies Beethoven riding the crest of his structural imagination in one of his most admirable works.

When all is said and done, therefore, comparative studies of the type suggested here in no way endanger Beethoven's historical or artistic stature: they rather add to a growing body of evidence that his justly celebrated originality derived not so much from any particular novelty of invention as from a matchless power of integration and sublimation of the widest possible variety of musical practices. Unflaggingly sensitive to the vicissitudes of the human condition, Beethoven was that rare musical artist who ranges freely over the whole cultural spectrum of his era yet in his supreme quest for unlimited spiritual freedom manages to transcend all convention. And this, one suspects, is why he who "preserved a human heart for all who are human" has himself been preserved "as a heritage to the whole world." [27]

---

[27] From Franz Grillparzer's funeral oration, as quoted in Michael Hamburger, ed. and trans., *Beethoven: Letters, Journals and Conversations* (Garden City, N. Y., 1960), p. 277.

ON BEETHOVEN'S
THEMATIC STRUCTURE

By DÉNES BARTHA

A CONTRIBUTION of Jens Peter Larsen to the series of essays
"18th-century Studies in Honor of Paul Henry Lang" bears the
title "The Viennese Classical School: a Challenge to Musicology." Speaking of style analysis as applied to the classic period, Larsen states:

> The studies in style problems have not been very conspicuous or revolutionary.....
> The greatest obstacle in this field is an old and deeply rooted tradition of regard-
> ing and judging music of the classic period with preconceived expectations of form
> in the manner of 19th century textbooks.... We shall find out that things look dif-
> ferent when we come close enough to form an impression founded on real observa-
> tion, not on traditional clichés.[1]

In this study, based on a thorough analysis of a hundred or so typical
themes by Haydn and Beethoven, I would like to challenge the traditional concept of phrase and period structure. To my knowledge, that
concept has not been seriously questioned since the long past days of
Koch, Momigny, and Riemann. Of course, many aspects of our classical
heritage have been dealt with by competent analysts and scholars: harmonic structure and motivic relationships by Schenker and his followers
(e. g., Jonas and Reti); thematic structure as related to eighteenth-century style by Wilhelm Fischer and Hans Gál; special aspects of historical
analysis by Tovey; the dynamism of *Entwicklungsmotive* by Ernst Kurth
and Kurt von Fischer; the long overdue revision of nineteenth-century
sonata-form concepts by Larsen, Leonard Ratner, and William Newman; the problem of "harmonic rhythm" by Jan LaRue — and so forth.
Nevertheless, until recent years the melodic and structural aspects of
classical themes have been rather badly neglected. While asymmetrical
structures have always held a particular fascination for analysts from
Riemann to the present, those other themes that have a tightly struc-

---

[1] *Current Musicology*, IX (1969), 109, 107.

tured symmetrical pattern — they are our specific concern here — have
long since been in disfavor with theorists and scholars. The most thorough investigation of rhythmic and metric structure published so far is
that of Grosvenor W. Cooper and Leonard B. Meyer,[2] but even this
excellent study has failed to yield a generally acceptable answer to the
question of thematic organization on a higher level than phrase and
period structure. In this respect I cannot but agree with a recent criticism of the "Chicago method" by Edward T. Cone:

> The classical phrase has often been analyzed as an alternation of strong and weak
> measures, on an analogy with strong and weak beats within a measure. . . . The
> larger rhythmic structure is treated simply as metric structure on a higher level. . . .
> I insist that on some level this metric principle of parallel balance must give way
> to a more organic rhythmic principle that supports the melodic and harmonic
> shape of the phrase and justifies its acceptance as a formal unit.[3]

Speaking from my own analytical experience, I would add that the
structural justification of the phrase concept demanded by Cone should
not be limited to the phrase level alone, because phrase is a rather
vaguely defined concept. In my opinion, on the larger levels of period,
double period, and thematic section even the refined analytical system of
Cooper and Meyer has failed to produce structure patterns of convincing
validity and logic.

In most of the analytical literature on classical music the key words
for thematic structure are still those that were used by such theorists of
the period itself as Koch and Momigny.[4] "Phrase" and "period" are the
principal terms from which such additional technical terms as "half-
period," "half-phrase," or "subphrase" were derived. These subdivisions
were usually units of two measures (Riemann's *Zweitaktgruppe*). Momigny was responsible for the division of periods into "antecedent" and
"consequent" halves.

In order to assess the traditional meaning of these terms, let us quote
the definition of the *Harvard Dictionary of Music* (1969) : "Period. In
traditional music . . . a group of measures comprising a natural division
of the melody; usually regarded as comprising two or more contrasting or complementary phrases and ending with a cadence." This is a
rather vague definition. In textbook parlance the term "period" has come

---

[2] Grosvenor W. Cooper and Leonard B. Meyer, *The Rhythmic Structure of
Music* (Chicago, 1960).

[3] Edward T. Cone, *Musical Form and Musical Performance* (New York, 1968),
p. 26.

[4] Their definitions are cited in detail by Leonard Ratner, "Eighteenth-Century
Theories of Musical Period Structure," *The Musical Quarterly*, XLII (1956), 439.

to convey a somewhat more closely circumscribed meaning: that of a strictly binary construction compounded of two phrases in the relationship of "question" and "answer," or "statement" vs. "counterstatement." Moreover, in traditional textbook definitions this binary character has mostly been associated with a contrast in cadences such as half-close, at the mid-caesura, against full close (possibly tonic) at the end of the period. We might add at this point that the eighteenth-century theorists, when speaking of "periods," did not expressly require such a specific cadential relationship; they mostly contented themselves with the rule that the two halves of a period should be differentiated in some way or another (cf. Koch). The *Harvard Dictionary* definition of the term "phrase" is even more vague in its wording: "Phrase. A division of the musical line, somewhat comparable to a clause of a sentence in prose. Other terms for such divisions are period, half-phrase, double phrase, etc. There is no consistency in applying these terms nor can there be. . . . Only with melodies of a very simple type, especially those of some dances, can the terms be used with some consistency. . . ."

The obvious lack of clarity in these definitions should have long since prompted our theorists to question the appropriateness of these age-old terms. Our great heritage of classical music comprises masterworks of absolutely convincing — if not always easily recognizable — structure; Jan LaRue speaks, for instance, of the "inevitability" of Beethoven's music. If that structure cannot be defined and assessed except in terms of such manifest vagueness and inconsistency as has been quoted above, our nomenclature is badly in need of revision and redefinition. And exactly this is the professed object of the present investigation.[5]

* * *

Concerning the principles and methods of this investigation, it seems appropriate at this point to advance some basic considerations. First: the author of this essay has been involved for years in the work of analyzing, comparing, and classifying thousands of Hungarian popular melodies, collected and prepared for publication in the series *Corpus Musicae Popularis Hungaricae,* an enormous undertaking that was started by Bartók and continued by Kodály until his death. The teamwork involved in this task was headed by the late Pál Járdányi. It finally arrived at a

[5] The title of the paper by H. Goldschmidt scheduled for the Beethoven Symposium in Vienna, June, 1970 — "Vers und Strophe in der Instrumentalmusik von Beethoven" — promises an analytical approach similar to mine. Unfortunately, it did not come to my notice until this article was well under way.

highly developed and specialized analytic technique of melodic structures
that had to be made completely independent of harmonic factors (so
dear to the mind of German scholars such as Riemann and Schenker),
the predominantly monophonic world of East European folk music being notoriously devoid of harmonic implications. Secondly: both terms,
"phrase" and "period," originate in grammar and prose speech; eighteenth-century music theorists were still aware of the fact that they had
been borrowed from Greco-Roman and Baroque rhetoric. Their applicability to classical music depends largely on whether we consider the language of that music mainly derived from prose rhetoric, or whether we
acknowledge its primary indebtedness to popular dance and song. As of
today, there seems to be an unmistakable tendency toward the latter attitude, notably by Ratner and the author of this essay,[6] but as early as
1915 a pioneer article of Wilhelm Fischer defined one prominent structure in classical themes as *Liedtypus*.[7] First he planned to call it *Tanz-
typus,* as opposed to the *Fortspinnungstypus* of Baroque concertos and
classical development sections. There is no substantial difference between
the two definitions.

The first stimulus to challenge the conventional notion of binary
period came to me in 1964-65 when I analyzed with my Budapest
students a series of contredanse-inspired finale-rondos in Joseph Haydn's
symphonies.[8] In Ex. 1 and Ex. 2 two characteristic Haydn finale themes
are quoted below. Further parallels would include a great many of
Haydn's *Sturm und Drang* works, originating from about 1771-73, and
most of his symphony finales from the Paris (Nos. 82-92) and the London (Nos. 93-104) series. Now let us see what are the stylistic-structural
criteria, the common denominators of these examples.

Ex. 1   Haydn, Symphony No. 44, finale, mm. 1-8

Ex. 2   Haydn, Symphony No. 98, finale, mm. 1-8

[6] Cf. Dénes Bartha, "Thematic Profile and Character in the Quartet-Finales of
J. Haydn," *Studia musicologica,* XI (1969).

[7] Wilhelm Fischer, "Zur Entwicklungsgeschichte des Wiener klassischen Stils,"
Studien zur Musikwissenschaft, III (1915).

[8] Cf. "Volkstanz-Stilisierung in J. Haydns Finale-Themen," *Festschrift Walter
Wiora* (Kassel, 1967), p. 375.

1. The conspicuous lack of a binary period structure. Instead, all the examples we shall study, including those of Beethoven, display a quaternary stanza structure of 4×2 or 4×4 measures, with motivic relationships between the four "verses" best symbolized as *AA'BC* or *AA'b-bC* in the case of a motivically halved third verse (see Ex. 2), while the typical pattern of a binary period is symbolized by *ABAC* or *ABAB'* relationships. The basic identity of these two- or four-measure subphrases (Bartók's term of "isometric verses" fits them perfectly) plus the rhythmic-motivic similarity of verses 1 and 2 inevitably suggests a model for this quaternary pattern: the typical four-verse stanza of Central European popular song and dance, very soon adopted by poets and musicians into thousands of folklore-inspired songs (*Lieder im Volkston,* as they were called in the eighteenth century) exhibiting the same four-verse stanza pattern, from the simplest ones to such unparalleled masterworks as Goethe's *Erlkönig.* Therefore, I would like to suggest for these musical structures the term "Quaternary Stanza Structure" (in the following, symbolized QSS), replacing the traditional concept of "period," which simply does not apply to this particular type of theme. (In our examples the verses are identified by the Arabic numerals 1, 2, 3, and 4.) Hence, the typical two-measure (or, in short meter, four-measure) unit will be termed "verse," replacing the somewhat clumsy term of "subphrase" or *Zweitaktgruppe.* But even further specifications can be derived from the given Haydn examples.

2. The cesuras or articulations between verses 1 and 2 and between 2 and 3 are clearly marked either by rests (see Ex. 1) or by melodic cadences (see Ex. 2). In marked contrast, the break between verses 3 and 4 is usually handled in a different way, resulting in a slight irregularity of the prevailing metric pattern (marked with an *x* in our examples). This technique of linking up verses 3 and 4 is rather similar to that of an enjambement between two poetic lines. (Our symbol for it shall be: verses 3-4: Enj.)

3. Against the prevailingly identical or closely related rhythmic-motivic patterns of verses 1 and 2 (and sometimes 3), verse 4 mostly displays an additional rhythmic irregularity, either through increased motion (designation: IM) that is in smaller note values, as for instance, in Ex. 1, or else through reduced motion (RM) utilizing larger note values or interspersed rests, as in Ex. 7, Ex. 8, and many others referred to later on.

4. Another characteristic feature of the QSS is the method of cutting

the third verse into two motivically identical or related halves (see Ex. 2). Numerous instances in the works of Haydn and Beethoven could be cited; particularly the latter exhibit a marked preference for this structural pattern in both small- and large-scale structures. A very Beethovenian version of this pattern — used only in large, compound-meter melodies — is the fragmentation of verse 3 into even smaller motivic units, as demonstrated in measures 9-12 of the "Ode to Joy" melody in the Ninth Symphony ("Deine Zauber binden wieder...") and in measures 9-12 of its probable model, Haydn's anthem melody "Gott erhalte Franz den Kaiser."

5. Since our analytical method is based on stanza structure, the notions of "verse" and "syllable" must inevitably be introduced into the analysis of instrumental music. Once the basic parallelism between the popular stanza pattern and the thematic structure of classical music is established, we can hardly avoid using some syllable-counting method for a metric definition of the four "verses." In vocal music this seems to be a self-explanatory procedure (down to the metric indices of our hymnals), yet many analysts of instrumental music still seem reluctant to adopt it. Nevertheless, Riemann's famous standard of *Vierhebigkeit* (four accents per phrase) and the Cooper-Meyer analytic method of rhythm and meter were both founded on this principle. The even pulsation of classical rhythm and meter presupposes a more or less regular alternation between accented (*Hebungen*) and nonaccented (*Senkungen*) notes, taken as the equivalents of syllables. As is widely known, German poetry has enjoyed the additional privilege of the so-called *Senkungsfreiheit:* the number of unaccented syllables has been less rigidly regulated then in most Romance languages. As a result, in German folksong (and poetry as well) iambs and anapests on one side, trochees and dactyls on the other, are allowed to alternate with remarkable freedom. For instance, in the thirty-two verses of the eight stanzas of *Erlkönig* the basic pattern of the iambic dimeter (e. g., Mein Sohn, es ist ein Nebelstreif") occurs only three times (verses 8, 9, and 13), whereas the remaining twenty-nine verses use not less than nine different versions of the sixteen possible permutations of mixing iambics and anapests within the framework of the four feet. A more thorough investigation of these questions of meter would lead us too far away from our central topic; it will have to be relegated to another essay. As for our present purposes, suffice it to say that a deeper understanding of the rhythmic-metric structure of classical music cannot afford to dismiss the notion

of "syllabic" analysis. A great many sonata and symphony themes of Haydn and Beethoven can be precisely defined in the terms of quaternary stanzas, consisting of single verses of six, seven, eight or more syllables organized into rows of iambic, trochaic, anapestic or other feet. If our versions of the themes found in Ex. 8 and the following examples are compared with the original scores of Beethoven, it may be noticed that each of our quotations provides a simplified skeleton, a reduction to the syllabic pattern, of what the score presents in a more elaborate and heavily ornamented form. Of course, these reductions have been done for purely analytical purposes, by way of eliminating or reducing an abundance of ornamental figures, passing notes, suspensions, etc. that were used by classical composers as a means of embellishing the simple melody, in order to conform to the demands of the Italian bel canto. The composers and theorists of the eighteenth century knew not only the difference between simple and figured melody but also the appropriate place to use each of these melodic styles.

* * *

In order to support and demonstrate our method of quaternary analysis let us proceed to a detailed study of a few Beethoven themes, always providing references to parallel and comparable phenomena in other works. Ex. 3 is taken from the Fourth Symphony (third movement, the

Ex. 3   Fourth Symphony, third mvt., trio, mm. 1-16

opening of the trio). It is to be described as follows:

1. It does not form a period.
2. QSS: *AA'BC*. Verses 3-4: Enj. Verse 4: IM.
3. Syllable count: 6, 6, 6, 7. Three iambic feet per verse (incomplete iambic dimeter; the fourth foot is supplied by the strings, while the melody itself is performed by the woodwinds).

The verse meter here is like that in the canon "Mir ist so wunderbar" in *Fidelio*, Act I. Another QSS theme that has the same pattern of feet with six syllables in each verse is the F major canon that appears in the Fourth Symphony, first movement, measures 141-48 (repeated in measures 149-56). It too is not a period. Its verses are of two measures each. Other characteristics of QSS are lacking.

Ex. 4   Fifth Symphony, first mvt., mm. 6-21

Ex. 4, from the first movement of the Fifth Symphony, has the usual QSS, here with the third verse halved ($b + b$). The first three verses are clearly separated by the sustained notes, while verses 3 and 4 are connected by enjambement. In Ex. 4 the subprimary level of the meter is shown above the melody, the more important primary level, below. On both levels reduced motion is evident in verse 4, creating an effect of retardation comparable to that in Goethe's *Wanderers Nachtlied* ("... kaum einen Hauch"). See also Ex. 8, below.

The tightly structured quaternary form of this famous theme (Ex. 4) may serve as a forceful argument for our contention that the preceding measures, 1-5, of this allegro, while tremendously impressive and moving as well as being motivically anticipatory of verse 1, really do not belong to the thematic structure proper. They fulfill the initial function of a curtain, fairly typical of Beethoven's mature style. Parallels with Ex. 4 can be found in the finale of the Sixth Symphony and in the finale of the piano sonata Opus 13, the *Pathétique*. In the former, measures 9-32 present a threefold statement of the same stanza theme, the preceding eight measures functioning only as a curtain. Not a period in the strict sense because of the unusual subdominant close in the middle, its strophic structure, which is emphasized by the similarly unusual double repetition, is in perfect accord with Beethoven's title, *Hirtengesang*. Of interest in the finale of Opus 13 is the fact that its opening theme may be viewed as of both periodic and QSS structure. (The *ABc-cA* layout of measures 1-8 has attached to it a refrain repetition of verses 3-4 in measures 9-12 and an athematic cadential appendix in measures 13-18.)

Ex. 5   Piano Sonata in F minor, Opus 2, No. 1, finale, mm. 35-42

The secondary theme in the last movement of the piano sonata Opus 2, No. 1 (see Ex. 5), may be described as follows:

1. It does not form a period.
2. QSS: *AA'A"B*.
3. Syllable count: 7, 7, 7, 6. The fact that it has one less syllable creates RM in verse 4 and establishes a remarkable kinship with the rhythmic-metric pattern of the primary theme (measures 1-12).

The seven-syllable metric pattern of this C minor theme is strongly reminiscent of several contredanse-inspired Haydn themes, most notably the primary theme of Symphony No. 88, first movement, though verse 4 there has IM. The theme of the finale of Symphony No. 78 also shows a marked likeness. (This theme — *ABA'B'* — is fashioned as a period.) It may be worth mentioning that Beethoven's Opus 2 was published with a dedication to Haydn.

In at least one theme by Beethoven himself the rhythmic pattern of its four verses is identical to the sonata theme quoted in Ex. 5: measures 9-20 of his Piano Trio in C minor, Opus 1, No. 3, follow this pattern, measures 1-8 being a nonthematic curtain, measures 21-30 a somewhat prolonged and structurally disrupted repetition of the first thematic statement. In the theme for the variations that make up the second movement of the piano sonata Opus 57, the *Appassionata,* the primary-level motion of verses 1 and 2 is metrically analogous to the themes in the earlier sonata and the piano trio. As to other aspects of the *Appassionata* theme, one might mention the structure of its last two verses — *b + b, b + c* (7 + 7, 7 + 3) — and the way in which the IM of measures 9-14 (IM on the subprimary level) beautifully counterbalances the RM in the last half-verse of verse 4 (measures 15-16). The basic structural unit of this theme is a four-measure phrase (i. e., verse) that closes on the tonic chord. Four such phrases are compounded into one complete stanza. The repetition of both half-stanzas (measures 1-8 and measures 9-16, both marked :‖ by Beethoven) appears somewhat unusual in art music, though not at all so in folksong and popular dance. Riemann's analysis [9] defines the theme as consisting of two different periods. Our quaternary interpretation, however, does more justice to the structural unity of the theme.

Our next example is taken from the second movement of the piano sonata Opus 10, No. 2 (see Ex. 6). This deeply emotional trio section, eighty measures long with an additional six-measure postlude, is a testi-

[9] Hugo Riemann, *Beethovens sämtliche Klavier-Solosonaten* (Berlin, 1918-19).

mony to Beethoven's refined use of QSS on two different metric and
formal levels. The excerpt in Ex. 6 (measures 1-16) gives but the primary level of QSS. Far from being a period, it is what Fischer terms a
Gegenperiode, since measure 8 closes on the tonic, measure 16 on the
dominant. The metric pattern in verses 1-3 (◡ - / ◡ - / ◡ - / -) is
that of "O Haupt voll Blut und Wunden" (cf. Mozart's Symphony in
G minor, K. 550, finale, measures 1-2, 5-6, etc). Verse 4 (measures 13-16) displays slightly increased motion, caused by inserting an
anapest into the verse (an example from poetry: "Wer reitet so spät
durch Nacht und Wind?"). In both verse 3 and verse 4 one metric beat
is missing from the treble line. Here Beethoven makes use of the license
formulated by contemporary theorists, Koch among others, who state
that a metric beat missing from a melody may be supplied by one of the
accompanying parts (measure 12: alto; measure 15: tenor); in Ex. 6
these supplementary notes are given in parentheses. The QSS pattern of
these sixteen measures seems to us hardly open to question.

Ex. 6   Piano Sonata in F, Opus 10, No. 2, second mvt., trio, mm. 1-16

But beyond this sixteen-bar limit the overall formal structure of the
whole trio section (without the postlude, measures 81-86) may very well
be analyzed along the lines either of QSS or of the so-called "two-
reprise" or bipartite dance form ||: A :||: BA :||. In dealing with this
piece, we would like to start out with the more traditional of these
analytic options, the second. It can be mentioned in advance that in this
instance Beethoven dismissed the simple repeat signs, as he was to do in
many later works, and replaced them with varied, written-out repetitions.
According to the conventional dance pattern, a diagram of the trio looks
like this:

A	A'	b + b	A''	b + b	A''	
16	16	4 + 4	16	4 + 4	16	= 80 measures
(1	2	3	4	3b	4b	= 6 verses)

But this is but one of the possible options for formal analysis. Keeping
in mind three telling features of the trio — (1) the *b + b* motivic halving of verse 3, (2) the enjambement between verse 3 and verse 4, in
measures 40 and 64 (that is, measures 78 and 102 of the whole movement), as opposed to the clear melodic breaks between verses 1, 2, and
3, and (3) the frequent occurrence of this type of refrain repetition of

verses 3-4 (the last half-stanza) in Beethoven's music — we simply cannot help recognizing the obvious parallelism between QSS plus Refrain and the traditional pattern of "two-reprise" dance form with written-out variations instead of mechanical repeat signs. In light of this recognition, the analysis of Riemann, who qualified A and A' as periods I and II, respectively, and bbA'' as a repeated period III, inevitably proves to be devious and illogical.

Another trio to which Beethoven gives a somewhat unusual structure is that in the Seventh Symphony, third movement, measures 149-222. Here the large-scale construction (disregarding the appended transitional section, measures 222-36) runs this way:

A	A'	$\|:$	$b + b$	X	A'' $:\|$	
16	16		8 + 8	10	16	= 74 measures
(1	2	$\|:$	3	Enj.	4 $:\|$	= 6 verses)

This layout is exceptional insofar as it tends to disrupt the traditional $\|: A :\|: BA :\|$ structure of dance form, not only by the insertion of the nonthematic transitional section between verses 3 and 4 (functioning as an enjambement), but also by its different handling of the two "reprises": the repetition of A in verse 2 is written out and varied, while the repetition of the second "reprise" (verse 3 — Enj. — verse 4) is asked for merely by repeat signs. Accordingly, in the second performance of the trio (measures 408-482) the repetition of A (verses 1 and 2) is again written out, while the merely symbolic directions to repeat the second "reprise" are simply omitted, as is usual in the da capos of minuets and other dances.

Two further examples demonstrating the basic equivalence of QSS plus Refrain (in all, a six-verse stanza) and the traditional dance form $\|: A :\|: BA :\|$ may be mentioned here. In the finale of the *Eroica Symphony,* measures 76-107 show the typical QSS-plus-Refrain pattern and can be diagramed as follows:

A	A'	$b + b$	A''	$b + b$	A''	
8	8	2 + 2	4	2 + 2	4	= 32 measures
(1	2	3	4	3b	4b	= 6 verses)

It becomes immediately evident that verse 2 and the second 3 and 4 are functioning here as mere replacements for the traditional repeat marks. In the preceding variations on the bass line of the same melody (measures 44-75 of the finale) Beethoven had indeed simply indicated the repetitions by such signs, as he did in his earliest use of the melody, in the contredanse WoO 14, No. 7. The dance origin of this theme suggests that accepting this dance-form interpretation is more appropriate than trying to enforce the QSS plus Refrain pattern of six verses that would have here to recognize verses of unequal length (four as against eight measures). However, the pattern of QSS may claim a certain relevance, too, by accounting for the typical halving of verse 3 into the subphrases $b + b$ and for the characteristic enjambement between verses 3 and 4 represented by the fermatas in measures 95 and 103. In the Seventh Symphony the variation theme of the second movement, measures 3-26, has, on a somewhat smaller scale than the *Eroica* example, a layout of QSS plus Refrain:

A	B	c + c	A′	c + c	A′	
4	4	2 + 2	4	2 + 2	4	= 24 measures
(1	2	3	4	3b	4b	= 6 verses)

The antique meter embodied in the single verses need not concern us here; in the music of Beethoven two short Adonic verses add up to a *vierhebig* 5 + 5 syllable verse. Suffice it to mention the emphatic equating of the song and dance qualities (very much in the spirit of old Greek poetry and music), the particular fitness of this stanza type of theme for unusual variations, the motivic halving of verse 3, and the echo-evoking pianissimo dynamics of the refrain repetition.

Once we admit the applicability of such a large-scale six-verse stanza concept (QSS plus Refrain) to the large dimensions of slow movements, we might be willing to admit its validity for such great melodies as the primary theme of the third movement of the piano sonata Opus 106, the "Hammerklavier." Measure 1 (the curtain, a later addition by Beethoven) and measure 26 (an appendix) can be dispensed with here. The remaining twenty-four measures, 2-25, add up to the following structure:

A	B	c + c	A′	c + c	A′	
4	4	2 + 2	4	2 + 2	4	= 24 measures
(1	2	3	4	3b	4b	= 6 verses)

All of the phrases and verses but A are anacrustic in meter; all of the breaks between verses and motives fall within measures rather than at bar lines. The usual metric differentiation of the fourth verse by means of IM or RM is replaced here by increased tonal tension: most of that verse is based upon a strongly emphasized Neapolitan harmony.

Ex. 7 presents a thematic unit that Riemann considered to be one period, but this, the opening of the piano sonata Opus 2, No. 3, seems to be a rather unusual period, since all three phrases close on the tonic.

Ex. 7   Piano Sonata in C, Opus 2, No. 3, first mvt., mm. 1-12

More appropriately it is termed QSS plus varied Refrain. It has typical QSS features, namely, the halving of verse 3 and the RM in verse 4. It seems remarkable that two out of three sonatas in Opus 2, dedicated to Haydn, exhibit QSS themes at the very outset; were these not meant as a special tribute to Haydn, who apparently initiated and greatly cultivated this structure? Otherwise, the most obvious uses of QSS customarily occur in finales, trios, and slow movements rather than in the opening allegros.

At the beginning of the scherzo (measures 1-18) of the Fifth Symphony an arresting instance of QSS appears. The orchestra underlines the quaternary question-answer structure (*ABA'B'*) by alternating the instrumentation from verse to verse. It is as though the listener were presented with an orchestral transcription of the half-stanza "Wer reitet so spät durch Nacht und Wind? / Es ist der Vater *und sein* Kind . . ." (in order to fit Beethoven's meter, we slightly changed Goethe's words in verse 2). Measures 13-14 are an irregular extension of the third verse and convey a twofold meaning: (a) with respect to harmony, they supply the only cadence (on a secondary dominant) other than the simple dominant, and (b) with respect to motif, they fulfill the typical enjambement function between verses 3 and 4. As to meter, the whole structure is an extremely refined version of the four-verse Ambrosian hymn stanza; each verse is a different version of the basic iambic dimeter, embellished and variegated through deliberately inserted anapests.

Ex. 8   Fifth Symphony, second mvt., mm. 1-8

The wonderful melody (Ex. 8) that opens the second movement of the Fifth Symphony can be regarded as a self-contained antecedent to the differently structured consequent of measures 11-22. Lack of room here prevents us from undertaking an analysis of the latter, nor will we discuss the appended echo of measures 9-10. Our job is to concentrate on the basic structure of measures 1-8. This can safely be regarded as a binary period, since the C major (III) cadence in measure 4 is a legitimate substitute for the dominant and measure 8 comes to rest on the tonic. However, a more thorough rhythmic-motivic analysis that looks beyond harmony, results in the recognition of a basic QSS: *AA'b-bC,* with all of the above-stipulated specific criteria of QSS (verse 3: halved; verses 3-4: Enj.; verse 4: RM). If anybody harbors doubts about the close motivic relationship of verses 1 and 2, he may be relieved of them by the famous sketch of Beethoven, entitled "Andante alla Menuetto" published many times since Nottebohm. The persistent dotted rhythm tends to obscure the relatively simple syllabic pattern of motion. In order to facilitate its recognition, we have marked the syllable count above the melody. Of course, the metric time span of each verse is identical (six eighths = two measures per verse), whereas the amount of rhythmic motion is differentiated from verse to verse, the fastest in verse 2 (nine syllables), the slowest in verse 4 (four syllables). This is no folksong but a highly sophisticated theme by one of the greatest masters of refined musical structures. Beethoven's procedure of rhythmic differentiation being somewhat comparable to the alternation of long and short verses in poetry, e. g., in Goethe's *Wanderers Nachtlied,* where the three verses "Die Vöglein schweigen im Walde / Warte nur balde / Ruhest du auch" are basically equal as to the time each fills; the short verses must be spoken much slower than the longest one. Or another example, by Wordsworth, of the same technique: "There was a time when meadow, grove and stream / The earth and every common sight / To me did seem / Apparelled in celestial light. . . ." I don't think we detract from the outstanding merit of Beethoven by pointing out these poetic parallels to his metric procedure.

Ex. 9   Piano Sonata in A, Opus 2, No. 2, finale, mm. 1-16

Several finale themes provide us with telling examples for the necessity of melodic reduction, that is, simplification, when we venture into the structural analysis of heavily ornamented themes. In the first sixteen measures of the finale of the piano sonata Opus 2, No. 2, the rich ornamentation of the melody, particularly the obtrusive arpeggios at the outset of the *A* sections, is strongly reminiscent of the *galant* style which is hinted at by Beethoven's tempo marking, Grazioso. Such elaboration tends to obscure the fairly simple metric-syllabic structure. Yet from the rhythmically reduced version given in Ex. 9 it appears that the meter of verses 1, 2, and 4 is closely related to the age-old pattern of certain Geneva Psalms (e. g., "O bien heureux, celuy'dont les commises"). The basic analytical information about this theme would include the following:

1. It does not form a period, since both of its segments close on the dominant.
2. QSS. *AA b-bA″*. (Note that verse 3 is halved.)
3. Verses 3-4: Enj. The left-hand figure is the more conspicuous in that it is used only at this spot (*) within the sixteen-measure theme.

Another closely related example of the same *galant* style and QSS structure is the theme at the outset of the finale of the piano sonata Opus 7. The enjambement between verses 3 and 4 is in the form of a fermata which in the performance practice of *galant* style permitted the player to improvise an *Eingang*. As in the theme from Opus 2, No. 2, *galant* ornamentation here, too, tends to overrun the underlying, simple dance melody and its *vierhebig* iambic-anapestic meter. The stripping away of its ornaments can make readily apparent the uncomplicated contredanse-like character of the melody.

The finale of Beethoven's First Symphony is the source of our next example. (Ex. 10a omits the adagio introduction and reduces the ornaments, passing notes, and runs in the melody to the bare substance.) This is one of the most Haydnesque melodies of the young Beethoven. Particularly the memory of Haydn's finale from Symphony No. 88 (Ex. 10b) must have lingered in Beethoven's mind very strongly when he conceived this movement exactly in the style and spirit of Haydn's famous contredanse-like finales. Beethoven himself may have felt it somewhat old-fashioned, for he prefaced it with a rather tongue-in-cheek slow introduction that must have elicited gales of laughter from every knowing audience when suddenly erupting into the allegro molto. Beethoven's allegro theme (measures 7-30) is usually analyzed as a compound of two periods; one simple statement (measures 7-14) and one repeated (measures 15-22 and 23-30). This method, however, does justice neither to the logical structure of the two sentences nor to the organic unity of the whole twenty-four-bar section. The first "period"

Ex. 10   First Symphony, finale, mm. 7-14
a.

b.   Haydn, Symphony No. 88, finale, mm. 1-8

is really an antiperiod, with a tonic cadence in measure 10 and one on the dominant in measure 14. In our interpretation this is but the first half (verses 1 and 2) of a six-verse stanza, the second half of which (measures 15-22) is followed by a varied repetition (that is refrain) in measures 23-30. The motivic pattern of the whole six-verse theme runs thus: *AA'b-bCb-bC*. Note the characteristic halving of verse 3 and the RM in verse 4. This QSS-plus-Refrain interpretation as well as the reduction to "syllabic" motion in the melody serves to indicate organic unity much better than any conventional period concept, which mostly fails in recognizing the motivic unity and metric identity of the different sections of the melody. Measures 7-14 move mostly in sixteenths, measures 15-30 mostly in eighths, but we must keep in mind that in Beethoven's sketch the thematic run of measures 6-7 and 10-11 originally had been notated in eighths.

A brief comparison with Haydn's procedure in his motivically closely related finale of Symphony No. 88 is rather instructive. Haydn's theme (measures 1-8), like Beethoven's, is an antiperiod (measure 4: tonic, measure 8: parallel), best viewed as equivalent to the half-stanza. But Haydn did not take pains to elaborate on a different but fundamentally related second half-stanza as did Beethoven some thirteen years later. Haydn simply repeats the initial reprise, resulting in the somewhat primitive pattern of *ABAB,* and then starts developing his motivic material in the second reprise of his rondo theme.

The next example, from the slow movement of the piano sonata Opus 2, No. 1 (Ex. 11), again omits the rich ornamentation, reducing the melody to its syllabic skeleton. In describing these sixteen measures as a theme compounded of two periods, Riemann relies on the dominant-tonic alternation of the cadences; this seems readily acceptable. Nevertheless, it does not account for the subdivision in the motivic structure of measures 9-12 and for the da capo of measures 13-16. The whole sixteen-measure complex can be better analyzed as a QSS: *AA′b-bA″*. In this analysis each of Riemann's periods corresponds to a half-stanza (two verses).

Ex. 11   Piano Sonata in F minor, Opus 2, No. 1, second mvt., mm. 1-16

It is worth comparing this high-level structure to the more primitive form of the same thematic material in Beethoven's early piano quartet from 1785 (Kinsky WoO 36, No. 3, second movement, adagio con espressione). Despite slight differences in the melodic line, measures 1-8 are essentially the same in both settings. The second period (measures 9-16) from WoO 36, however, is lacking the tight structural organization of the sonata version, particularly with regard to the third verse, measures 9-12, which is an undifferentiated four-measure unit in WoO 36, whereas in the sonata it gets the motivically halved character, so typical of verse 3 within the framework of a QSS. Moreover, in WoO 36 Beethoven wants both halves of the thematic section (measures 1-8 and 9-16) to be repeated, a procedure reminiscent of Haydn's finale in Symphony No. 88. This simple repetitive procedure might be appropriate in folksong and popular dance, but it is much less so in art song or instrumental music. It seemed satisfactory to the inexperienced young Beethoven in 1785, but ten years later he eliminated these repetitions.

Earlier we called attention to the basic similarity of the "Ode to Joy" theme in the Ninth Symphony to Haydn's Austrian anthem, "Gott erhalte Franz den Kaiser." This likeness can now be detailed. The two melodies share the same trochaic dimeter and the same syllable count, eight and seven syllables alternating. As to the QSS of each. the third verse is not halved but rather cut into shorter subsections. (In the Beethoven theme the customary enjambement between verses 3 and 4 is provided by a syncopated anticipation.) The "Ode to Joy" melody may be diagramed as QSS plus Refrain:

A	A′	b + b′ + b″ + c	A″	b + b′ + b″ + c	A″	
4	4	1 + 1 + 1 + 1	4	1 + 1 + 1 + 1	4	= 24 measures
(1	2	3	4	3b	4b	= 6 verses)

The Haydn anthem has the following layout:

A	A	$b + b + c$	$d + d + e$	$d + d + e$	
4	4	$1 + 1 + 2$	$1 + 1 + 2$	$1 + 1 + 2$	$= 20$ measures
(1	2	3	4	4b	$= 5$ verses)

In Beethoven's piano sonata Opus 2, No. 3, in the course of the last movement there is an episode in F major, measures 103-150, that can be likened to these melodies, since its meter and prosody are closely akin to theirs. For forty-four of its forty-eight measures it follows the plan of QSS plus Refrain, while its last four measures contain the slight disruption of a turn into a minor variant having a sequential development.

* * *

We have tried to deal systematically with the structural aspect of classical themes, particularly on a dimensional level larger than phrase or motive and smaller than say, sonata (or rondo) form as a whole, for the most part concentrating on symmetrical structures of eight or sixteen measures (or twenty-four, thirty-two, forty-eight, and so on). Until now, surprisingly little analytical work has been done on this particular level. Analysts have mostly relied on the concept of the "period," more or less following the rather dogmatic formulations of the past century. Thorough analysis has demonstrated that in many instances that concept simply does not work. Looking for an appropriate substitute, my students and I came upon the concept of the quaternary stanza, as derived from folk-song and popular dance, then widely accepted into classical poetry of the *folklore imaginé* variety. This introduction of the stanza concept into music is not without precedent. Henry Hadow and Gerald Abraham have used it in describing the structure of short piano pieces by Schumann.[10] Both associated this penchant of Schumann toward stanza structure with the composer's predilection for the poetry of Heine, many of whose poems he set in masterful fashion. Thus so far, I am in full agreement with them. But I cannot agree with Hadow and Abraham in feeling that Schumann's structural procedure strongly contrasts with that of Beethoven. "There are very few of Beethoven's instrumental melodies to which it would be possible to adapt metrical words; there is scarcely one of Schumann's which could not so be treated" (Hadow). In view of the overwhelming testimony to the contrary provided by our examples

[10] W. Henry Hadow, *Studies in Modern Music* (London, 1892); Gerald Abraham, *A Hundred Years of Music* (London, 1938).

above, this opinion is no longer tenable.

In the analysis of classical themes the concept of quaternary stanza structure can fulfill a double function: it can account for (1) architectonic structures within the period concept, and well beyond it, and (2) the use of specific metric patterns, partly within and partly beyond the limit of the phrase (i. e., verse). A detailed and systematic investigation of verse meter in Beethoven's music has had to be bypassed this time, since it would have required an article almost the length of a book. Guided primarily by the characteristics of the stanza in European popular song and dance, it has been possible to work out a series of structural specifications that proved, surprisingly, to fit a great many themes of Beethoven and Haydn. There has been no opportunity yet to start a similar systematic investigation of Mozart along these lines, but in all probability the method will be workable with Mozart as well.

The philosophical aspect of this analytical method touches at the basic question of the relations between folk music and classical music. It happened exactly in Beethoven's mature life that Goethe, when reviewing the famous folksong collection *Des Knaben Wunderhorn,* wrote these prophetic words: "Folksong, after having fulfilled its purpose, may elicit new and significant melodies." Friedrich Blume, who quotes this sentence, feels compelled to add that "this prophecy has been fulfilled in the music of the Viennese classic masters beyond expectation, in a way Goethe never had anticipated." [11]

This idea of Goethe — a higher synthesis of folksong and art music — seems to have fallen out of favor in the past 150 years, albeit one of the great pioneers of modern musicology, Guido Adler, upheld it into this century, professing that "the art of the Viennese masters stands firmly on the ground of folk music." Recent opinions of respected and competent authorities, however, strongly opposed it, Alfred Einstein by stressing the aristocratic character of Mozart's music and Arnold Schoenberg in questioning the folkloristic tendencies of modern music (*Symphonien aus Volksliedern,* 1947). Chauvinistic distortions (e. g., those by Kuhač and Hadow) that seek to reveal folksong motifs have also played a part in discrediting the view that folk music is an important source of great art. Nevertheless, there is a basic relationship between these two domains. In my opinion, the common denominator lies not in motivic fragments but in structural similarity. Walter Wiora recently advocated this idea in his significant book *Europaeische Volksmusik und*

[11] Friedrich Blume, "Klassik," *Die Musik in Geschichte und Gegenwart,* VII, col. 1044.

abendländische Tonkunst (1957). With this work we seem to return to the original concept of Goethe. Wiora says, "Poets and musicians very often create small-scale works of art that at first appear to be very simple and naïve, and yet, they are products of individual inspiration." This is exactly the concept of *folklore imaginé*, and certainly it holds true for a great many classic works, be they conceived on a small or larger scale. Perhaps our analytical concept of quaternary stanza structure, with all its specifications given above, will be able to provide an important tool for two impending tasks: to relieve our great classic heritage of music from the anachronistic burden of sterile late-Baroque rhetoric, and to establish its intimate basic relationship to one of its main sources, popular song and popular dance.

SCHUBERT'S BEETHOVEN

By EDWARD T. CONE

ACCORDING to Johann Leopold Ebner, Schubert was once on the point of destroying one of his own songs because a friend had called his attention to a few measures that resembled a familiar passage from Beethoven. The year was 1817, and the song was *Die Forelle*. Shortly after he had finished it, the young composer showed it to a group of friends, one of whom recognized in it an unconscious quotation from the *Coriolan* Overture. "Schubert saw this at once, too, and wanted to destroy the song, but we would not allow it and thus saved that glorious song from destruction." [1] The passage in question is probably measures 64-65, which should be compared with measures 19-20 of the Beethoven overture.[2]

If the story is true, then Schubert must have been unaware that he had already (in 1815) committed a much more patent offense in his Second Symphony: the line and harmonic structure of the main theme of the first movement (measures 10-23) almost exactly parallel those of the corresponding theme of Beethoven's First Symphony (measures 13-33), with their I-II-V-I. And later he must have been equally unconscious of numerous references of the same kind scattered throughout his compositions.

There is, however, another possibility. Ebner may have taken seriously what Schubert meant as a facetious gesture. It is probable that the composer regarded his debt to Beethoven in quite a different light from that indicated by the anecdote. His friends attested that he idolized the older composer and freely acknowledged his influence. And although some of his quotations may have been unconscious (after all, he often

---

[1] Quoted in Otto Erich Deutsch, *Schubert, Memoirs by His Friends* (New York, 1958), p. 47. Ebner (1791-1870), writing in 1858, insisted that *Die Forelle* was actually composed in 1816, as opposed to the more generally accepted, later date (see p. 49).

[2] Deutsch is certainly wrong in suggesting the accompaniment of Beethoven's measure 52 as the source of the trouble and comparing it with Schubert's accompaniment (*ibid.*, p. 49). The resemblance is minimal.

seemed unaware of quoting from himself!), it is hard to believe that others were not wholly intentional. Thus, when one finds in each of the last three piano sonatas, composed almost simultaneously during the summer of 1828, a reference to the music of the master, then one begins to suspect that Schubert may have been deliberately trying to pay tribute to the memory of the illustrious colleague who had died only a short time before.

The C minor Sonata makes only a bow in Beethoven's direction, but it is one that reveals more than mere politeness. Schubert's opening is taken almost note-for-note from the theme of Beethoven's Thirty-Two Variations in C minor. It should be noted that, although Beethoven uses a familiar chaconne bass, Schubert does not. What he copies is Beethoven's melodic line, rising C-D-E♮-F-F♯-G-A♭ — at which point a typically Schubertian expansion postpones the V-I cadence common to both themes. It is as if Schubert deliberately eschews Beethoven's use of the traditional bass, in order to throw into greater relief the more characteristic melody. And in order to make his point more clearly, he punctuates the arrival at E-natural by an ascending scale like Beethoven's. Such overt quotations end with the completion of the theme, but I find a veiled reference to Beethoven's coda, too, in Schubert's: measures 255-57 of the sonata present a transposed variant of Beethoven's final melodic idea, measures 299-300 (Ex. 1).

Ex. 1

The foregoing correspondences could be dismissed as unconscious, or even coincidental, were they not supported by stronger and more pervasive resemblances in the other two works. It has often been pointed out that the main themes of the finales of Schubert's Sonata in B-flat and Beethoven's quartet in the same key, Opus 130, have many points in common. These include the dance-like 2/4 meter, the introductory G and its continuation as a pedal, the interpretation of this G as V of II, and the ensuing establishment of the tonic. What is not often observed is the fact that the two movements have certain unusual formal elements in common.

The repetition of Beethoven's exposition is a clue that the movement can be read as a sonata form. From this point of view the new material that, after a brief transition, follows the exposition (measures 109-55) is a "new theme" in the development; its restatement after the recapitulation (measures 353-99) is then part of the coda, like the return of the corresponding theme in the first movement of the *Eroica*. Here is a brief outline of the movement as a whole (omitting transitions):

Exposition	Development Section	Recapitulation	Coda
‖:A B:‖	C Development of A	A B	Return of C and A

But the rounded song form of the first theme and the balanced periodic construction of the third suggest a rondo. The unwary listener, deprived (as almost invariably) of the repeated exposition in performance, and concentrating only on themes and broad key areas, would hear:

Theme:	A	B	C	Development	A	B	C	A	Coda
Key:	I	V	bVII		IV-I	I	IV-I	I	

Now, this scheme, with its exposition and recapitulation of three thematic and key areas rather than two, is close to the one used by Schubert:

Theme:	A	B	C	A_1	interrupted	A_2	B	C	A	Coda
Key:	I	V	V	I	by development	I	I	I	I	
			minor-major					minor-major		

Instead of two new key areas, Schubert's exposition uses two versions of the dominant; and the development is differently placed. Otherwise the two patterns are superficially similar enough to lead one to suspect that the later movement might have been modeled on the earlier one. But that would be an error. Schubert here varied a form that he had already used before — notably in January, 1826, when the String Quartet in D minor was finished; the Beethoven movement was not composed until later the same year. Schubert's quartet finale can be taken as the "regular" pattern from which the sonata slightly diverges:

Theme:	A	B	C	A	Development	B	C	A	Coda
Key:	I	III	V	I		VI	I	I	

Versions of this form are to be found in the finales of Schubert's two other mature quartets, those in A minor and G major; also in the B-flat Piano Trio, and in the Piano Sonata in C minor itself (here with the development preceding the return of the first theme, as in the Beethoven quartet). All these differ somewhat from one another, but all agree in showing an amalgamation of the rondo with Schubert's own trithematic, tritonal sonata exposition.[3]

Here we have the real point of difference between Schubert's design and Beethoven's. The parallelism between the presentation of themes in Schubert's rondos and the tripartite expositions of his sonata forms indicates that he considered his exposition complete only with the conclusion of the third theme with its new key area. (Further evidence is the fact that in the example from the B-flat Sonata themes *B* and *C* are in the same key, differing only in mode.) For Beethoven, as the position of the double bar and repeat sign attests, the exposition was basically bitonal, and the third theme was part of the development. Nevertheless, Schubert, who, as we know, eagerly studied every new composition by the great man, may have recognized in the layout of the Opus 130 movement a real, although superficial, resemblance to a pattern which he had made his own. (And did he also feel in the periodic structure of the themes, and in the episodic and sequential developments, a relaxed sense of form unusual for Beethoven but highly suggestive of his own music?) When he based his finale in B-flat on Beethoven's recent example in the same key, he may have been making an elegant gesture of homage.

Only in the finale of the A major Sonata do we find among these last sonatas a complete movement directly based on a Beethoven original. The clues here are so obvious that it is surprising that the relationship has not been noted more often. Perhaps it is because the Beethoven movement, the finale of the piano sonata Opus 31, No. 1, comes from one of the most neglected of the thirty-two. Otherwise, certain clear quotations could not have been overlooked: the rhythmic and harmonic motif of Schubert's measures 61-67 (to name only its first appearance) refers to Beethoven's measures 37-42; the pianistic figuration of the same passage, to Beethoven's measures 49-52; the contrapuntal design of Schubert's measures 41-45, to Beethoven's measures 200-205. There is even a subtle relationship between the main themes of the two rondos: displace the Beethoven by one half-measure, transpose it, and the parallels become apparent (Ex. 2). Where the two do not coincide they counterpoint each other.

These comparatively superficial borrowings are signs of a much deeper indebtedness, for with amazing fidelity Schubert has traced out and copied the entire formal pattern of Beethoven's rondo. All major

---

[3] See Felix Salzer, "Die Sonatenform bei Schubert," *Studien zur Musikwissenschaft,* XV (1928), 86-125.

Ex. 2

sections, many individual phrases, and even single measures of the earlier movement are reflected in the later. One can only conclude that Schubert was deliberately using the Beethoven as a formal model. The following schematic description should make the correspondences and differences clear:

Beethoven		Schubert	
Measures		Measures	
1-16	Theme *A,* I (G major).	1-16	Theme *A,* I (A major).
1-8	*a*	1-8	*a*
9-12	*b*	‖:9-16:‖	‖:*b*:‖
13-16	*b*		

In Beethoven's rondo, the theme totals sixteen measures, two statements of *b* (a four-measure phrase) balancing one of *a* (an eight-measure period). In Schubert's, one entire statement of *b* balances one of *a,* so that the repetition of the second half creates a ratio of 1:2.

17-32	Variation of *A.* Melody in left hand with trip- let counterpoint above, revert- ing in *b* to eighths. The variation ends, like the theme, on I.	17-32	Variation of *A.* Melody in left hand with trip- let counterpoint above, revert- ing in *b* to eighths. The varia- tion ends, after a repetition of *b,* with a deceptive cadence on V of VI.
32-42	Developmental bridge, based on *A,* moving to a threefold cadence on V of V. The trip- let accompaniment returns.	32-46	Developmental bridge, based on *A,* moving to a fourfold cadence on V of V. The trip- let accompaniment returns.

Schubert's greater expansiveness, perhaps already suggested by the repetition of *b,* is beginning to show itself.

42-52	Theme *B,* V (D major). It is derived from the preceding theme (Ex. 3).

    42-46   A four-measure phrase, moving V-I in the new key. The triplets are retained.

    46-50   Twofold repetition of the last two measures of the preceding phrase.

    50-52   Twofold repetition of the cadential measure.

52-66   Transition, evolving from a cadential figure. D major is converted into a V⁷.

46-106   Theme *B,* V (E major). It is derived from the preceding movement (see the trio of the scherzo).

    46-61   Three five-measure phrases moving I-V, V-VI, VI-IV in the new key. The triplets are retained.

    61-67   Cadential figure on IV.

    67-79   Three four-measure phrases moving IV-♮VII, ♮VII-V, V-I.

    79-106   Instead of the cadential figure on I, balancing the preceding passage on IV, a long interpolation moving to an expansion of ♮VI, after which a return is made to I.

    106-15   Now the previously expected cadential figure on I, slightly longer than that on IV.

116-25   Transition, based on *A,* converting E major into a V⁷.

Ex. 3

The discrepancy between Schubert's and Beethoven's proportions is nowhere more striking than here in the second themes. Beethoven's theme is the elaboration of single phrase, and his retransition grows out of its cadence. Schubert's theme is basically a roughly balanced two-part form: I-IV, twenty-one measures; IV-I, nineteen measures — but it is interrupted by an interpolation of twenty-seven measures! After an elaborate cadence, the retransition enters as a separate idea.

66-82	Theme *A*, I, continuing for a time the triplets of the preceding section.
82-132	Development, based on *A*.
82-125	The first phrase of the theme, now in the left hand, in minor. It leads to an imitative contrapuntal section cadencing on ♭VI, then in turn on minor IV and minor ♮VII. The last cadence is truncated, going into a series of sequences leading to a half-cadence on V.
125-32	Confirmation of V in preparation for the return.

126-41	Theme *A*, I, continuing for a time the triplets of the preceding section.
142-211	Development, based on *A*.
142-68	The first phrase of the theme, now in the left hand, in minor. It leads to antiphonal statements (left and right hands) cadencing in turn on V, on II, on IV (a deceptive substitute for VI), and definitively on III.
168-200	Another huge expansion, this time of III, in constantly expanding phrases, the last of which, through repeated interruptions, mounts up to fifteen measures.
200-211	Confirmation of III, which is turned at the last minute into V⁷ of VI.

Here again the contrast is revealing. Schubert's development would have been shorter than Beethoven's (thirty-three measures to fifty) had it not been for the twenty-seven-measure interpolation on III.

132-64	Recapitulation of *A*, I.
132-48	Complete statement, retaining the triplet accompaniment.
149-64	A second complete version, in part identical with the variation of the exposition.
164-78	Bridge. Fourteen measures as against the ten of the exposition.

212-44	Recapitulation of *A*, VI-I.
212-20	Statement of *a* only, in major VI, modulating to I (through an extra measure).
221-44	A complete version of *A*, in part identical with the variation of the exposition.
244-58	Bridge. The same length as before.

Beethoven characteristically takes the opportunity afforded by the altered key relationship of the recapitulation to present his material in a new light through a fresh modulatory development. Schubert, here as so often elsewhere, merely transposes a corresponding passage from the exposition.

178-88	Theme B, I. As before.	258-327	Theme B, I. As before, but ending on V⁷, followed by a pause.

178-88   Theme B, I. As before.

188-224   Cadential figure merging into a transition as before. This passage is now extended by a new development leading to a quasi cadenza over a dominant pedal.

224-42   Theme A, I, broken by pauses. It ends with a trill over V.

258-327   Theme B, I. As before, but ending on V^7, followed by a pause.
There is no transition corresponding to the one following the exposition.

328-48   Theme A, I, broken by pauses. It ends on V, followed by another pause.

Schubert's interrupted recapitulation is more nearly complete than Beethoven's and harmonically more elaborate, arriving on V through a turn toward the tonic minor and ♮VI. But the two passages are undeniably similar in effect.

243-75   Coda, Presto.

243-48   The trill over the dominant is retained; hence the first move of the coda, as in the theme itself, is V-I.

248-62   Cadences derived from A.

262-75   Final cadence, reminiscent of the opening of the sonata.

349-82   Coda, Presto.

349-67   The dominant on which the theme ended is not retained. The coda enters on I, moving to V.

368-75   Cadences derived from A.

375-82   Final cadence, reminiscent of the opening of the sonata.

Beethoven's quotation of his first movement is less obvious than Schubert's, but still unmistakable. The use of this device by both composers, in each case following the disintegration of the main theme and a speed-up of the tempo, clinches the connection between the two rondos.

If, as I hope, the reader has been convinced by the foregoing that Schubert did indeed deliberately follow Beethoven in the layout of his movement, the question that will naturally occur to him is "Why?" Why did Schubert feel the need of such a guide, and why did he choose this particular rondo? The latter half of the question is, I believe, the more easily answered. Schubert's theme, in spite of its parallels with Beethoven's, could hardly have been written with the earlier one in mind, for its origin is to be found among Schubert's own compositions. It is a vastly superior reworking of the theme of the second movement of the early (1817) Sonata in A minor, Opus 164. It is also closely related to the opening of the song *Im Frühling,* which, although written earlier, was published in September, 1828, and may thus have been fresh in the composer's mind. So the resemblances to the Beethoven theme are probably fortuitous. But if it is granted that Schubert was looking for a suitable Beethoven rondo, it is reasonable to suppose that he hit upon this one because it was in a major key, its tempo was close to his own, and its main theme strongly resembled the one he had decided to use. If he had already thought of returning to the opening of the sonata in its concluding pages, then Beethoven's coda may have added a further inducement to choose this model; on the other hand, it may have been Beethoven's example that suggested such an ending in the first place.

What remains to be explained is why he should have sought a model at all. Very likely Schubert was impelled by the same kind of insecurity that, during the last year of his life, drove him to apply to Sechter for counterpoint lessons. He felt that he had failed to master certain technical problems and needed help in solving them. He chose Sechter to teach him counterpoint; he chose Beethoven to teach him disciplined composition — although in a different manner.

Schubert had always had trouble in controlling the rondo. It is to his finales, and especially to his rondo finales, that his reputation for rambling redundancy is due. (His most successful finale, that of the Great C major Symphony, is of course in sonata form.) Now, these rondos are hardly ever complete third- or sonata-rondos; if they were, they would reach well beyond heavenly lengths! One favorite form has already been described, the *ABCA*-Development-*BCA*. (Sometimes one finds a less elaborate version with a bitonal exposition, as in the finale of the Cello Quintet.) Another favorite is the second-rondo, *ABACA*. Both forms are subject to a hypertrophy that sometimes causes the individual sections to swell to gigantic size. Look for a moment at the finale of the Fantasy-Sonata in G, Opus 78 (1826). It is basically a second-rondo, but it is 411 measures long. Themes *A* and *B* are elaborate, fully developed, self-contained structures; section *C* is a complete first-rondo in its own right, whose digression in turn comprises two statements and two developments of a new theme! The whole can be outlined as *ABA(CDC)A*. An even more swollen example, which the reader may examine for himself, is the Rondo for Violin and Piano, Opus 70 (1826); exclusive of the andante introduction, it contains over 650 measures!

Small wonder, then, that Schubert rarely ventured into the third-rondo, and should want some company when he did. One early attempt, the Rondo for Violin and Strings of 1816 (D. 438), shows the same tendency toward thematic self-sufficiency that marks the examples just described, and it is further expanded by the frequent recurrence of a closing theme (*C* in the following diagram): *ABC*-Transition-*ADD'C*-Transition-*ABC,* in which the two statements of *BC* occur in dominant and tonic, respectively. Opus 70 also points toward the third-rondo when its second theme returns in the tonic, greatly abbreviated, to introduce the coda. Of all the examples before 1828, perhaps the finale of the A minor Piano Sonata, Opus 42 (1825), most nearly achieves the canonical form. Yet even here the proliferation of members diffuses the sense of pattern of the whole. Consequently one is not sure what "counts" as a theme — for example, is the passage beginning at measure 47 a new theme or part of the first? One never knows, as one hears the movement, what proportions to expect. In a word, the form is unclear — not necessarily to the analyst, who can study the movement as a whole, but certainly to the listener, who has to take it as it comes.

These, then, are the problems of which Schubert may have been conscious when confronted with the task of writing yet another finale that he wished to cast in rondo form, and they may explain why he entrusted his design to a more experienced master. The fact that he did succeed here in the composition of a convincing sonata-rondo vindicates his procedure; yet the contrast between the proportions of Beethoven's 275 measures and Schubert's 382 (398 with the repeats) suggests that the younger composer's more relaxed sense of form could never produce an exact imitation of the older man's concentrated structures. Schubert's realization of this fact may explain why the finale of the B-flat Sonata, probably the last of the three to be finished, offers a compromise between his own type of rondo and the conventional one. By placing his development between the two halves of his first theme he achieved the pattern of recurrence typical of the third-rondo without increasing the number of statements of a somewhat unwieldy subject.

The hypothesis that Schubert was deliberately patterning a movement of his own on one of Beethoven's is supported by evidence that he had done exactly the same thing not long before, and for another rondo — probably his most successful example of the form. The Rondo in A for Piano Duet, Opus 107, was written during the spring of 1828; its model was the finale of Beethoven's Piano Sonata in E minor, Opus 90. As in the previous case, Schubert's close adherence to Beethoven's formal procedures is the best indication of the relationship; but, as before, there are superficial resemblances too. Both movements are in major and in 2/4; Schubert's "Allegretto" turns out, in performance, to be almost identical with Beethoven's "Nicht zu geschwind"; the instrumentation of Schubert's opening is a four-hand transcription of Beethoven's solo writing; and the chromatic progressions found in corresponding positions in the two initial themes are the same: V^7 of V, V, V^7 of IV, IV, in measures 9-12 of each.

More fundamental is the fact that both themes exhibit the same uncommon form. This can be outlined as $aa'bb'aa'$, in which a and a' are four measures each, b and b' eight measures. These proportions are unusual. Why should the middle of a song form, already as long as the first section, be repeated? The fact is that we are not dealing here with a true three-part form, since all the phrases end on the tonic chord. (In the Beethoven, all the phrases save the two a's end melodically on the tonic as well. In the Schubert, only the even phrases — a', b' — arrive at the tonic.) The basic pattern, then, is a two-part form, since harmony and melody are both complete at the close of b'. The following return to aa' is in the nature of a reminiscence — a codetta, as it were.

It seems hardly possible that Schubert arrived independently at this almost unique design, for the two themes coincide, not only in form, but in pianistic registration as well. In both examples, all the even phrases are partially or completely set off by the doubling of the melody in the upper octave. It is, therefore, likely that, having the general idea of his musical subject in mind, Schubert searched for an appropriate Beethoven model — one that agreed with his projected rondo in tempo, movement, and general spirit. When he found it, he proceeded to cast his own theme in the mold he discovered there.

The parallel description of the two movements will again show how closely Schubert followed his guide, and where he departed from him.

	Beethoven		Schubert
Measures		Measures	
1-32	Theme A, I (E major).	1-32	Theme A, I (A major).
33-40	Bridge.	33-54	Bridge, two balanced periods.
	Based on a single motif, it	33-43	VI moving to V, I.
	moves from VI to V of V.	44-54	VI moving to V of V, V.

Schubert's lyrical expansion contrasts here with Beethoven's concentrated, motivically developed modulation.

41-69	Theme B, V (B major).	55-91	Theme B, V (E major).
41-59	The theme begins on V of the new key, which it elaborates harmonically.	55-68	A fully rounded theme in the new key: $cc'cc'dd'$.

60-69   It arrives at its tonic with a new thematic statement (closing theme) that will be important in the development. But scarcely has the new tonic been established than it is turned into a V⁷, and we are in the transition back to A.

69-91   An equally rounded closing theme: *eeff'* with an extended cadence. The material of *e* will be important in the development.

92-102 An extended transition over a dominant pedal.

Once more Schubert's tendency to expand his second group and his transitions is evident.

70-101 Theme *A*, I, complete.

102-39 Development.

102-13 Transitional passage based on the cadence of *A*, repeated in major, then in minor with an extension modulating toward VI.

114-39 Development of closing theme with highly chromatic modulations arriving finally on V⁷.

103-34 Theme *A*, I, complete.

135-75 Development.

134-51 Transitional passage based on the cadence of *A*, repeated with a turn to minor, then modulating to ♮III. A new version appears in the bass, modulating toward ♭II (N).

152-75 Development of closing theme with highly chromatic modulations arriving finally on V⁷.

Schubert's modulations at one point make more than a perfunctory gesture in his master's direction. Compare his juxtaposition of C minor and C-sharp minor in measures 157-61 with Beethoven's in measures 117-22.

140-71 Theme *A*, I, complete.

172-80 Bridge, extended by one measure and ending on V⁷.

176-83 Theme *A*, I, in a statement restricted to *aa'*.

184-94 Bridge, with proportions as before. But instead of moving first to I and then to V, it moves twice to I.

Thus the conciseness of Schubert's recapitulation of *A* is balanced (and perhaps explained) by the redundancy of his transition, which, keeping its original shape in spite of the loss of its modulatory function, now reiterates a single progression: VI-V-I.

181-211 Theme *B*, I, extended by a modulation ending on V $\begin{smallmatrix}6\\5\end{smallmatrix}$ of ♮VI.

206-41 Theme *B*, I, ending with a deceptive cadence on ♮VI.

212-29 An interpolated development based on Theme *A*. A highly chromatic passage leads to an extended V^7.

242-68 An interpolated development based on the closing theme. Expanded VI and N lead to an extended V^7 based on the transition of measures 92-102.

230-53 Theme *A*, I.
Only *aa'bb'*, the melody occurring alternately in the left and right hands. The cadence is elided, for the last two measures initiate the coda.

269-92 Theme *A*, I.
Only *aa'bb'*. For the first time the melody is given to the secondo.

252-92 Coda.
An extension of *A*, based on a development of the last two measures, leads to a pause followed by a quasi cadenza. An abbreviated statement of *A* introduces a ritardando that is continued in an imitative passage. An accelerando leads to the final cadence.

293-310 Coda.
A reference to the closing theme leads to an authentic cadence on I. It is followed by an imitative ritardando passage based on *A*, which creates a plagal cadence.

Contrasting each of the two Schubert rondos as a whole with its Beethovenian model, one can descry at least one source of Schubert's heavenly lengths: the expansion of the second half of the exposition. Where Beethoven follows a lyrical principal theme by a concise bridge, a motivically developed second theme, and a brief retransition growing out of the cadence, Schubert dwells lovingly on each of these elements in turn, producing proportions entirely different from those of the original. In the sonata finale, he subjects the development to the same kind of treatment, interpolating into it an episode derived from the main subject, yet independent enough to constitute a theme in itself. In the four-hand rondo he follows Beethoven's development section more closely, to the advantage of the movement's formal concentration.

Schubert's use of Beethoven's Opus 90 late in his career throws interesting light on a work of his early youth, the Piano Sonata in E minor (D. 566) of 1817. This work had a strange publication history. The *Gesamtausgabe* of 1888 printed only the first movement, a moderato. But one of the autographs contained two other movements as well. Of these, one (the second of the three), an allegretto, appeared in 1907. It was not until 1928 that the third, a scherzo, was published, together with a complete history and description of the manuscript sources by

Adolf Bauer.[4] Finally, in 1948, a hypothetical fourth movement was added, the Rondo in E, Opus 145, to form a "complete" version, which was edited by Kathleen Dale and published by British and Continental Music Agencies of London. Mrs. Dale, backed by good scholarly opinion such as that of Ludwig Scheibler and Gerald Abraham, felt that there was reason to believe that the rondo, for years improperly attached to a partly spurious adagio, was the missing finale.

On broadly musical and specifically stylistic grounds, I find the reconstruction unsatisfactory. The second and fourth movements (allegretto and allegretto molto, both in 2/4) are far too much alike in tempo and general spirit to fit together happily as members of the same work. The scherzo seems both too heavy pianistically and too adventurous harmonically for the comparatively mild movements that precede it. The evidence of the manuscript would seem to be in its favor, but Bauer pointed out significant differences between the autographs of this movement and the preceding ones: "The first two movements exhibit a number of emendations; but the third movement, the scherzo and trio, is almost without correction and appears to have been written down in a single spurt." [5] It may well be, then, that the scherzo was never intended as part of the sonata and was only adventitiously attached to it.

A survey of Schubert's instrumental compositions reveals no other example of a work in which a first movement in minor is followed by a second in tonic major, although the reverse does occur. The finality of the minor-major succession suggests a two-movement work when supported, as in the present instance, by the elaborate sonata form and brisk tempo of the second movement. This is the unique case of a fully developed, formally divided (by double bar and repeat) sonata form among Schubert's second movements. (The only other possible contender, the slow movement of the Sonata for Violin and Piano, Opus 137, No. 3, is hardly more than an elaborate three-part song form.) The present example, that is to say, sounds more like a finale than like a slow movement.

Now, Beethoven had published just such a sonata not long before. Opus 90, which had appeared in 1815, was in two movements, of which the first was in E minor and the second in E major. Is it far-fetched to suppose that Schubert was modeling his entire sonata on Beethoven's?

[4] "Scherzo aus der Klaviersonate E-moll (Juni 1817) von Franz Schubert," *Die Musik,* Vol. XXI, No. 1 (Oct. 1928), pp. 13-16, and supplement.

[5] *Ibid.,* p. 15.

There are other connections between the two works. In the first movements, the bass progression in measures 3-7 of the Schubert reflects that of Beethoven's measures 17-24, and Schubert's approach to the I $^6_4$ at the end of his development presents a simplified version of Beethoven's progression at the corresponding point. In the second movement, 2/4 in each case, Schubert's "Allegretto" is again very likely the equivalent of Beethoven's "Nicht zu geschwind," and Schubert's pianistic layout imitates that of Beethoven — characteristics that this movement shares with the piano duet.[6] The second half of Schubert's main theme, moving chromatically down from B to G-sharp reflects a similar motion at the corresponding point of Beethoven's. Other resemblances are less exact, but all suggest the same inference. Schubert was writing a two-movement sonata in emulation of Beethoven's.

According to this hypothesis, then, the scherzo is an independent movement, even though it appears in the same manuscript; and the E major Rondo has no connection with the sonata beyond the fortuitous identity of key. The sonata consists solely of an E minor moderato followed by an E major allegretto. Even if one rejects the reasoning that has led to this conclusion, one may still find the composition more convincingly viable in this form than in any other.

---

[6] The resemblance of this movement to Beethoven's was pointed out by Abraham in his notes accompanying the publication of the four-movement version, but he drew no inference therefrom.